T0301543

The International Monetary Fund

The International Monetary Fund

Distinguishing Reality from Rhetoric

Graham Bird

Professor, Claremont McKenna College, USA and Claremont Graduate University, USA; Emeritus Professor, University of Surrey, UK

Dane Rowlands

Professor and Director, Norman Paterson School of International Affairs, Carleton University, Canada

Edward Elgar
PUBLISHING

Cheltenham, UK • Northampton, MA, USA

Published by
Edward Elgar Publishing Limited
The Lypiatts
15 Lansdown Road
Cheltenham
Glos GL50 2JA
UK

Edward Elgar Publishing, Inc.
William Pratt House
9 Dewey Court
Northampton
Massachusetts 01060
USA

A catalogue record for this book
is available from the British Library

Library of Congress Control Number: 2015952666

This book is available electronically in the **Elgar**online
Economics subject collection
DOI 10.4337/9780857939708

ISBN 978 0 85793 969 2 (cased)
ISBN 978 0 85793 970 8 (eBook)

Typeset by Servis Filmsetting Ltd, Stockport, Cheshire
Printed and bound in Great Britain by TJ International Ltd, Padstow

Contents

Preface

There is no shortage of opinion about the International Monetary Fund (IMF). Some see it as the agent of austerity and as being manipulated by wealthier countries for their own commercial and political gain. In a similar vein the Fund is sometimes viewed as acting as a debt collector for private capital markets. From this viewpoint the IMF appears to be no friend of the developing and emerging economies that have, since the mid-1970s and until recently, been its principal clients. Instead it is presented as often forcing poor countries to pursue programs that require macroeconomic overkill and slow down growth and development.

In sharp contrast there is an alternative view that sees the Fund as bailing out countries by providing large amounts of soft finance, rather than forcing them to bite the adjustment bullet. From this perspective the Fund's activities delay appropriate economic reform, cause international financial crises by encouraging private markets to lend excessively, and create international financial instability.

In a somewhat ironic way both 'right wing' and 'left wing' critics of the IMF have on occasions argued that the IMF should be closed down, claiming that it is doing more harm than good. Although they reach the same conclusion, they reach it via very different routes. When they do not opt for complete closure, critics argue for substantial reform of the institution, though here their reform agendas often differ quite dramatically.

The challenge for researchers is to try and evaluate the alternative arguments and to distinguish the reality from the rhetoric. This is the challenge that we try to meet in this book. In part, meeting the challenge means undertaking a careful theoretical analysis of the issues involved. But it also means trying to test the arguments empirically. This book is essentially empirical. Is it the case that IMF resources are systematically filtered to friends of the US and other powerful countries and excluded from the rest? Do different countries turn to the IMF in different or similar circumstances? Does the degree to which programs with the IMF are implemented depend on the power of special interest groups to resist economic reform or upon underlying economic factors? Do IMF programs in poor countries exert a negative impact on economic growth? Do programs in emerging economies have a catalytic effect on other international capital flows, encouraging private markets to lend more than they otherwise would have done? Our main purpose in what follows is to assess these and other questions against the evidence.

We should offer a word of warning at the outset. The IMF is a complex institution. It has a wide and diverse membership. It is open to economic, political and legal influences. There are underlying issues affecting its governance and the balance of power in its decision-making. Historical institutional factors influence its contemporary operations. In these circumstances it is most unlikely that there will be unambiguous answers to questions that may initially appear straightforward. Moreover the Fund has multilateral, regional and bilateral roles that may be interconnected, introducing yet another source of complexity.

In this book we studiously try and avoid making sweeping generalizations that we find to be unsupported by the empirical evidence. There is a danger in adopting this cautious and balanced approach. Sweeping generalizations and an unconstrained use of rhetoric makes things easier to comprehend and more fun to read. How annoying it is when economists insist on pointing out that there are nuances, and revert to their preferred phrase that 'it all depends'. Whilst recognizing the danger that empirical conclusions that are ambivalent may be frustrating, we have chosen to try and be informative and accurate. This book is not a polemic on the IMF. It is an attempt to offer an objective and scientific analysis of key aspects of the Fund's operations. We believe that in assessing the Fund's operations and in considering reform proposals there is a clear need for such empirically informed analysis.

While many of the chapters report original research that we have not published elsewhere, some chapters reproduce work that has already been published in academic journals. Where we do this, we cite the original source and acknowledge the willingness of the publishers to reproduce it. Our approach was to consider what topics needed to be covered in the book. Where we had recently undertaken and published research on a topic that we felt should be included, there seemed little point in replicating it. Where we identified gaps not addressed by our previous work, we undertook new research to fill those gaps and thus provide a more coherent and comprehensive story. The book's contents are therefore determined by the issues that we thought should be covered and not by what articles were already out there that we could conveniently reproduce.

The list of people who have helped us either directly or indirectly in writing this book is long and we apologize for not acknowledging them individually. Some of them work for the IMF, or have worked for it, and may prefer to retain their anonymity. However, special thanks must go to those with whom we have collaborated on some of the research that appears here, namely, Ozlem Arpac, Alex Mandilaras and Jim Mylonas.

We see the IMF as an important global institution and one with tremendous power to do good in the world. Our hope is that the contents of this book will make a useful contribution to contemporary debates about the Fund's future and reform.

Acknowledgments

Some of the chapters in this book originally appeared as papers in academic journals as follows.

Chapter 2: IMF quotas: constructing an international organization using inferior building blocks, *Review of International Organizations*, 2006, 1, 153–171 (Graham Bird and Dane Rowlands).

Chapter 3: Should it be curtains for some of the IMF's lending windows?, *Review of International Organizations*, 2007, 2, 281–299 (Graham Bird and Dane Rowlands).

Chapter 4: The episodic and unpredictable nature of IMF lending: an empirical analysis, *The World Economy*, 2010, 1280–1301 (Graham Bird and Dane Rowlands).

Chapter 6: Stop interrupting: an empirical analysis of the implementation of IMF programs, *World Development*, 2008, 36(9), 1493–1513, (Ozlem Arpac, Graham Bird and Alex Mandilaras).

We are grateful to the publishers of these journals for permitting us to reproduce the papers in this volume. In the case of Chapter 6 we are also grateful to our co-authors for allowing us to include the paper in this volume.

1. Introduction and overview: the purposes and operations of the IMF

1.1 INTRODUCTION

The International Monetary Fund (IMF or 'the Fund') is the world's premier international financial institution. In 2015 it had a total of 188 member countries spanning all geographical regions of the world and all levels of economic development from the richest economies to the poorest. For many years after it was established in 1946 it was not the subject of widespread academic study. Isolated studies certainly existed covering various aspects of the Fund's operations, but there was not a large or comprehensive research literature to which reference could be made.

This paucity of academic research did not prevent people from having firmly held views about the institution. The views were diverse and frequently diametrically opposed. Those on the political 'right' saw the Fund as bailing out countries that had been seriously mismanaged by providing them with relatively 'soft' low cost financial assistance. To these critics, the IMF often caused more problems that it cured by sustaining such regimes and postponing necessary economic reform. In contrast, those on the political 'left' saw it as imposing austerity measures on vulnerable countries and as having a negative impact on economic growth and development. They perceived the Fund as an institution dominated by advanced countries and as representing their political and commercial interests usually to the detriment of poorer countries.

Lively as the debate about the IMF was, it tended to be polemic in style and grounded in ideology rather than analysis. Claims and counter claims were made with, at best, only passing reference to empirical evidence. When evidence was cited, it was usually partial, selective and anecdotal.

The contemporary situation is different. Polemics still features in debates about the IMF, but there is now a substantial scientific literature upon which to draw. This later research has attempted to analyse the Fund's role and operations both theoretically and empirically.

In this book we aim to contribute to the contemporary debate about the IMF by offering empirically based analyses of the Fund's operations. To do this we draw together some of our previously published work on various aspects of the IMF's activities but we also present new and previously unpublished material.

1.2   THE PURPOSES AND EVOLUTION OF THE IMF

The IMF was conceived at the Bretton Woods conference in 1944 as part of a global response to the Great Depression of the 1930s. The basic idea was to set up an international financial institution that would help avoid the beggar thy neighbor policies that had characterized that period. The Fund was seen as providing short to medium term finance to member countries facing balance of payments difficulties, in order to allow them to pursue policies of economic adjustment that did not rely on competitive devaluation and protectionist trade policies. In the words of the IMF's Articles of Agreement, a central purpose was to make the resources of the IMF available to members under 'adequate safeguards' and to provide them with the opportunity to 'correct maladjustments in their balance of payments without resorting to measures destructive of national or international prosperity.'

In principle, the rationale for the Fund's existence was to offset elements of 'market failure'. These included information failures, externalities and contagion, coordination failures, financing gaps, and the inability of market operators to produce the 'public good' of conditionality or to provide an international lender of last resort that would supply adequate international liquidity in the event of crises. In the years during which the Fund has existed, opinions have varied as to how important these elements of market failure are, and therefore how important the IMF is. At times when markets have seemed to be working adequately, the need for the IMF has been questioned. When markets have more conspicuously failed the importance of the IMF has been highlighted.

During the Bretton Woods era there were few challenges to the IMF's existence. After all, the Fund had been designed to manage that system. But with the system's demise in 1973 some observers argued that it had outlived its usefulness. In the immediate post Bretton Woods era, economic adjustment was supposed to rely more heavily on the flexible exchange rates adopted by the world's largest and wealthiest economies. Private international capital markets (particularly in the context of petro dollar recycling) were seen as providing balance of payments finance and, as a result of these developments, there was a reduced need for the increased international reserves that might otherwise have been created by allocations of the IMF's newly introduced Special Drawing Rights. In addition, in the late 1970s, there was a move away from multilateralism in international monetary relations, as the European Monetary System was set up in 1979. Much of the initial rationale for the IMF seemed to have disappeared, and indeed for the next 30 years the IMF's traditional lending concentration on its higher-income members evaporated, to be replaced by agreements with low and middle-income countries. Indeed, at the beginning of the 1980s, all the IMF's programs were with low-income countries (LICs) that tended not to have access to international capital markets.

Things then changed. The overvalued US dollar suggested that freely operating foreign exchange markets did not necessarily guarantee that equilibrium rates would be generated. Furthermore, the debt crisis in the developing world suggested that private international capital markets could be susceptible to periods of both over-lending and under-lending. Relatively large Latin American economies became clients of the Fund and the IMF took on the role of trying to help resolve the debt crisis. In the global conditions of the 1980s the IMF rapidly re-acquired international relevance and prominence. Over this time period its portfolio of agreements settled into a pattern that comprised low-income countries (often on a fairly prolonged or frequent basis) and, more infrequently, emerging economies in circumstances where they had lost access to international capital markets.

The Fund's comeback continued during the early 1990s as it was confronted with the challenge of assisting countries that had embarked on a transition from centrally planned to market-based economic systems. Then, in the later 1990s it was faced with the East Asian financial crisis. In the latter case, a debate ensued between the Fund's supporters who argued that the crisis reinforced its underlying *raison d'être*, and detractors who argued that it had helped to cause the crisis by offering a financial safety net that had in turn encouraged private capital markets to underestimate risk. The latter arguments found expression in the claim that IMF lending involved a severe moral hazard; a claim that was emphasized strongly in the Meltzer Commission report (Meltzer, 2000). Critics also argued that the design of programs in East Asia was inappropriate, involving excessive conditionality and much more emphasis on compressing domestic demand through fiscal austerity than was required (see, for instance, Stiglitz, 2002). Between these two poles of disaffection, the Fund played a prominent (though still controversial) role in the debt forgiveness initiatives that emerged at the turn of the millennium.

Following the trials and tribulations at the end of the 1990s and beginning of the 2000s the world economy became relatively benign for many countries that had previously used IMF resources. The absence of significant international financial volatility fostered further debate about whether the IMF was needed any longer. There was an increasing groundswell of opinion amongst influential financial journalists and a number of well-respected central bank officials (including the Governor of the Bank of England) that the Fund was becoming less and less relevant. The reduction in the Fund's lending activity was not simply because of an exogenous decline in the number of countries seeking its help, but also because it seemed to be rather ineffective in exercising preventative multilateral surveillance (Bird and Willett, 2007).

The lower profile of the IMF in the middle of the 2000s is reflected by Table 1.1 which shows the decline in both the number of IMF arrangements and in the total amount of IMF lending. However, obituaries of the Fund proved to be premature. The global financial and economic crisis that erupted in 2008 enhanced the Fund's profile and increased its relevance both in terms of its systemic purpose and its bilateral function in assisting individual member countries that had been particularly adversely affected by the crisis. There was a sharp increase in IMF lending. The Eurozone crisis in the late 2000s saw Greece, Portugal and Ireland negotiating programs with the IMF, the first time that high-income countries had sought IMF assistance since the mid-1970s.

Not surprisingly, the pattern of IMF activity, and the waxing and waning of its prominence, corresponds closely with major international financial events. Although an important part of the Fund's functions can reasonably be seen as seeking to avoid and avert crises, the reality has been that its role as an international financial trouble-shooter has been most prominent when severe economic distress has been faced by relatively large individual economies or by the world economy as a whole (see Bird, 1999). On top of this the IMF has experienced its own existential issues irrespective of global financial crises.

In this book we take the basic rationale for the IMF as given. Even at times when the world economy is enjoying a period of relative tranquility it remains vulnerable to economic and financial shocks and instability and, in these circumstances, the IMF fulfils a useful function. Societies opt not to close down fire services just because there has been a period when no major fires have occurred. Nor do they completely disband air and sea rescue services immediately after weather conditions improve. Rather than deliberating as to whether the world needs the IMF, we are keen to examine key elements of its bilateral dealings with member countries under the auspices of its stabilization and adjustment programs.

1.3   THE LAYOUT OF THE BOOK

1.3.1   IMF Quotas

Many of the IMF's activities are based, albeit often quite loosely, on countries' quotas. The Fund has sometimes referred to quotas as the institution's

Table 1.1 IMF lending by type of program

Financial Year	Number of Arrangements					Amount committed under Arrangements as of April 30 (in millions of SDRs)				
	Stand-by	FCL	EFF	PRGT	Total	Stand-by	FCL	EFF	PRGT	Total
1997	14	–	11	35	60	3,764	–	10,184	4,048	17,996
1998	14	–	13	33	60	28,323	–	12,336	4,410	45,069
1999	9	–	12	35	56	32,747	–	11,401	4,186	48,334
2000	16	–	11	31	58	45,606	–	9,798	3,516	57,920
2001	17	–	8	37	62	34,906	–	8,697	3,296	46,901
2002	13	–	4	35	52	44,095	–	7,643	4,201	55,939
2003	15	–	3	36	54	42,807	–	4,432	4,450	51,689
2004	11	–	2	36	49	53,944	–	794	4,356	59,094
2005	10	–	2	31	43	11,992	–	794	2,878	15,664
2006	10	–	1	27	38	9,534	–	9	1,770	11,313
2007	6	–	1	29	36	7,864	–	9	1,664	9,536
2008	7	–	2	25	34	7,507	–	351	1,090	8,949
2009	15	1	–	28	44	34,326	32,528	–	1,813	67,668
2010	21	3	2	30	56	56,773	52,184	205	3,244	112,406
2011	18	3	4	31	57	59,048	68,780	19,804	3,345	151,390
2012	13	3	6	28	51	30,804	70,328	67,331	3,912	162,788
2013	7	3	5	25	41	5,130	73,162	67,152	2,929	152,490
2014	6	3	7	18	35	15,763	73,162	53,804	1,874	148,721

Note: Figures reflect amounts of arrangements in effect at end of financial years ending April 30.

Sources: IMF Annual Report (2004, 2007, 2011, 2014), Washington, DC: IMF.

5

'building blocks'. It is therefore important to investigate whether they form an appropriate foundation for determining the way in which the Fund is financed and the way in which it allocates its resources to member countries. Quotas also have important implications for the balance of power within the institution since they help determine the distribution of voting rights and therefore affect decision-making. In Chapter 2 (previously published as Bird and Rowlands, 2006) we examine various aspects of IMF quotas and argue that an underlying problem with them is that one common formula has been used to help determine different dimensions of the Fund's activities (voting, subscriptions and drawing rights). These dimensions of the IMF's operations are likely to be at odds with one another. However, pointing to the problems associated with quotas has turned out to be much easier than formulating agreed modifications that overcome them. The reform of IMF quotas has proved to be an ongoing challenge.

1.3.2   The Range of IMF Lending Facilities

Another organizational issue relates to the number and nature of the IMF's lending windows. Table 1.1 gives an indication of the range of facilities available. Over the years facilities have been extended, abandoned or modified. It is therefore interesting to explore whether the facilities have fulfilled distinct or overlapping functions. In Chapter 3 (previously published as Bird and Rowlands, 2007b) we compare lending under the non-concessional and concessional facilities. We also investigate whether there are discernible differences in the use of the IMF's principal non-concessional facilities, stand-by agreements and Extended Fund Facility (EFF) credits.

We discover that in the years following the introduction of the EFF in 1974 there were significant differences in the economic circumstances in which the two non-concessional facilities were used. But we also find that these differences diminished over time; by the early 2000s they no longer existed. This result suggests that either the IMF's lending facilities have not always been used appropriately and for the purposes for which they were designed, or that a degree of redundancy has sometimes been allowed to persist. It also suggests that from time to time there may be unused potential for reforming the design of individual lending facilities. In this regard it is interesting to observe that there was a spate of reform to the design of lending facilities in the aftermath of the global economic crisis at the end of the 2000s; although the Fund opted to retain the EFF alongside its more frequently used stand-by facility.

The policy challenge facing the Fund is to ensure that its contemporary portfolio of lending windows allows it to cope with the particular and potentially diverse circumstances under which countries turn to it for

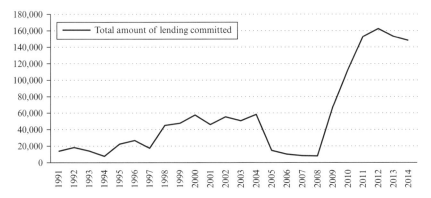

Note: Figures reflect amount of arrangements in effect at end of financial years ending April 30.

Source: IMF Annual Report (2000, 2004, 2011, 2014), Washington, DC: IMF.

Figure 1.1   Total amount of IMF lending (in millions of SDRs)

assistance (Bird, 2003). In designing individual IMF lending facilities it is therefore important to understand the factors that influence participation in IMF programs. Chapters 4 and 5 address this issue.

1.3.3   Participation in IMF Programs

In Chapter 4 (previously published as Bird and Rowlands, 2010) we turn to the temporal pattern of aggregate IMF lending that is reflected in Figure 1.1 and Table 1.1. In principle, the aggregate demand for IMF resources may be influenced by the size and distribution of current account balance of payments deficits, the size and distribution of holdings of international reserves, access to private international capital markets, levels of external debt and the cost of borrowing from the IMF comprising both the rate of charge on IMF credit, and perhaps more significantly, the perceived cost in terms of the conditionality associated with IMF programs.

In Chapter 4 we build on earlier research by Bird (1995) and more particularly by Ghosh et al. (2007). We confirm the episodic and volatile nature of non-concessional lending. We go on to calculate a series of bivariate correlations between various measures of IMF lending and the variables that theory suggests could be relevant, but find no simple and stable relationships. Finally we undertake a multivariate regression analysis aimed at explaining aggregate IMF lending using new IMF lending in a given year as our dependent variable.

We discover that while the bivariate correlations exhibit considerable instability, these seem to mask some apparently stable and significant relationships. Global economic growth is found to have a significant and lagged negative association with new IMF lending. Real international interest rates are positively (though weakly) associated with IMF lending. Finally, and in the period 1990–2007, we find that an increase in short term debt increases the following year's level of IMF lending. However, our regression results suggest that the relationships between IMF lending and other variables (international reserves, long term debt and current account deficits) are not significant.

The predictive power of our underlying econometric model is only modest, identifying the big increase in IMF lending in 2002, as well as the jump in lending in 1990, but failing to anticipate the large increases in 1993, 1995 and 1998.

While it seems possible to isolate a number of factors that exert a significant influence over aggregate IMF lending, there is substantial evidence that the relationships identified are unstable over time in ways that are difficult to predict. This volatility makes it hard to anticipate the adequacy of the IMF's lending capacity and suggests that it is important to have institutional mechanisms that allow this capacity to be altered relatively quickly as circumstances require.

Aggregate IMF lending is of course nothing more than the sum of lending to individual countries. It is therefore important to understand the distribution of IMF lending across countries. What factors determine whether or not individual countries participate in IMF programs?

In Chapter 5 we begin by reviewing the large literature that exists on participation. We then go on to make our own estimations of an econometric model that attempts to incorporate all the variables that theory and previous studies suggest may be significant.

Countries may be expected to consider turning to the Fund when their balance of payments has become unsustainable. The reasons for this external unsustainability are likely to differ between countries. For example, low-income countries may be vulnerable to current account shocks whereas emerging economies may be more vulnerable to shocks emanating from the capital account. In both cases domestic economic mismanagement may also be an important factor although the precise nature of the mismanagement is unlikely to be identical across all countries. The underlying economic problems that countries encounter may sometimes be deep-seated and difficult to correct in the short to medium term, or they may be temporary and self-correcting. It is therefore to be expected that some countries will have a long-lasting relationship with the IMF while others may participate in IMF programs only infrequently and for shorter periods of time (Bird, 2004).

Faced with an unsustainable balance of payments various responses may be possible, and some governments may be more inclined than others to seek IMF assistance. In determining whether or not to turn to the Fund domestic politics seem likely to play a role. As a consequence, countries that have similar economic characteristics may make different decisions with regards to borrowing from the IMF. Once the decision has been made to refer to the IMF, based on a contingent combination of the demand side economic and political factors discussed above, the IMF will have to determine its response. An important question is the extent to which this response is influenced by political factors. It seems reasonable to assume that politics will play a significant role on the supply side of participation in IMF programs as well as on the demand side. There is little doubt that the US and other wealthy (particularly European) economies are able to exert considerable influence within the IMF and will be motivated to try and use this to further their own political and commercial interests.

Chapter 5 offers a comprehensive attempt to test empirically all the potential economic and political influences on IMF participation. Our results emphasize the need for a disaggregated approach. We discover significant differences between concessional and non-concessional programs, as well as between regions and over time. While we find evidence that political factors are significant in some cases, our general conclusion is to counsel caution in assuming that US or advanced country influence provides a dominant explanation of participation in IMF programs. In many of our estimations previous programs with the IMF remains the best single predictor of current programs. No one model of participation fits all cases. While a general test of goodness of fit may seem to imply that there is much about participation in IMF programs that we are unable to explain, our analysis of false positives and negatives in Chapter 5 suggests that a substantial proportion of this is to do with the precise timing of programs.

1.3.4 The Implementation of IMF Programs

Having reached and signed an agreement with the IMF there is then the issue of whether the program is actually implemented. What factors affect implementation? We deal with this issue in Chapter 6 (previously published as Arpac, Bird and Mandilaras, 2008).

To begin with there is the not inconsequential problem of measuring implementation. There is no single way of doing this. One approach examines the extent to which loans are disbursed. A second examines whether programs are irreversibly interrupted. The third refers to the Fund's assessment of implementation according to its monitoring of arrangements as captured by its MONA database. There are deficiencies associated with each of these measures. For example, a low level of disbursement may reflect an improvement in economic performance. Meanwhile, the MONA database only covers programs coming up for review by the Fund's Executive Board, and thereby excludes cancelled or interrupted programs. Excluded programs are likely to exhibit poor implementation, and, therefore, the MONA index overstates implementation. Although the first two measures are quite closely correlated, the third is not closely correlated with the other two.

In Chapter 6 we adopt irreversible interruption as our measure of implementation. We then draw on underlying theory in order to guide our empirical estimation. This in part focuses on the marginal benefits and costs of implementation (see Bird, 2007).

The benefits arising from an IMF agreement are largely associated with the additional resources coming either directly from the IMF or indirectly via any catalytic effect that IMF programs have on other financial flows (we discuss this later). The costs are associated with the economic and political sacrifices related to implementation as perceived by the authorities. Both the benefits and the costs may turn out to be different from those that were envisaged at the time that the program was agreed, such that the political economy of implementation may differ from that of participation.

Other theoretical work has emphasized the importance of special interest groups (SIGs) that are opposed to the economic reforms embedded in programs (see, for example, Drazen, 2002; Khan and Sharma, 2008; and Mayer and Mourmouras, 2004). The more powerful these opposition groups are, the less likely it becomes that the authorities will be able to fully implement the program. These approaches are related since, with more external financing, the authorities may be in a stronger position to compensate those opposed to reform. On this basis, implementation may be expected to vary positively with the amount of financing and negatively with the strength of SIGs opposed to reform. In addition, the degree of implementation may in theory depend on the size of the problems that need to be corrected, and the incidence of shocks that blow a program off course.

Chapter 6 goes on to review the available literature before offering additional estimations testing the significance of a range of economic and political variables that theory and the extant literature identifies. Our results suggest that trade openness, the number of veto players and the amount of resources committed by the Fund are significant determinants of implementation, with the other variables being insignificant. Our overall conclusion is that the implementation of IMF programs will not be understood by examining economic factors on their own. Political influences are important, but they may have country specific elements that are missed by any one basic model. A full understanding of the implementation of IMF programs requires that large sample studies are augmented by structured case studies. Some of these are investigated briefly in Chapter 6. A more detailed analysis of Turkey's dealings with the IMF may be found in Arpac and Bird (2009). Since the IMF is concerned not only about the technical design of programs but will also be anxious to improve the record of implementation, the message would seem to be that it should pay close attention to the political environment in which governments seek to deliver on the commitments they make.

1.3.5 The Effects of IMF Programs

Macroeconomic effects
In debating the role of the IMF it is clearly important to know what impact IMF programs have on the countries that use IMF resources. A large part of the literature on the IMF has historically focused on the conditionality embodied in IMF programs and the effects of programs on various indicators of economic policy and macroeconomic outcomes (for an example of the early work on conditionality, see Williamson, 1982). In the early studies no distinction was made between programs that were implemented and those that were not, so that the effect of implementation was not evaluated. Nor was an attempt made to distinguish the effects of conditionality from those that were a consequence of the additional resources provided by IMF programs. The literature on IMF conditionality has been surveyed by Bird (2007), Dreher (2009), and Stone (2008).

Underlying all evaluation studies are fundamental methodological problems in isolating the impact of the Fund as opposed to other factors. There is no ideal way of doing this. Various approaches have been used including 'before and after' comparisons, 'with and without' comparisons, and 'performance versus target' comparisons. However, things other than IMF involvement change over time. Countries will differ in ways apart from their involvement with the Fund. In the case of performance versus target comparisons, targets may have been set unrealistically (Bird, 2005). A range of econometric and simulation techniques have also been used in an attempt to overcome the problem of estimating a counterfactual and dealing with selection bias. These methods have included the Generalised Evaluation Estimator (GEE) developed by Goldstein and Montiel (1986), Heckman two stage filters, instrumental variables (IV), and propensity score matching. None of these techniques is entirely satisfactory (see, for example, Atoyan and Conway, 2006). The GEE approach requires reliable policy reaction functions to be specified in order to calculate the counterfactual. The Heckman procedure relies on being able to find variables that appear in a selection equation but not in the structural model, and, in similar vein, the IV approach requires good instruments; variables that are strongly correlated with the likelihood of having a program but not with the macroeconomic outcome that is being investigated. The propensity score matching approach sets out to estimate a reasonably well-fitting participation model and to find program and non-program countries with similar propensity scores.

Evaluation is made yet more difficult by the fact that the design of conditionality has itself changed over time (see, for example, Bird, 2009, for a description and analysis of these changes). It started in the 1950s as being relatively parsimonious and involving a limited number of reasonably conventional macroeconomic policies as 'performance criteria' or 'prior actions'. Until the beginning of the 1980s IMF conditionality tended to be characterized as involving tight fiscal and monetary policy and exchange rate adjustment. In the 1980s and 1990s it became much more wide-ranging and began to incorporate a relatively large number of structural conditions in addition to the more conventional macroeconomic ones. This proliferation of conditions may have reflected an increasing consensus within orthodox economics at the time which prioritized policies of economic liberalization. However, concerns that conditionality was becoming excessive, and that this excess undermined ownership and implementation, led to a rethink. Bird (2001a) raised the possibility that there could be a conditionality Laffer curve; beyond some point the beneficial effects of conditionality might decline as the amount of conditionality rose. At the beginning of the 2000s, and perhaps reflecting an implicit acknowledgment of this view, the Fund embarked on an initiative based on 'streamlining' conditionality. This streamlining was intended to provide a clearer focus built on the institution's traditional competences and to foster stronger 'ownership' by the country's government as a means of improving implementation.

In the aftermath of the global financial and economic crisis at the end of the 2000s, the Fund undertook a major overhaul and modernization of conditionality. This reform, in part, involved redesigning its lending facilities. The use of structural conditions as performance criteria (where implementation had exhibited a particularly poor record) was discontinued. Ever since the Fund's involvement with countries as part of the East Asian crisis there had also been concerns that the strictures of conditionality were dissuading countries from borrowing from the IMF, as they preferred instead to accumulate a larger stock of their own reserves as a form of self-insurance. Bird and Mandilaras (2011) provided some empirical justification for these concerns. To the extent that it was the case, it implied that the benefits of reserve pooling were being lost. It also implied that the perceived costs of conditionality might induce countries to try and run balance of payments surpluses in a way that would add to global economic imbalances.

The mixed findings of evaluative studies relating to the macroeconomic effects of IMF programs on the balance of payments, inflation and growth, as well as on income distribution and poverty, have allowed commentators to draw opposing conclusions, particularly when the evidence has been used partially and selectively. Thus, ul Haque and Khan (1998) claimed that on balance conditionality worked, while the Meltzer Report (Meltzer, 2000) claimed that it did not. Bird (2001b) attempted to explain why such disparities existed with regards to the key macroeconomic variables, while Garuda (2000) showed why reaching conclusions about the distributional effects of IMF programs is far from straightforward.

We do not explore all of the issues associated with the impact of IMF programs and IMF conditionality in detail in this book. To cover the topic adequately would probably require a book in its own right. Fortunately much of the literature has been reviewed extensively elsewhere (Bird, 2007; Dreher, 2009). Instead, and more narrowly, Chapter 7 focuses on the effects of IMF programs on economic growth. As noted earlier, the Fund's Articles of Agreement state that one of the central purposes of the IMF is to facilitate economic adjustment in member countries without them having to resort to measures that are destructive of national prosperity. Testing the effect of IMF programs on economic growth enables us to assess how well this objective is being fulfilled. Moreover, sustained economic growth seems to be a reasonably reliable passport toward graduation away from the need for IMF programs. A negative effect on economic growth would therefore have the effect of making it more probable that countries would have to return to the IMF at a later date.

Chapter 7 draws on the earlier analysis of participation reported in Chapter 5 that allows us to identify countries with broadly similar propensities to participate in IMF programs. By using this empirical approach to distinguish between countries that did and did not have programs, we are able to address some of the more serious problems that arise from the selection problem mentioned earlier.

While a number of studies have been published that examine the effects of IMF programs on economic growth, we try and add value by using participation equations that better fit individual groups of countries, and in particular we discriminate between middle-income and low-income countries. We also distinguish between the effects of concessional and non-concessional programs and allow for other contingent factors including the size of programs and the degree of implementation. As with many other aspects of the IMF's operations we discover rather nuanced results. However we do find that claims that IMF programs have been universally detrimental to economic growth are not supported by the evidence. Indeed, in the case of low-income countries our evidence shows a positive effect.

The claim that IMF programs always involve severe austerity misrepresents the reality. In discussions about the reform of IMF programs it is therefore unwise to make this assumption.

1.3.6   Effects on Other Lending: The Catalytic Effect of IMF Programs

For many years the IMF has claimed that one of the most important effects of its programs is to provide a 'seal of approval' that encourages other capital markets to lend more than they otherwise would have done; the so-called catalytic effect of IMF programs. In one of its 'fact files' the IMF states that programs 'can help unlock other financing, acting as a catalyst for other lenders. . .programs serve as a signal that a country has adopted sound policies. . .and this increases investor confidence.' Thus, the Fund argues that catalysis operates via conditionality (Dhonte, 1997; Mussa and Savastano, 2000). More recently Morris and Shin (2006), and Corsetti et al. (2003) have developed theories of catalytic finance and have argued that IMF programs encourage others to lend by alleviating liquidity shortages.

There is an increasing amount of research that explores both the theory underpinning the catalytic effect and the empirical evidence relating to it. Cottarelli and Giannini (2002) summarize the channels through which catalysis may work and also survey the early empirical literature. The theory underpinning catalysis emerges as ambiguous (see, for example, Bird and Rowlands, 1997). An increase in interest rates and depreciation in the exchange rate may act to stimulate capital inflows, but such policies may alternatively lead to expectations of future financial problems and further depreciation and therefore have a negative effect. The potentially beneficial effects of conditionality may also be undermined by a lack of credibility associated with poor implementation.

A problem in investigating the catalytic effect is that international capital movements are themselves not fully understood and different types of capital flow are likely to be affected by different things; it is therefore difficult to be confident about the impact of Fund programs. Certainly it seems reasonable to assume that capital markets may be as likely to see IMF involvement as an indicator of current economic weakness as much as one of future strength.

The empirical evidence on the catalytic effect of IMF programs has expanded since early studies in the mid- to late-1990s. The results are mixed (see, for example, Rowlands, 2001; Bird and Rowlands, 2002; Edwards, 2006; Eichengreen et al., 2006; and Mody and Saravia, 2006). In Chapter 8 we attempt to provide a comprehensive analysis of the catalytic effect both from a theoretical and empirical perspective, whilst also providing a succinct summary of the existing literature. We disaggregate between different types of international capital, different IMF facilities, different time periods, different records relating to previous IMF programs and implementation, and the amount of IMF financing. We also try to distinguish between the effects of conditionality and financing. Furthermore, we allow for the possibility that the relationship between IMF programs and other flows may not be linear and may depend on the seriousness of the economic problems that bring countries to the Fund in the first place.

Our econometric investigations reported in Chapter 8 show that the sign and size of the catalytic effect varies depending on the details of the sample. This observation helps to explain why different studies that examine only a specific and narrow sample report different results. However, our general conclusion is that the catalytic effect is more often likely to be negative than it is to be positive. IMF programs may bring with them a net additional inflow of external finance but some of the IMF resources substitute for other forms of capital.

In work that is related to that reported in Chapter 8 (Bird and Rowlands, 2007a, 2009), we have distinguished between private capital flows and foreign aid. IMF programs do seem to be positively associated with additional inflows of aid for poor countries. But this may not be because of a catalytic effect in the conventional sense but more a reflection of a coordinated approach between aid donors and the IMF, with aid and IMF programs being essentially joint products. Similar findings concerning the relationship between IMF programs and foreign aid have been reported more recently by Bal Gunduz and Crystallin (2014).

There are important policy conclusions that lead on from the research on the catalytic effect. IMF programs that are under-resourced are unlikely to be successful (Bird and Rowlands, 2004). Shortages of finance will force countries to place greater reliance on faster acting adjustment policies that are difficult to implement for both economic and political reasons, and this emphasis on adjustment is likely to impair their success. There are, in turn, implications for the lending capacity of the IMF. For low-income countries the idea that aid agencies delegate the responsibility for designing and overseeing macroeconomic policy to the IMF may mean that the Fund is more important as a facilitator than as a financier in this group of countries. However, it may also have an important role to play in providing short term financing designed to protect development from the impact of temporary shocks to which LICs are vulnerable, such as the global economic crisis at the end of the first decade of the 2000s.

1.4 CONCLUDING REMARKS

In terms of international monetary relations, the IMF is the most significant and pivotal international financial institution. It has therefore received a great deal of attention both in the media and amongst academics. To understand its role and operations, and to facilitate serious policy discussion, it is important to have a sound basis of research that has firm empirical foundations.

Undertaking research into the IMF presents a daunting challenge since both economics and politics are involved. There are also important legal dimensions to the Fund's activities that need to be borne in mind. Similarly, a range of complementary research methodologies may be adopted, incorporating quantitative analysis using large sample regression techniques and qualitative ones using case studies and interviews. These methods can be connected in various ways. For example, regression analysis may be used to identify outliers that can then be examined in more detail to see why they deviate from a general pattern. Case studies can add flesh to the bones of large sample results.

Although the IMF has potentially important systemic and multilateral functions in terms of overseeing international monetary arrangements, for example in encouraging international adjustment to maintain global economic imbalances at sustainable levels and regulating the amount of international liquidity, we do not directly deal with these issues in this book. Instead we focus on the stages in what we have elsewhere referred to as the 'life cycle' of IMF programs (Bird and Rowlands, 2003). The book uses large sample regression techniques to empirically examine the determinants of participation in IMF programs, their implementation, and their effects on economic growth and capital flows. However, we do augment this quantitative approach with additional qualitative analysis.

If any one simple overall conclusion emerges from the chapters that follow, it is that it is misguided to provide simple overall conclusions. The analysis and empirical results that we present provide a warning against accepting sweeping generalizations about the IMF. While it may be more exciting to find straightforward and unambiguous answers to important questions concerning the IMF, it is also important to understand why unambiguous answers are misplaced and to be aware of the complexities involved. Our hope in writing this book is that it helps to identify the complexities and therefore to provide a better foundation for understanding and then reforming the IMF.

REFERENCES

Arpac, O. and Bird, G. (2009). Turkey and the IMF: A case study in the political economy of policy implementation. *Review of International Organizations*, 4(2), 135–157.

Atoyan, R. and Conway, P. (2006). Evaluating the impact of IMF programs: A comparison of matching and instrumental variable estimators. *Review of International Organizations*, 1(2), 99–124.

Bal Gunduz and Crystallin, M. (2014). Do IMF supported programs catalyze donor assistance to low income countries. *IMF Working Paper*, WP/14/202. Washington, DC: International Monetary Fund.

Bird, G. (1999). Crisis averter, crisis lender, crisis manager: The IMF in search of a systemic role. *The World Economy*, 22, 955–975.

Bird, G. (2001a). IMF programmes: Is there a conditionality Laffer curve? *World Economics*, 2(2), 29–49.

Bird, G. (2001b). IMF programs: Do they work? Can they be made to work better? *World Development*, 29, 1849–1865.

Bird, G. (2003). Restructuring the IMF's lending facilities. *The World Economy*, 26(2), 229–245.

Bird, G. (2004). The IMF forever: An analysis of the prolonged use of fund resources. *Journal of Development Studies*, 40(6), 30–58.

Bird, G. (2005). Over-optimism and the IMF. *The World Economy*, 28, 1355–1373.

Bird, G. (2007). The IMF: A bird's eye view of its role and operations. *Journal of Economic Surveys*, 21(4), 683–745.

Bird, G. (2009). Reforming IMF conditionality: from streamlining to major overhaul. *World Economics*, 10(3), 81–104.

Bird, G. and Mandilaras, A. (2011). Once bitten: The effects of IMF programs on subsequent reserve behavior. *Review of Development Economics*, 15(2), 264–278.

Bird, G. and Rowlands, D. (1997). The catalytic effect of lending by the international financial institutions. *The World Economy*, 20(7), 967–991.

Bird, G. and Rowlands, D. (2002). Do IMF programmes have a catalytic effect on other international capital flows? *Oxford Development Studies*, 30, 229–249.

Bird, G. and Rowlands, D. (2003). Political economy influences within the life cycle of IMF programmes. *The World Economy*, 26(9), 1255–1278.

Bird, G. and Rowlands, D. (2004). Financing balance of payments adjustment: Options in the light of the elusive catalytic effect. *Comparative Economic Studies*, 46, 468–486.

Bird, G. and Rowlands, D. (2006). IMF quotas: Constructing an international organisation using inferior building blocks. *Review of International Organizations*, 1, 153–171 (Reprinted as Chapter 2, this volume).

Bird, G. and Rowlands, D. (2007a). The IMF and the mobilisation of foreign aid. *Journal of Development Studies*, 43(5), 856–870.

Bird, G. and Rowlands, D. (2007b). Should it be curtains for some of the IMF's lending windows? *Review of International Organizations*, 2(3), 281–299 (Reprinted as Chapter 3, this volume).

Bird, G. and Rowlands, D. (2009). Financier or facilitator: The changing role of the IMF in low income countries, in J. Boughton and D. Lombardi (eds), *Finance, Development and the IMF*: Chapter 6. Oxford: Oxford University Press.

Bird, G. and Rowlands, D. (2010). The episodic and unpredictable nature of IMF lending: An empirical analysis. *The World Economy*, 33(10), 1280–1301.

Bird, G. and Willett, T.D. (2007). Multilateral surveillance: Is the IMF shooting for the stars? *World Economics*, 8(4), 167–189.

Corsetti, G., Guimaraes, B., and Roubini, N. (2003). International lending of last resort and moral hazard: A model of IMF catalytic finance. *NBER Working Paper* 10125.

Cottarelli, C., and Giannini, C. (2002). Bedfellows, hostages or perfect strangers? Global capital markets and the catalytic effect of IMF crisis lending. IMF Working Paper 02/193. Washington, DC: IMF.

Drazen, A. (2001). Conditionality and ownership in IMF lending: A political economy approach. *IMF Staff Papers*, 49 (special issue), 36–67.

Dhonte, P. (1997). Conditionality as an instrument of borrower credibility. *Papers on Policy Analysis and Assessment* 97/2, Washington, DC: International Monetary Fund.

Dreher, A. (2009). IMF conditionality: Theory and evidence. *Public Choice*, 141, 233–267.

Edwards, M.S. (2006). Signalling credibility? The IMF and catalytic finance. *Journal of International Relations and Development*, 9, 27–52.

Eichengreen, B., Kletzer, K. and Mody, A. (2006). The IMF in a world of private capital markets, *Journal of Banking and Finance*, 30, 1334–57.

Ghosh, A., Goretti, M., Joshi, B., Thomas, A., and Zalduendo, J. (2007). Modeling aggregate use of fund resources: Analytical approaches and medium-term projections. *IMF Working Paper*, WP/07/70.

Khan, M. and Sharma, S. (2008). IMF conditionality and country ownership of programs. *IMF Working Paper*, 01/142.

Mayer, W. and Mourmouras, A. (2004). IMF conditionality and the theory of special interest politics. *Comparative Economic Studies*, 46, 400–422.

Meltzer, A.H. (2000). *International Financial Institution Advisory Commission.* Washington, DC: United States House of Representatives.

Mody, A., and Saravia, D. (2006). Catalyzing capital flows: Do IMF-supported programs work as commitment devices? *Economic Journal*, 116(513), 843–867.

Morris, S., and Shin, H.S. (2006). Catalytic finance: When does it work? *Journal of International Economics*, 70, 161–177. Mussa, M. and Savastano, M. (2000). The IMF approach to economic stabilization, in B.S. Bernanke and J.J. Rotemberg (eds), NBER Macroeconomics Annual 1999: 79–122. Cambridge, MA: MIT Press.

Rowlands, D. (2001). The response of other lenders to the IMF. Review of International Economics, 9, 531–546.

Stone, R.W. (2008). The scope of IMF conditionality. *International Organization*, 62, 589–620.

Stiglitz, J. (2002). *Globalization and Its Discontents*. New York: W.W. Norton.

ul Haque, N.U. and Khan, M.S. (1998). Do IMF-supported programs work? A survey of the cross-country empirical evidence. *IMF Working Paper*, 98/169.

Williamson, J. (ed.) (1982). *IMF Conditionality*. Cambridge, MA: MIT Press.

2. IMF quotas

2.1 INTRODUCTION

Among the most fundamental issues currently facing the International Monetary Fund (IMF) are its role as a financing and adjustment institution, its economic crisis management duties, and its own internal governance. All of these issues have featured prominently in recent discussions about the IMF and have resulted in lively, if not downright heated, debate. Reports such as that of the Meltzer Commission (*The Meltzer Report*, 2000) have received close attention not only amongst policymakers and academics but also within the media. Critical commentaries of the Fund's role in crisis countries have generated wide interest and have been latched onto by those opposed to certain aspects of globalization.[1]

One central element of the Fund's operations, however, has avoided this upsurge in public interest and inspection. Despite its pivotal role in determining the IMF's governance structure, resource capacity, and lending behavior, membership quotas have attracted little attention outside of the Fund's own formal internal review process. It has been only relatively occasionally that the topic has cropped up in the academic literature (see, for example, Bird, 1987). More recently, however, and particularly in the context of governance, IMF quotas have received closer inspection (Buira, 2002; Kelkar, Yadav, and Chaudhry, 2004; and Kenen et al., 2004). Obscured by seemingly complex equations and often mired in important but technical debates about the merits of different measures of aggregate income or balance of payments variance, it is easy to see how the topic would test the attention of even seasoned IMF watchers. And yet quotas are presented by the Fund as its building blocks (IMF, 2002a). Are IMF quotas good or bad building blocks?

This chapter focuses on the practical and political economy dimensions of IMF quotas and their reform. As indicated by recent experience with the Twelfth General Review of Quotas, in which a consensus for change failed to emerge, the question of quotas is at the heart of institutional reform at the Fund, and consequently it is politically highly charged. Central to the debate over quotas is the fact that they attempt to play multiple roles, requiring any reform to strike a balance between conflicting ideals and opposing constituents. We examine the various roles played by the quota system, identify some of its deficiencies, and illustrate how the linkages between its functions both necessitate and confound the reform process. We then examine whether and how the reform impasse may be overcome, arguing that it is necessary to contemplate fairly profound changes to the Fund's institutional structure.

The layout of the chapter is as follows. By way of background, Section 2.2 provides a brief history and summary of IMF quotas. Section 2.3 examines two of the three key roles for quotas: determining the Fund's resource base and its members' borrowing capacities. It also briefly discusses the role of quotas in allocating Special Drawing Rights (SDRs). Section 2.4 investigates the implications of quotas for the governance of the IMF. Section 2.5 examines the linkages between these functions and the implications for reform from a political economy perspective. Section 2.6 offers a few concluding remarks.

2.2 IMF QUOTAS: THE BACKGROUND

Quotas are significant to the Fund's operations because they affect voting rights, subscriptions, the size of ordinary drawing rights and access to special facilities, as well as the distribution of Special Drawing Rights (SDRs).[2] However, from the outset of the Fund's operations in 1946 the formula used to calculate quotas was spurious, since agreement had already been reached about the total amount of quotas and the relative sizes of the quotas for the most powerful countries. A trial-and-error process was then used to devise a formula—the Bretton Woods formula— that generated the desired results.[3] In the early 1960s the Bretton Woods formula was re-specified, and four supplementary formulas were added in an attempt to reflect, among other things, the financing needs of small primary commodity-exporting nations. In addition, the equations were calculated using two different sets of data to take into account more subtle and improved current account balance of payments measures. Thus, from 1963 to 1983 the calculated quotas were based on a fairly complex relationship between ten different equations.[4] In 1983 the system currently used for calculating quotas came into effect, modifying the equations once more and eliminating the five not based on improved current account data.

Following the Eleventh General Review completed in 1998, and reflecting the concerns of some of the Fund's principal shareholders, an independent review of quota formulas was undertaken by a panel of eight external experts. This Quota Formula Review Group (QFRG) submitted its report in 2000.[5] However, its recommendations, which involved adopting a much-simplified formula, based on GDP averaged over three years and external variability comprising both current receipts and capital flows, were not warmly received (i.e., effectively rejected) by the Fund's Executive Board which agreed to carry forward the work of the panel (IMF, 2000a). Consideration of alternative formulas has constituted a part of the Fund's work program since then.[6] But there is no suggestion that consensus is any closer.

In addition to occasional refinements to the quota formulas, which affect calculated quotas, the 'actual' quotas themselves also undergo frequent review and adjustment. These can occur because of special events that need to be accommodated, such as the accession to membership of the IMF, or because of economic developments that dramatically alter the financial significance of a country, as in the case of Saudi Arabia in the 1970s. In these cases it is often just the quota for a single country or small group of countries that is adjusted.

More generally, however, there are periodic reviews of the full range of quotas that take place at least once every five years, of which the Twelfth General Review is the most recent. These reviews are the mechanism by which major changes in actual quotas are made, occasionally leading to substantial changes in total quotas as well as to a realignment of relative shares. Of the General Quota Reviews that there have been the first, second, third, tenth and twelfth (concluded in 2003) did not recommend any enlargement in overall quotas. The remaining eight (including one extraordinary review in 1958/1959) recommended quota increases averaging just over 44 percent, with a range from 30.7 percent (1965) to 60.7 percent (1959). When quotas have been generally increased, this has usually been based in part on existing actual quotas and in part on the calculated quotas derived from the quota formulas.

In terms of institutional governance, individual country quotas are the major determinant of relative voting power at the IMF. Furthermore, individual quotas affect countries' contributions and access to IMF resources, while collectively they determine the aggregate resource base of the IMF. As a consequence, quotas have important political economy dimensions, and frequently generate vigorous debate.

The struggle over quota assignments is well illustrated by the recent Twelfth Review. During the course of this review the Fund failed to come up with a definitive solution to the quota formula problem, and simultaneously failed to reach a consensus regarding a change in total subscriptions. Despite seminars, staff papers and the work of its own QFRG, the IMF's Executive Board failed to reach a conclusion at its October 2001 and June 2002 meetings. Indeed, an important feature of the Board's discussions of quotas has been the wide divergence of opinion.

Disagreements can exist because the formal equations are not the objective and authoritative or, for that matter, legally binding (Lister, 1984: 54) determinant of quotas. The Fund's major financial contributors have not been prepared to commit to a completely objective and binding formula for quota calculations. In the context of the Twelfth General Review, the US was reluctant to expand the resource base of the IMF or to see its share of votes decline. The US view, albeit somewhat caricatured, is that private capital markets should be the principal source of financing for emerging economies and that the IMF should not be lending long term to developing countries. Indeed, while conceding to a quota increase at the end of the 1990s, the US Congress made their acceptance conditional on the establishment of a commission to examine the role of the IMF and other (International Financial Institutions IFIs). Congress selected as the Chairman of the Commission someone who had publicly expressed doubts about the continuing need for the IMF. European economies have generally been associated with a more accommodating view but were reluctant to cede their influence. Developing countries would have welcomed an increase in their share of total votes and an enhanced role in IMF governance as well as greater access to IMF resources, but might have been unenthusiastic about increasing their obligations to the Fund. Moreover, many of the poorest countries draw from the Fund under the concessionary Poverty Reduction and Growth Facility and the resources for this do not come from quota-based subscriptions. An increase in quota assignments may thus have required these countries to contribute more in the form of subscriptions without really affecting the resource base from which they usually draw. A critical problem is that the quota system is simply charged with too many, potentially inconsistent, functions. We examine these in the following two sections.

2.3   RESOURCE ADEQUACY AND ACCESS

Quotas affect (but no longer wholly determine) each country's access to Fund resources on an individual basis. Collectively the subscriptions based on them provide a significant proportion of the resources available to the IMF through its General Resources Account (GRA), though these funds are not used for its concessionary lending window. Thus quotas arguably operate on both the supply and demand sides of IMF resource use, with critical implications for resource adequacy.

In identifying the tensions that have emerged in the IMF's quota system, it is instructive to examine how access to IMF resources has evolved. The IMF was initially established in the form of a credit union where most members were seen as being equally likely to require the kind of temporary financial assistance that the IMF was designed to provide. The theory and early practice of operating the Bretton Woods fixed exchange rate system suggested that wealthier industrial members were as likely to draw on IMF resources as the poorer members. Clearly the amounts drawn by the former would be larger due to their relative economic size, but then their contributions would also be larger. In fact, from 1947 to 1978, the single largest purchaser of IMF resources was the UK, accounting for over a quarter of all purchases. Industrial countries accounted for over 60 percent of all purchases. As there were mechanisms to encourage economic adjustment built into both IMF conditionality (as it eventually emerged) and the fixed exchange rate system, no country was envisaged as being perpetually a net contributor or client. Balance of payments problems were viewed as cyclical rather than endemic. The exception to this rule was the United States, whose dominant role as a supplier of finance was incorporated into the IMF's financial and governance structure. There were various reasons for the collapse of the Bretton Woods system in 1971–1973 (these are summarized in Bird, 1985) but amongst them was the failure to accommodate a balance of payments adjustment process for the US.

It took only a few years for the post-Bretton Woods IMF to become bifurcated. After 1976, industrial countries became absent from the list of credit-tranche agreement clients.[7] Effectively there emerged two types of members: rich country lenders and poor country borrowers. This division made the quota structure increasingly untenable and unsuitable as a means of determining simultaneously contributions and access. It also inevitably complicated questions of governance as well. Lenders may be expected to adopt different positions than debtors and will be unwilling to cede control to them.

In practice the IMF accommodated this division by breaking, or at least bending, the connection between quotas and borrowing limits. This innovation reflected the increased financial volatility that emerged after the early 1970s. While quotas had initially been based on national income, reserves, imports, export variance, and trade dependence, actual balance of payments structures and imbalances were often more dependent on financial flows that were not part of the quota calculation. Countries with substantial current account deficits, the presumed trigger for an IMF agreement under the Bretton Woods system, could avoid crises by relying on private or non-IMF official financing. However, when these alternative sources dried up, countries were forced to ask the IMF to fill a far larger financing gap than the quota structure had foreseen. The IMF responded to this new situation by increasingly lending above the original 100 percent of quota limit.

The crises in emerging markets in the 1990s illustrated just how disconnected the relationship had become. It became difficult to maintain the pretence of carefully planned and regulated credit limits, or to claim that quotas were appropriate to the task.[8] Beginning with the Tequila Crisis in 1994–95, financial crises triggered large IMF programs that bore little connection to the original lending limits. Funding requirements were only loosely linked to the volatility measures on the current account that were represented in the quota calculations. The clearest signal of the break between quotas and resource access came in the form of the Supplemental Reserve Facility, established at the end of 1997 in the midst of the Asian Crisis, which had no resource use limits linked to quotas.

In an extensive review of access to GRA resources the IMF (2003: 3, 6) still claimed that in the period after 1994 over 90 percent of arrangements fell within the normal access limits. But 85 percent of the Fund's commitments at the end of 2002 were concentrated in five arrangements with exceptional access. Of these cases, Argentina's use was over five times its total quota. Turkey borrowed resources over 15 times its quota (IMF, 2002c: 166–169). Thus, while claiming that quotas remained relevant, the Fund in fact adopted a pragmatic response to the borrowing needs of its members, unconstrained by quotas.

The fact that standard quota calculations have become completely inadequate as a measure of the real borrowing needs of members is reflected in the reforms suggested by the QFRG. The QFRG argued that financial openness and volatility should be part of the quota formula. However, it proved easier to acknowledge the need for reform in principle than to come to an agreement on the specifics of reform. Moreover, the formula revision favored by the QFRG highlighted the fact that reforming quotas to reflect the needs of its borrowing members necessarily implied unnecessary changes in access for advanced countries for whom IMF support is irrelevant. More importantly, however, quota changes to reflect borrowing needs imply more contentious changes to individual country subscriptions to the Fund, overall resource levels in the GRA, and, perhaps most significantly, voting power.

The absence of formal access limits that has emerged as a pragmatic response, however, must also be regarded with some concern. For as long as they operated, limits provided greater predictability in terms of financing packages, eased resource management problems for the Fund, and may have played a useful role in sending appropriate signals to financial markets. They may also have constrained the Fund's vulnerability to political manipulation both by key shareholders and large borrowers. Without a credible mechanism for denying exceptionally large loans, the IMF can be subjected to greater pressure to lend liberally to favored nations, as perhaps the loans to Argentina and Turkey illustrate. The debacle between the IMF and Argentina in the early 2000s illustrates, however, that when these loans become too large the IMF is compromised in its ability to disengage from a program for fear of jeopardizing its portfolio.[9]

Moreover, the quota system should have helped ensure that the Fund had sufficient resources to meet the demand from countries in balance of payments difficulties. If access limits are relaxed, what happens when the demand for IMF resources exceeds the supply of resources provided by quota-based subscriptions? The chances of this happening may be minimized in as much as the demanders of IMF resources are developing and emerging economies whereas the suppliers are advanced economies. But large loans to emerging economies can strain the IMF's liquidity and compromise the Fund's ability to handle financial crises without supplementary bilateral financing, thereby politicizing a process that was supposed to have been institutionalized.

In response to real or potential shortages, the IMF has made alternative arrangements to increase its resources beyond those generated by quotas. These arrangements include the General Arrangements to Borrow (GAB) and the New Arrangements to Borrow (NAB), which provide a means of supplementing IMF resources by borrowing from wealthier nations deemed sufficiently sound financially. The IMF also has the right to borrow from private markets, though it has never exercised this (see Bird and Rowlands, 2001).

In theory the IMF could also seek to enhance its resources through the allocation of Special Drawing Rights (SDRs). However, the initial idea that SDRs would become the principal reserve asset in the international financial system, and would be created on a regular basis to meet systemic reserve needs, has not materialized. National currencies, and in particular the US dollar, have continued to perform the role of the principal international reserve asset, and flexible exchange rates, combined with increased private capital flows, have undermined the need for SDRs in a systemic role. Regular allocations of SDRs have not occurred.

Moreover, SDRs were originally allocated on the basis of quotas since these were assumed to stand as a proxy for the demand to hold reserves. The implication was that countries would hold on to the SDRs they were allocated. In practice, poor countries have generally spent them and richer countries have generally acquired them. Thus the theoretical justification for using quotas as the basis for SDR allocation turned out to be misplaced. Some observers have suggested that SDRs should be allocated more exclusively to low-income countries to provide them with additional financial assistance, breaking away from the use of quotas (Bird, 1994). Others have simply viewed the role of quotas in determining allocations as irrelevant given the severely diminished role of SDRs. Having been overtaken by innovations in the international financial system, and crippled by conflict over their distribution, SDRs cannot be seen as a realistic means of supplementing the Fund's resource base.

So are IMF resources adequate or inadequate? G24 publications regularly emphasize the decline in IMF quotas relative to world trade, falling from 17 percent of total imports in 1950 to 4 percent in 2000 (Buira, 2002, 2004). The IMF's management sometimes alludes to a trend toward inadequacy; though some argue that this represents the bureaucratic pursuit of self-interest (Vaubel, 1991, 1994, 1996). In February 2002 the Fund's Executive Board requested its Treasurer's Department to quantify resource adequacy (IMF, 2002b). In general its report identifies a declining trend in resource adequacy since 1972, as measured by the ratio of total quotas to the GDP of members, calculated quotas, current payments, reserves, and the variability of current receipts. The report also notes that a similar conclusion is reached when other measures (such as Gross Financing Need) are used. Furthermore, the report claims that the unpredictability of claims on IMF resources (IMF, 2002b, point 31, and Rowlands, 1998) and the increase in private capital flows makes the current resource base too low to handle potential risks. Consequently, and with specific reference to the decline in the ratio of quotas to members' GDPs, the report recommends an increase in quotas to ensure that the IMF's own resources are adequate to meet the challenges of managing the international financial system.

However, there are counter arguments. The IMF recognizes that its immediate resource adequacy (liquidity) is linked to usable resources; the holdings of currencies of members deemed to be financially strong, minus current resource commitments. Its own calculated liquidity ratio (the ratio of usable resources to its liquid liabilities) shows high volatility but no declining trend over the period 1984–2002 (IMF, 2002c).[10]

Figure 2.1 shows the ratio of industrial country quotas (a proxy for usable resources) to various current account balance of payments measures, including world trade (total world exports), the total of all developing country current account deficits, and the total of all developing country current account deficits above 5 percent of GDP. Aside from the large drop in the ratio in the mid-1970s, there has been no discernible trend thereafter. Furthermore, the underlying question about the IMF's resource adequacy is adequate for what? However, it is perhaps unsurprising that G24, envisaging an enhanced lending role for the Fund, also views IMF resources as inadequate, whereas the US and others who envisage a truncated lending role view its resources as adequate or even excessive. Much will depend on one's perception of the relative importance of market failure in the context of private capital markets, and institutional failure in terms of the way in

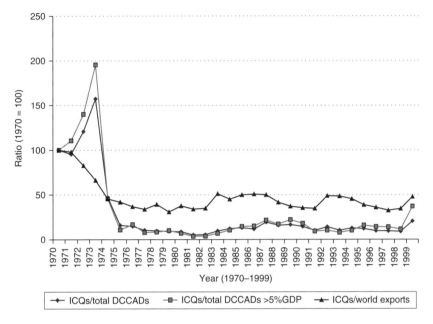

*Figure 2.1   Industrial country quotas (ICQs) to current account measures
ratio*

which the Fund conducts its affairs. The issues are not straightforward
and we do not examine them here. For a review of them see Bird and Joyce
(2001).

Where does this leave us? The de facto separation of its members into
lenders and borrowers has eroded the original credit union nature of the
modifications that have taken place to deal with resource constraints and
access limits have occurred in a pragmatic, but largely piecemeal way. The
dangers of this response are twofold. First, dealing with resource constraints through ad hoc borrowing agreements and bilateral contributions
introduces delays and additional political constraints on IMF operations.
These restrictions may be particularly costly during crises. Second, it
complicates resource management and accountability.

The overall conclusion with regards to the adequacy of the IMF's
resources and access to them cannot be separated from the broader debate
about the role of the Fund. However, little objective support for the quota
system emerges. Apart from the fact that actual quotas have deviated
sharply from those calculated on the basis of the quota formulas, they
have failed to generate the access to IMF resources deemed necessary in
large crisis country cases. They have failed to ensure that the Fund has

adequate resources in the sense that there have been efforts to supplement
them, and they have failed to generate the distribution of SDRs that was
either originally intended or that some critics would favor. Reforming the
quota system to meet the imperatives of access and resource management,
however, would have implications for the governance of the IMF as well.
In order to understand why the quota structure has not been modified in
the light of its obvious financial shortcomings, it is necessary to understand the political dimensions of quotas.

2.4   IMF AND GOVERNANCE

The IMF's organizational structure is currently based on quotas. The
ultimate decision-making body at the IMF is the Board of Governors,
comprising a governor (and an alternate) for each member country. Each
member has 250 basic votes plus one vote for every 100,000 SDRs of their
quota.[11] The distribution of votes is shown in Table 2.1. While the 250
basic votes technically generate a bias in favor of small countries, this does
nothing in practice to reduce the dominance of the advanced economies in
overall voting rights. Basic votes as a percentage of total votes have fallen
from about 10 percent up until the mid-1970s to barely 2 percent in 2002,
thus reducing the voting power of small, developing countries.

The day-to-day running of the IMF is managed by its Executive Board,
consisting of 24 members elected in constituencies. Eight of these consist
of single countries that have their own permanent seat (United States,
Japan, Germany, France, United Kingdom, Saudi Arabia, China, and

Table 2.1   The distribution of votes at the IMF

Consistency	Votes
Total votes in OECD-dominated constituencies	1,537,691
United States	371,743
Japan	133,378
EU single country constituencies	345,602
OECD-dominated constituencies	686,968
Total votes in Non-OECD-dominated constituencies	621,985
Non-OECD single country constituencies	193,751
Non-OECD constituencies with a dominant country	148,929
Non-OECD constituencies without a dominant country	279,305
Total of all votes (April, 2002)	2,159,676

Source: Calculated from IMF annual reports.

Russia). The remaining countries are organized into 16 multiple-country constituencies. Of these, five are dominated by a single member with more than half of the combined votes of the constituency (Brazil, Canada, India, Italy and Switzerland). Four have either clearly dominant members (Belgium, Netherlands, Argentina) or a reasonably dominant member (Australia). The remaining seven constituencies have a greater dispersion of votes amongst members. It is through their dominance of the multiple constituencies that the influence of European countries within the Fund is further enhanced (Kenen et al., 2004).

This governance structure is more complex in reality. Informally the IMF's decisions are made by consensus with few actual votes taken. On the one hand, the apparently smooth operation of the Fund in most decision-making areas may be attributable to the common beliefs and attitudes of its Governors and Board members given their origins in central banks and finance departments. On the other hand, the consensus principle does not mean strict unanimity. As Van Houtven (2002: 23) argues, consensus is determined by the Chair of the Board, and is meant to ensure that all key players and groups are broadly accepting of a decision. This consensus is also in part engineered inasmuch as technical aspects of debates are shaped by IMF staff who are clearly aware of the distribution of influence and power in the Executive Board. Moreover, the constituencies that contain both developed and developing countries may help to forge a consensus between initially opposed groups (Van Houtven, 2002: 68) although they could also, in principle, be a conduit for coercion. However, while the nature of the consensus process and extent to which it constrains actual decision-making is largely unknown (De Gregorio et al., 1999: 80), it may be safe to conclude that it cannot be entirely divorced from underlying voting power. Consensus is facilitated by the fact that the formal rules could be invoked. For most decisions a simple majority is sufficient.

For strategically more important decisions, however, special majorities are required.[12] It is in these areas that the element of power embedded in voting shares is most apparent. Two majority levels for key decisions are used: one at 70 percent and the other at 85 percent. Quota changes are among the decisions governed by the 85 percent requirement.[13] In fact this was the first key decision singled out for a special majority in the initial conception of the IMF (Lister, 1984: 82). The only country to wield an individual veto over these most critical changes is currently, and tradition-ally, the United States with just over 17 percent of the votes, although, as a group, the European Union also has an effective veto. Despite the general use of consensual decision-making, the contentious nature of quotas is therefore easily understood in terms of the formal voting rights that underpin the IMF as an organization.

The politics of IMF governance creates various dilemmas. Given they represent 85 percent of the total membership of the Fund, developing countries believe that they have an inappropriately small voice within the institution. As noted above, the emphasis on consensual decision-taking is not a substitute for voting rights. This line of argument has been clearly articulated by the G24, where it is suggested that the bias in favor of advanced countries undermines the legitimacy and representativeness, as well as ultimately the effectiveness of the IMF, since the majority of members feel that they exert insufficient influence over the Fund's operations (Buira, 2004). But the arguments have also been endorsed outside the G24 (see Kenen et al., 2004). Advanced countries point out that actual quotas disproportionately favor developing countries by comparison with the calculated quotas, and even developing countries may be wary of increasing their voting rights if this simultaneously encourages advanced economies to become any further disengaged from the IMF, bypassing the Fund in favor of other decision-making bodies that they dominate, such as the G7. The external review of quotas, for which developing countries pushed, recommended a new formula that would have increased the voting share of advanced economies. With increasing membership, advanced countries have sought to retain their veto and their powerful position within the governance of the IMF by manipulating the majorities required for key decisions. It is not therefore the objectivity of the quota system that determines the governance of the IMF but rather power politics. The quota system has simply been the instrument through which the power politics has been played out.

The IMF governance structure and reform process allows past political influence to become perpetuated within and through the Fund. Consequently the Fund's political structure puts at risk the institution's role in international financial governance. This danger is most clearly seen in the frequent abandonment of the IMF as the venue of choice in discussions relating to international financial reform. This process is especially true when the financial system faces unprecedented events, such as the breakdown of the fixed exchange rate system, the debt crisis, or other financial crises. The Financial Stability Forum, G20, and the plethora of discussion groups and arrangements associated with the Bank for International Settlements, all attest to the perceived deficiencies of the IMF as a forum for discussing, and sometimes overseeing, fundamental reform.[14]

So governance at the IMF also appears to be far from ideal, certainly in terms of criteria such as legitimacy, representativeness and accountability, and is in as much need of reform as the Fund's financial operations. The concern is that in remedying these governance-related deficiencies, the future effectiveness of the Fund may be endangered. Although effectiveness may also be impaired if developing countries feel under-represented, as Van Houtven (2002: 8) points out, there is no quota formula that is sensible from a financial perspective and that would also solve the governance issue. What has emerged is an ad hoc compromise in which the politics of IMF governance drives the quota system and the economic consequences of this are then handled by expediency. Is it possible to do better than this?

2.5 REFORMING IMF QUOTAS: BROAD PRINCIPLES

There is no simple solution to the reform of quotas. There will be underlying conflicts of interest, and progress will depend on compromise. Given the multiplicity of roles performed by quotas, it is not surprising that consensus for reforming the quota system has been impossible to achieve. The system initially balanced the responsibilities and privileges of IMF members. With the division of this membership into those that borrow and those that provide resources, this balance disappeared. In some cases individual countries must weigh up the potentially contradictory effects of a quota increase on their contributions of hard currency on the one hand, and their nominal access to resources on the other. An increase in the share of developing country quotas would increase their relative voting rights but also their obligations. The lender–borrower fault lines that generate tension over resource provision and access largely coincide with divisions over governance and international financial management. Despite the sometimes significant differences within these two broad groups of members, problems with the quota structure have increasingly become defined as a zero-sum game based on differentiated roles and relative power. Such fundamental conflict within the decision-making structure of the IMF has prevented meaningful restructuring and is likely to lead to a continuing reform impasse. Can the impasse be overcome? Without proposing specific and detailed reforms, it may be useful to identify some broad principles upon which reform may be based. These principles are hardly new. They were, for example, enunciated and examined in some detail by one of us in the 1980s (Bird, 1987). More recently the same basic ideas have been reaffirmed by others (see, for example, Kelkar et al., 2004).

If we take as a starting point the IMF's mandate to promote international monetary and financial stability, it is possible to identify some of the factors that need to underpin its structure. Fund resources need to be adequate to handle its financing responsibilities, with each member's obligations being grounded in their capacity to provide these resources. Access to IMF resources, and by extension SDR distribution, however, should reflect financial needs. Finally, governance must be such as to allow all members to feel that their views are taken into account and represented, but at the same time must be sensitive to both financial and political power and the need for effective operation.

2.5.1 Subscriptions and Resource Adequacy

A member's subscription should reflect its ability to provide resources and should be firmly based on wealth. Beneath some level of GDP per capita, poor countries could either be exempt from making subscriptions to the Fund altogether or could be asked to make only nominal contributions in terms of their own domestic currencies. Paying such a subscription might make them more committed to the institution but could create additional domestic fiscal problems. Poor countries are by definition short of foreign exchange and it may seem illogical that they have to contribute it to the Fund in exchange for access to credit. Therefore, in terms of providing useful resources, while minimizing resource burdens on the poor, GDP could serve as the sole or at least the primary determinant of contributions.[15]

In terms of designing a subscription system, it may be useful to think of three groups of member countries. One group consisting of relatively poor countries should not be required to make any subscription in the form of hard currency. At the other end is the group of wealthy industrial countries that have not made any significant drawing on the Fund for over 25 years;[16] their contributions should constitute the vast majority of the IMF's resources. A third group lies between these two; it consists of countries within the income range in which occasional (and occasionally very large) drawings from the IMF occur. These countries could provide an intermediate level of financing, including hard currencies.

A related issue in restructuring subscriptions to the IMF is to determine the overall amount of resources that the Fund needs. With a link to GDP, contributions would automatically rise in step with global economic growth. However, this might not always guarantee that the Fund would have adequate resources. But, as noted earlier, determining adequacy requires a clear definition of the role of the IMF. Is it an adjustment or a financing institution? What is its role in the context of crises?

Should the IMF have enough resources on a permanent basis to handle crises that only occur periodically, or should the Fund's resource base be temporarily expanded as needed through the GAB, NAB or private borrowing? If resources are permanently in place, some may fear that the IMF will push loans, especially if institutional welfare depends on the quantity of lending. On the other hand, a delayed response to crisis may mean that it is managed less efficiently.

It is reasonably easy to deal with the resource provisioning of the IMF while minimizing the burden of membership on poorer members. By manipulating the level and allocation of quotas, and the proportion of quotas paid in domestic currency, it is possible to generate any combination of IMF resource levels, relative voting shares, and access for countries that need to borrow. But identifying an adequate resource base first requires a consensus about the role of the Fund, which in turn affects political considerations and questions of resource access.

2.5.2 Access

Should the IMF be a fully-fledged international lender of last resort? Should it completely fill the financial vacuum created when there are outflows of private capital? These questions strike at the very heart of the debate over the Fund's role and it is impossible to supply a definitive statement about access to IMF resources until they are answered.

To fulfill its current Articles, the IMF must ensure that access depends on balance of payments need. To all intents and purposes, however, the IMF has already broken the connection between quotas and access. The question is therefore whether retaining the notion of quota-based access limits has any value, or should each case be decided on its own merits?

Even a modified quota formula may be too restrictive. On the one hand, it is difficult to anticipate all future circumstances in the context of a transparent and simple formula. On the other hand, leaving everything to the circumstances of the time may be excessively flexible and may leave IMF lending open to whimsy and serendipity. The difficulty is in balancing the need to provide sufficient resources to avoid damaging the international financial system or compromising the welfare of the people it is supposed to serve, with the need to provide administrative accountability, predictability, and protection from undue interference.

Any system would have to lie between the two extremes of lending programs that are credible but restrictive and flexible but arbitrary. This would most likely require introducing an access formula that would endeavor to reflect the sources of balance of payments vulnerability both in terms of current account and capital account shocks. It would also contain a scale factor in terms of GDP or total trade. Perhaps, however, any resulting formula should only be a management tool. It should provide a benchmark against which the size of IMF lending to individual countries could be judged. Lending above these limits could occur, but, to avoid excessive political influences on lending, this would need to be overseen by some form of independent review panel. This oversight could be conducted ex ante, but this would generate undue delay. A better alternative might be to encourage the Independent Evaluation Office to audit cases where lending was significantly in excess of quota limits. Systemically the Fund should also focus on how best to catalyze others to lend, either private capital markets or aid donors, since this would reduce claims on its own resources.

2.5.3   Governance

The IMF plays a critical role in the international financial system. It disburses some money on a concessional basis, and can, in principle, affect the operation of private capital markets and the delivery of official capital flows. It also helps to create rules for behavior in international financial and monetary matters. Its programs blend policy conditionality with adjustment financing. Control over these functions is certainly a non-trivial matter for members.

   To the extent that they provide the bulk of usable resources in the GRA and the concessional facilities, advanced creditor economies will demand ultimate control. If they are pressured to give it up, they may simply withdraw their support for the IMF which relies on them for its resources. As former British Prime Minister Thatcher stated, 'there was no way in which I was going to put British deposits into a bank which was totally run by those on overdraft' (cited in Bakker, 1996: 52).

   But the IMF does more than simply provide resources. It establishes the rules under which these resources will be provided, as well as the general rules for the conduct of the international financial system. The developing and emerging market countries have a clear stake in how the IMF functions, and considerable experience to bring to the discussions. They should not be sidelined. The failure of the IMF to balance its financial role with its consultative and systemic management role has led to its diminished stature in both. These roles must be reconciled or separated.

   While the tradition of the IMF has been to seek consensus and thereby dilute the degree to which its governance is fractured into an adversarial system, problems still arise in building political and governance structures on a voting system nominally anchored in economic-based formulas. From amongst the advanced economies, the US, that has traditionally maintained a dominant role within the IMF, will be reluctant to relinquish it. The same may be said of Europe. One can envisage a stand-off that will stymie the Fund's operations. Changing nothing may consign the Fund to irrelevance because of its inability to adapt to new global financial realities, while significant changes risk the disengagement of key players upon whose presence the system relies. Clearly this dilemma is difficult to resolve. There is no straightforward technically superior solution. And even if there were, it would need to be politically acceptable, reflecting both the reality of the current distribution of power in the international system as well as the distribution of voting power in the Fund's own current governance structure. Options include, first, restoring the significance of basic votes to a level that was initially intended, accounting for 10 percent or 11 percent of total votes. A second option, favored by the G24 and other outside experts (Kenen et al., 2004) is to reduce the relative votes of European countries and raise those of developing and emerging economies. The logic for this is that European countries exercise disproportionate influence relative to GDP. Much of their trade is intra-European, and 12 European countries now share the same currency, the euro. European countries could, for example, be divided into two constituencies within the Executive Board representing the euro and non-euro areas. European countries may resist such proposals and may have to be offered political incentives to entice them to agree (Kenen et al., 2004 discuss what these might be). Another related possibility would be to revisit the composition of constituencies in order to enhance the influence of developing and emerging economies within them.

There is little alternative to political compromise. A management and governance structure has to be found which allows developing countries to have an effective voice and exert an influence on discussions that affect them but also allows advanced economies to retain the degree of control associated with their creditor status. The current quota system is unsatisfactory in this regard, and finding an alternative has been made more difficult by the other functions that quotas seek to achieve. A challenging task has thereby in effect been made impossible. By reforming subscriptions, access, and resource adequacy it may become easier to resolve the governance issue. If not, the IMF will likely lose its role in international financial management to institutional arrangements that better reflect the current global views on power and legitimacy.

But, of course, current governance structures will constrain reform. The hope must be that growing recognition of the deficiencies of the current quota system and the implications of these for the future relevance of the IMF will eventually galvanize a momentum for reform.

2.6   CONCLUDING REMARKS

Following a period of relative neglect, a number of external and internal reports on IMF quotas has been written since the end of the 1990s. However, there has been no progress in reforming the quota system. The report of the Quota Formula Review Group found little favor within the Executive Board—or indeed elsewhere—and the Fund's staff were sent away to think again following their initial attempts to come up with more acceptable formulas. The whole question of the specific design of quota formulas can appear arcane and irrelevant. This is unfortunate since quotas are, to quote the *IMF Survey*, September 2002, the basic building blocks of the IMF. Subscriptions, drawing rights and votes within the Fund are influenced by quotas.

The existing quota system is deficient in a number of ways. Actual quotas differ from calculated ones, so that objectivity and transparency are lost. On important occasions quotas miscalculate the demand for IMF resources and they may not ensure resource adequacy. Moreover, they provide a distribution of voting rights that many countries regard as inappropriate for a global institution.

The analysis in this chapter emphasizes that the debate about quotas in fact cuts to the very essence of the Fund's operations. It should be given a much higher profile than it has been. At the same time, given the design flaws of the existing quota system, it is difficult to see how current problems can be overcome by simply modifying existing quota formulas. As currently constituted, quotas are being asked to do too much. One instrument will not achieve all the targets that it has been set.

More fundamental reform that goes beyond tinkering with formulas is needed if the Fund's role as the premier international financial institution is to be maintained and enhanced. The solution suggested here is to split up the various functions that, at present, one quota is being asked to perform. Existing quotas were designed when the IMF was envisaged as a credit union. It no longer is and quotas should be reformed to reflect this. Countries should contribute to the Fund according to their ability to pay based on GDP, and should have access to Fund resources according to their balance of payments need. In terms of governance, all countries that are affected by the decisions made should be able to contribute a reasonable input into influencing those decisions. However, equity needs to be constrained by expediency. Poor countries may gain little if a more powerful voice is purchased at the cost of losing the support of the advanced economies for the Fund's operations. It is difficult to envisage the Fund's major shareholders giving up their control. Political pragmatism will dictate the outcome.

If quotas are indeed the building blocks of the Fund, they are inferior building blocks and an IMF which uses them will be relatively unstable and insecure. They provide a weak foundation for the Fund's operations. It is important that the quota system is reformed. Putting off decisions and rolling over current arrangements is not the answer and will tend to gradually erode the Fund's role in the world economy. Undeniably reform is difficult since it relates to fundamental issues, including the lending capacity of the Fund, its governance, and the governance of the international financial system. But side-stepping the underlying issues has led to a series of ad hoc and possibly ill thought out palliatives. If reforming the IMF is part of a new international financial architecture, the Fund needs to address its own financial architecture, and the reform of quotas is a key component of this.

NOTES

1. Bird (2001) provides a summary and discussion of the principal issues involved in the current debate about the IMF.
2. SDRs are the IMF's unit of account linked to four major currencies and also constitute a financial resource created by the IMF and distributed, on occasion, to its members. Members of the IMF pay subscriptions equivalent to their quotas. Up to 25 percent of the subscription is paid in the form of international reserve assets specified by the IMF (SDRs or widely accepted foreign reserve currencies such as US dollars, Euros, Japanese yen or pounds sterling) with the rest being paid in the member's own currency. Each member of the IMF has 250 basic votes plus one additional vote for each SDR 100,000 of quota. Access limits to IMF resources via the range of facilities that it offers are based in part on quotas. Similarly, allocations of SDRs are set in proportion to member countries' quotas.
3. See Mikesell (1994) for a fascinating first-hand account. Lister (1984: 53) points out that even after these computational gymnastics the deviation of actual from the computed quotas were enormous, with the highest difference being 75 percent.
4. The final calculated quota was the higher of the revised original Bretton Woods formula and the average of the two lowest of the additional formulae. See IMF (2001a: 7–8, and Annex II).
5. For a more detailed and technical review of quota issues, see IMF (2000a, b). Jha and Saggar (2000) provide a valuable and more independent overview and suggest their own alternative formula.
6. See IMF (2001a, b).
7. The first 25 percent of a country's quota, called the reserve tranche, can be accessed by a country without negotiating an IMF program. The remaining 75 percent of the quota is paid in the country's domestic currency, and for most developing and emerging market countries is thus not very useful for dealing with balance of payments problems. Loans of hard currencies above the reserve tranche amount are considered to be from the upper tranche purchases that are not accessible without a negotiated program.
8. IMF (1998) lays out very clearly just how complex the IMF's lending facility structure became, and how lending under these facilities was linked (or not) to quotas.
9. Excessive lending also damages the IMF's reputation and has wider implications for international finance. In the case of the Argentina program, private lenders have challenged the preferred creditor status of the IMF, presumably because they see reckless IMF lending as jeopardizing their own repayment prospects.
10. The calculation has only been made since 1984, however, so a longer time series is not available.
11. Thus, for example, Angola, with a quota of SDR 286,300,000 has 3,113 votes (2,863 + 250).
12. See Lister (1984) for a discussion of how these special majorities have evolved.

13. For a list of decisions governed by special majority, see De Gregorio et al. (1999: 80–81).
14. In the case of the G20, for example, it was seen as a necessary development given the perceived lack of legitimacy for the G7 in dealing with fundamental questions of international economic and financial management (see the G20 website). The perceived need was to construct a forum that balanced the voices of advanced and developing countries. In the end, however, the composition of the G20 was remarkably similar to that of the IMF's Executive Board, which was clearly dismissed as an inappropriate venue for such important discussions. See also Kenen et al. (2004).
15. There is still a technical question of which GDP measure to use, noting that purchasing power parity adjustments tend to increase the measured GDP of poor countries (Buira, 2002; Kelkar et al., 2004).
16. Though given the enormity of the current US fiscal and current account deficit, and the potential for substitution away from the US dollar, we should be cautious in assuming that large industrial countries will never need IMF assistance.

REFERENCES

Bakker, A.F.P. (1996). *International Financial Institutions*. London: Longman.

Bird, G. (1985). *World Finance and Adjustment*. London: Macmillan.

Bird, G. (1987). Financing the Fund and reforming quotas. In Bird, G. *International Financial Policy and Economics Development*. Basingstoke: Macmillan.

Bird, G. (1994). Economic assistance to low income countries: Should the link be resurrected? *Essays in International Finance*, 193. Princeton, NJ: Princeton University Press.

Bird, G. (2001). A suitable case for treatment: Understanding the on-going debate about the IMF. *Third World Quarterly*, 22(5), 823–848.

Bird, G. and Joyce, J.P. (2001). Remodelling the multilateral financial institutions. *Global Governance*, 7(1), 75–93.

Bird, G. and Rowlands, D. (2001). Catalysis or direct borrowing: the role of the IMF in mobilising private capital. *The World Economy*, 24(1), 81–98.

Bird, G. and Rowlands, D. (2002). Do IMF programmes have a catalytic effect on other international capital flows? *Oxford Development Studies*, 30(3), 229–249.

Buira, A. (2002). A new voting structure for the IMF. *G24 Research Paper*.

Buira, A. (2004). The governance of the IMF in a global economy. G24 Research Paper.

De Gregorio, J., Eichengreen, B., Ito, T., and Wyplosz, C. (1999). *An Independent and Accountable IMF*. Geneva: ICMB International Center for Monetary and Banking Studies.

G20 website, www.G20.org.

International Financial Institution Advisory Commission (IFIAC) (2000). *Report of the IFIAC (The Meltzer Report)*. Washington, DC: US Government Printing Office.

IMF (2000a). *Report to the IMF Executive Board of the Quota Formula Group*. (EBAP/00/52, 5/01/00 and Supplements 1, 2 and 3 all May 1, 2000).

IMF (2000b). *Staff commentary on the external review of the quota formulas* (EBAP/00/66, June 7, 2000).

IMF (2001a). Alternative quota formulas: Considerations, www.imf.org/external/np/tre/quota/2001/eng/aqfc.pdf (accessed 19 October, 2015).

IMF (2001b). *External review of quota formulas—quantification* (EBAP/01/29, April 13, 2001).

IMF (2002a). Alternative quota formulations: Further considerations, www.imf. org/external/np/tre/quota/2002/eng/050302.pdf (accessed October 19, 2015).

IMF (2002b). Twelfth general review of quotas—further considerations, www. imf.1org/external/np/tre/quota/2002/eng/080902.htm#f1 (accessed October 19, 2015).

IMF (2002c). IMF annual report. Washington, DC: IMF.

IMF (2003). Review of access policy under the credit tranches and the Extended Fund Facility, January 14, 2003, www.imf.org/external/np/tre/access/2003/ pdf/011403a.pdf (accessed October 19, 2015).

Jha, R. and Saggar, M. (2000). Towards a more rational IMF quota structure: Suggestions for the creation of a new international financial architecture. *Development and Change*, 31(3), 579–604.

Kelkar, V., Yadav, V., and Chaudhry, P. (2004). Reforming the governance of the International Monetary Fund. *The World Economy*, 27(5), 727–744.

Kenen, P.B., Shafer, J.R, Wicks, N.L., and Wyplosz, C. (2004). *International Economic and Financial Cooperation: New Issues, New Actors, New Responses.* Geneva reports on the world economy, number 6. International Center for Monetary and Banking Studies, and Centre for Economic Policy Research.

Lister, F. (1984). *Decision-making Strategies for International Organizations: The IMF Model.* Denver, CO: University of Colorado.

Mikesell, R.F. (1994). The Bretton Woods debate: A memoir. *Essays in International Finance*, No 192, Princeton, NJ: International Finance Section, Princeton University.

Rowlands, D. (1998). Quantitative approaches to sovereign risk analysis: Implications for IMF responses, in S. Schmeidl and H. Adelman (eds), *Early Warning and Early Response*. Columbia: Columbia International Affairs Online (CIAO), Columbia University Press.

Van Houtven, L. (2002). *Governance of the IMF: Decision making, institutional oversight, transparency and accountability*. Pamphlet Series No. 53. Washington, DC: IMF.

Vaubel, R. (1991). The political economy of the International Monetary Fund, in R. Vaubel and T.D. Willett (eds), *The Political Economy of International Organisations: A Public Choice Perspective*: 204–244. Boulder, CO: Westview.

Vaubel, R. (1994). The political economy of the IMF: A public choice analysis, in D. Bandow and J. Vasquez (eds), *Perpetuating Poverty: The World Bank, The IMF and the Developing World*. Washington, DC: The Cato Institute.

Vaubel, R. (1996). Bureaucracy at the IMF and the World Bank: A comparison of the evidence. *The World Economy*, 19(2), 195–210.

3. The IMF's lending facilities

3.1 INTRODUCTION

Questions are increasingly being asked about many aspects of the International Monetary Fund's organizational structure. Common amongst them are those that relate to governance; including the structure of the Executive Board, quotas and voting rights. However, rather less attention has been paid to the range of lending facilities or windows through which the IMF makes its loans. In some ways this is surprising since one dimension of the claim that the Fund has exhibited 'mission creep' may be seen in the proliferation of IMF lending windows. From a situation in the early 1950s when all IMF lending was conducted via stand-by arrangements, by the end of the 1990s there were six facilities under which client countries could, in principle, borrow from the Fund.

From amongst them the most frequently used windows, in addition to conventional stand-bys (SBA), were the Extended Fund Facility (EFF) and the Poverty Reduction and Growth Facility (PRGF). The implicit logic of having an array of facilities must be that they serve different purposes. Certainly PRGFs differ from SBAs and EFFs in as much as assistance is granted at concessionary rates and only to low-income countries. Furthermore, the Fund's rubric relating to each of its facilities suggests that they meet different needs. Thus whereas stand-bys are aimed at achieving macroeconomic stabilization via measures designed to manipulate aggregate demand and the exchange rate, extended facilities are intended to go beyond this and help achieve structural adjustment. They are designed to strengthen the long term balance of payments. But are the Fund's intentions matched by reality? Is it possible to pick up discernible differences in the economic characteristics of countries that draw from the IMF under different facilities? Up to now there is no study that has sought to answer this question in a formal fashion.

Existing research into IMF lending has focused on it in aggregate and has attempted to better understand the factors that determine IMF arrangements in general. Early studies concentrated on economic determinants, but more recently political and institutional factors have also been incorporated. The methodological approach has been to combine

IMF arrangements from a range of facilities to construct the sample and little attention has been paid to the selection of the particular facility under which an arrangement takes place. The question therefore arises as to whether the circumstances in which countries use different IMF facilities themselves differ. Answering this question has both methodological and policy implications. From a methodological point of view, if the circumstances differ then aggregating arrangements from under a number of facilities together in large sample studies of IMF lending may obscure facility-specific relationships. If the circumstances are broadly similar then, while the findings of large sample studies of IMF lending may be more secure, at the same time, a policy issue arises, since the Fund's justification for retaining a range of facilities is that they meet different needs and are appropriate in different circumstances. If, in fact, there seem to be no, or at least only few discernible differences in the circumstances in which different facilities are used, the wisdom of keeping the current portfolio of lending windows intact is called into doubt. Might there be scope for reorganization and rationalization? This issue has been considered by the IMF fairly recently (IMF, 2000) but the report contained only informal empirical analysis. Relatively modest reforms were forthcoming and these did not fundamentally alter the facilities upon which we focus here.

Based on an analysis of IMF programs over the period 1978–2000, in this chapter we seek to discover whether there are statistically significant differences in the circumstances in which member countries of the IMF borrow under the Extended Fund Facility and the Poverty Reduction and Growth Facility as opposed to conventional stand-bys. We consider not only economic factors but also political ones, and we therefore build on the recent research into the determinants of IMF arrangements.

The chapter is organized in the following way. Section 3.2 provides a brief account of the evolution of IMF facilities, and reports the Fund's rationale for their separate status. Section 3.3 presents some descriptive statistics to show the extent to which the facilities upon which we concentrate have been used in the period since toward the end of the 1970s. Section 3.4 offers an informal theoretical framework within which the possible influences over the use of different facilities may be analysed. The section goes on to use this framework to suggest possible reasons for the variations in the usage of facilities reported in Section 3.3. Section 3.5 draws on the theoretical framework more formally as the basis for a regression analysis of the use of individual facilities. In essence this section tests whether the empirical evidence is consistent with the claims made by the IMF as reflected by the description of the facilities that it presents in its official documentation. Finally, Section 3.6 offers some concluding remarks which consider the policy implications of our findings. It reviews the logic of the

Fund's current portfolio of lending windows, but in particular critically examines the case for retaining SBAs and EFFs in their current form.

3.2 THE IMF'S LENDING FACILITIES: BRIEF DESCRIPTION AND HISTORY[1]

By way of background, this section provides a brief description of the Fund's financial facilities, and the circumstances in which they were introduced. The IMF has recently reviewed its facilities, and a detailed and current description of them may be found in the associated papers available on the Fund's website (www.imf.org).

Since 1952 the Fund has used stand-by arrangements to make financing available to member countries with a balance of payments need. The typical SBA is for 12–18 months, with financing being conditional on the borrower fulfilling specified performance criteria; conditionality is phased over a series of credit tranches, which become progressively stricter. Loans must be repaid within 3 and a quarter to 5 years.

In an attempt to assist developing countries deal with the problem of export instability the Fund introduced the Compensatory Financing Facility (CFF) in 1963. The facility has been retained although it has also been modified on a number of occasions.[2] In 1968, the Buffer Stock Financing Facility (BSFF) was set up as a way of offsetting the balance of payments consequences of participating in buffer stock schemes.

The problems encountered by developing countries also lay behind the introduction of the Extended Fund Facility (EFF) in 1974, which aimed to provide medium-term finance to help with structural adjustment, particularly for economies 'suffering serious payments imbalance relating to structural maladjustments in production and trade and where price and cost distortions have been widespread and characterized by slow growth and an inherently weak balance of payments position which prevents pursuit of an active development policy'. Also in the 1970s the Fund introduced, as a temporary measure, the Oil Facility (1974–76) to help countries deal with the balance of payments consequences of the four-fold increase in the price of oil in 1973. To help poorer countries, a Subsidy Account was introduced supported by a Trust Fund financed by gold sales, which allowed the rate of charge on drawings under the Oil Facility to be reduced.

The Trust Fund was used again in the late 1980s to help establish the Structural Adjustment Facility (SAF) and then the Enhanced Structural Adjustment Facility (ESAF). These facilities were therefore different from stand-bys, the CFF, the BSFF and the EFF inasmuch as they were not financed from the General Resources Account (GRA) of the IMF and were on concessionary terms. However, they were similar in terms of the trend toward increasing conditionality. Indeed the SAF, which was perceived as having fairly weak conditionality, was quickly supplemented and soon replaced by the ESAF where conditionality often incorporated not only the traditional elements of monetary, fiscal and exchange rate policy, but also structural conditionality relating to the micro economy and openness.

The 1990s witnessed a further proliferation of lending facilities, with the introduction of the low conditionality Systemic Transformation Facility (STF; 1993–95) to assist countries in transition (CITs), and the Supplemental Reserve Facility (SRF) in 1997, 'to supplement resources made available under SBAs and the EFF in order to provide financial assistance for exceptional balance of payments difficulties owing to a large short-term financing need resulting from a sudden and disruptive loss of market confidence.' Two years later in 1999 the Fund introduced—but subsequently discontinued—the Contingent Credit Lines (CCL) which had been intended to provide a 'precautionary line of defence' for countries with 'strong economic policies' against balance of payments problems resulting from international financial contagion.

The Fund had come a long way from the days when stand-bys were seen as an adequate modality for dealing with all balance of payments difficulties. Had it come too far? In 2000 it began a full review of its array of lending facilities. Critics—one of the authors included (Bird, 1995)—had for some time been suggesting that there was scope for rationalization or, in the terminology preferred by the Fund, 'streamlining' (or even 'house-cleaning'). What emerged from this review?

The Fund decided to discontinue the BSFF, not unreasonably since no drawing had been made under the facility for 16 years, and no commodity agreements existed for which BSFF financing was eligible, and to remodel its compensatory lending window by removing the newer contingency element; 'complexity and rigidity' had meant that this element had been little used.[3] Some Executive Directors apparently favored eliminating the CFF altogether on the grounds that it is difficult to measure the extent of an export shortfall and the extent to which it is temporary, that resources are provided 'up front' in a way that 'can weaken economic reform incentives', and that adjustment is difficult to ensure outside an SBA or EFF (or indeed an ESAF, which was modified and renamed the Poverty Reduction and Growth Facility in 1999). However, the majority of Executive Directors on the Fund's Board favored retaining the CFF provided it was confined 'to cases where arrangements are in place or in which the balance of payments position is deemed satisfactory apart from a temporary export shortfall or cereal import excess'.

The Executive Board also opted to retain the EFF, but confirmed that users of this facility would be expected to have only 'limited access to private capital' and 'an appropriately strong structural reform program to deal with the embedded institutional or economic weaknesses'. The EFF was now presented as an appropriate facility for those countries graduating from a PRGF program or for CITs without 'enough' access to capital markets.

This brief historical tour of the IMF's lending windows provides a sense of how facilities and programs have evolved. New problems as perceived by the IMF lead to new lending facilities. However, it also hints at an element of institutional inertia in terms of the range of lending windows. An important question is whether or not the current configuration of facilities is appropriate. Do they all fulfill a distinct function? We shall attempt to answer this question later in this chapter. In the next section, however, we provide some descriptive statistics on the use made of the Fund's facilities.

3.3   DESCRIPTIVE STATISTICS

Table 3.1 provides data on the use of stand-bys, EFFs and SAFs/ESAFs/PRGFs over the period 1978–2005. The EFF had been introduced in 1974, but only three EFF programs were arranged until 1979 (two in 1976 and one in 1977). Table 3.1 reveals that, in terms of the number of arrangements, EFFs were relatively popular between 1979 and 1983. Then, for about ten years, they were little used with no more than three arrangements in any one year being made, and with some years when there was only one or none (1985–89). The period between 1993 and 2000 saw an increase in the use of extended arrangements but from 2001 to 2005 they were again little used.

There are generally many more SBAs than EFFs. In some years, and in terms of non-concessionary lending, only stand-bys have been arranged (1978, 1985, 1987, 2002, 2004, 2005). Having said this, there have also been isolated years or short periods when the relative popularity of SBAs as compared with EFFs has diminished somewhat. This was the case in the early 1980s and again in the brief period 1997 to 2000. Indeed in 1999 there were only five SBAs compared with four EFFs.

Given the longer duration of EFFs it is unsurprising to find, as shown in Table 3.1, that the amount of resources committed under EFFs is generally much larger than that under SBAs, although there are exceptions to this pattern (as in 1999).

Table 3.2 provides data on the use of facilities in a slightly different way by examining arrangements 'in effect' rather than 'approved'. Given the

Table 3.1   IMF arrangements approved during financial years ended April 30, 1978–2005

Financial year	Number of arrangement					Amounts committed under arrangements (in millions of SDRs)				
	Stand-by	EFF	SAF	PRGF	Total	Stand-by	EFF	SAF	PRGF	Total
1978	18	–	–	–	18	1,285	–	–	–	1,285
1979	14	4	–	–	18	508	1,093	–	–	1,601
1980	24	4	–	–	28	2,479	797	–	–	3,276
1981	21	11	–	–	32	5,198	5,221	–	–	10,419
1982	19	5	–	–	24	3,106	7,908	–	–	11,014
1983	27	4	–	–	31	5,450	8,671	–	–	14,121
1984	25	2	–	–	27	4,287	95	–	–	4,382
1985	24	–	–	–	24	3,218	–	–	–	3,218
1986	18	1	–	–	19	2,123	825	–	–	2,948
1987	22	–	10	–	32	4,118	–	358	–	4,476
1988	14	1	15	–	30	1,702	245	670	–	2,617
1989	12	1	4	7	24	2,956	207	427	955	4,545
1990	16	3	3	4	26	3,249	7,627	37	415	11,328
1991	13	2	2	3	20	2,786	2,338	15	454	5,593
1992	21	2	1	5	29	5,587	2,493	2	743	8,825
1993	11	3	1	8	23	1,971	1,242	49	527	3,789
1994	18	2	1	7	28	1,381	779	27	1,170	3,357
1995	17	3	–	11	31	13,055	2,335	–	1,197	16,587
1996	19	4	1	8	32	9,645	8,381	182	1,476	19,684
1997	11	5	–	12	28	3,183	1,193	–	911	5,287
1998	9	4	–	8	21	27,336	3,078	–	1,738	32,152
1999	5	4	–	10	19	14,325	14,090	–	998	29,413
2000	11	4	–	10	25	15,706	6,582	–	641	22,929
2001	11	1	–	14	26	13,093	−9	–	1,249	14,333
2002	9	–	–	9	18	39,439	–	–	1,848	41,287
2003	10	2	–	10	22	28,597	794	–	1,180	30,571
2004	5	–	–	10	15	14,519	–	–	967	15,486
2005	6	–	–	8	14	1,188	–	–	525	1,713

Source: IMF Annual Report, 2005.

longer duration of extended arrangements, this interpretation enhances the role of EFFs relative to SBAs. Indeed, in 1999, there were more EFFs 'in effect' than there were stand-bys. Table 3.3 gives information on outstanding IMF credit and shows that under the General Resources Account, SBAs and EFFs dominate. Table 3.3 also shows that whereas, according to this criterion, in 1996 SBAs were about twice the size of EFFs, by 2001 there was little to choose between them. However, by 2004 EFFs accounted for only 20 percent of outstanding IMF credit whereas SBAs accounted for 60 percent.

Table 3.2   IMF arrangements in effect as of April 30, 1995–2004

Financial year	Number of arrangements as of April 30					Amounts committed under arrangements as of April 30 (in millions of SDRs)				
	Stand-by	EFF	SAF	PRGF	Total	Stand-by	EFF	SAF	PRGF	Total
1995	19	9	1	27	56	13,190	6,840	49	3,306	23,385
1996	21	7	1	28	57	14,963	9,390	182	3,383	27,918
1997	14	11	–	35	60	3,764	10,184	–	4,048	17,996
1998	14	13	–	33	60	28,323	12,336	–	4,410	45,069
1999	9	12	–	35	56	32,747	11,401	–	4,186	48,334
2000	16	11	–	31	58	45,606	9,798	–	3,516	58,920
2001	17	8	–	37	62	34,906	8,697	–	3,298	46,901
2002	13	4	–	35	52	44,095	7,643	–	4,201	55,939
2003	15	3	–	36	54	42,807	4,432	–	4,450	51,689
2004	11	2	–	36	49	53,944	794	–	4,356	59,094

Source: IMF Annual Report, 2004.

The recent trend appears to be away from using the EFF. To some extent this may reflect the 'streamlining' of conditionality that has been pursued since 2002 and the decision by the Fund to limit structural conditionality to reforms viewed as necessary to achieve macroeconomic targets. By being more parsimonious with structural conditionality, one of the original identifying features of the EFF has been de-emphasized.

Tables 3.1, 3.2 and 3.3 also provide data on the use of the Fund's concessionary facilities. The PRGF has been heavily used by comparison with the EFF in terms of the number of arrangements under it. But, unsurprisingly given the low-income status of countries eligible for concessionary loans, the amounts committed and outstanding under PRGFs are generally lower than under EFFs and much lower than under SBAs.

What factors might, in principle, explain the pattern of usage of IMF facilities revealed in Tables 3.1, 3.2 and 3.3?

3.4   THEORETICAL FRAMEWORK AND INTUITIVE ACCOUNT

There is a substantial literature that examines the determinants of IMF programs. Early contributions focused on economic factors and evaluated the part played by domestic macroeconomic policy and performance and external shocks (for a review of this literature see Bird, 2007). Given the limited success of these studies in explaining IMF lending,

Table 3.3   *Outstanding IMF credit by facility and policy, financial years*
ended April 30, 1995–2004 (in millions of SDRs and percent of
total)

	1995	1996	1997	1998	1999	2000	2001	2002	2003	2004
	(In millions of SDRs)									
Stand-by arrangements[a]	15,117	20,700	18,064	25,526	21,213	21,410	17,101	28,612	32,241	42,070
Extended arrangements	10,155	9,982	11,155	12,521	16,574	16,808	16,108	15,538	14,981	13,783
Supplemental reserve facility	–	–	–	7,100	12,655	–	4,085	5,875	15,700	6,027
Compensatory financing facility	3,021	1,602	1,336	685	2,845	3,032	2,992	745	412	119
Systemic transformation facility	3,848	3,984	3,984	3,869	3,364	2,718	1,933	1,311	644	154
Subtotal (General Resources Account)	32,140	32,268	34,539	49,701	60,651	43,968	42,219	52,081	65,978	62,153
SAF arrangements	1,277	1,208	954	730	565	456	432	341	137	86
PRGF arrangements[b]	3,318	4,469	4,904	5,505	5,870	5,857	5,951	6,188	6,676	6,703
Trust fund	102	95	90	90	89	89	89	89	89	89
Total	36,837	42,040	40,488	56,026	67,175	50,370	48,691	58,699	72,879	69,031
	(Percent of total)									
Stand-by arrangements[a]	41	49	45	46	38	43	35	49	47	61
Extended arrangements	28	24	28	22	25	33	33	26	21	20
Supplemental reserve facility	–	–	–	13	19	–	9	10	21	9
Compensatory financing facility	8	4	3	1	4	6	6	1	1	_c
Systemic transformation facility	10	9	10	7	5	5	4	2	1	_c
Subtotal (General Resources Account)	87	86	85	89	90	87	87	88	91	90
SAF arrangements	3	3	2	1	1	1	1	1	_c	_c
PRGF arrangements[b]	9	11	12	10	9	12	12	11	9	10
Trust fund	_c	_c	_c	_c	_c	_c	_c	_c	_c	_c
Total	100	100	100	100	100	100	100	100	100	100

Notes:
a   Includes outstanding credit tranche and emergency purchases.
b   Includes outstanding associated loans from the Saudi Fund for Development.
c   Less than one-half of 1 percent of total.

Source: IMF Annual Report, 2004.

subsequent research incorporated political and institutional variables (for example, Anderson, Harr, and Tarp, 2006; Barro and Lee, 2005; Bird and Rowlands, 2001; Thacker, 1999). In a related paper, we have attempted to provide a detailed account of the circumstances in which countries turn to the Fund for assistance and negotiate a program (Bird and Rowlands, 2006). Economic factors may combine to make a country's balance of payments unsustainable. These may, in principle, include fiscal deficits, rapid monetary expansion, currency overvaluation, excessive indebtedness, rapid inflation, terms of trade shocks, and a weakening capital account. Governments then need to decide on their response and on whether to involve the IMF. This is where political factors are likely to become relevant. What cost will a government attach to involving the Fund as compared with policy changes outside the auspices of the Fund? Political factors may also influence the final outcome if, as some scholars claim, the Fund's negotiating stance is influenced by powerful shareholding countries in general, and by the US in particular (see, for example, Anderson et al., 2006; Barro and Lee, 2005; Stone, 2002; Thacker, 1999). Thus a 'left leaning' government may be less likely to have an IMF program either because it is reluctant to adopt the policies that the IMF favors or because influential advanced economies are reluctant to endorse IMF assistance (Bird and Rowlands, 2001).

At present, however, the empirical research has failed to identify a model of IMF arrangements that offers a complete explanation of them, and seeking a better understanding remains 'work in progress'. As we argue elsewhere (Bird and Rowlands, 2006), there are likely to be different groups of circumstances that account for referral to the IMF and for IMF arrangements. This is supported by other research that finds significant differences between prolonged users and infrequent users of IMF resources (Bird, Hussain, and Joyce, 2004).

While our analysis in this chapter is informed by the body of work alluded to above, our focus is a little different. Rather than seeking to explain IMF arrangements in general, we examine whether individual components of a reasonably general model vary in significance according to the facility under which an arrangement is made.

Instead of allowing this to be a purely empirical exercise, we now consider whether our investigation can be guided by some theoretical priors? These, in part, can be derived from the stated intentions of the facilities as presented by the IMF. On these grounds we would anticipate that both the EFF and SAF/ESAF/PRGF arrangements would be more significantly associated with structural weaknesses than are SBAs. While standbys would be linked to the need for short term stabilization, extended IMF lending would be linked to long term inflation and protracted low economic growth. For SAF/ESAF/PRGF arrangements we should also anticipate an association with per capita income, since concessionary lending is only available to low-income countries.

But political factors may also be expected to be important. Countries with a record of political instability, for example, may be unwilling or unable to commit to the longer term program of policies that would be embodied in extended arrangements. Similarly in these circumstances the IMF may be reluctant to commit its resources and may prefer to keep countries on a short leash by using a sequence of stand-bys instead. While 'left leaning' governments may perhaps reluctantly accept the need for short run stabilization in a situation where the balance of payments has become unsustainable, they may be less willing to commit to the structural conditionality that a longer term extended arrangement involves, unless the subsidized rate of charge on PRGF arrangements provides them with an additional financial incentive to do so. Furthermore, governments (and perhaps the IMF as well) may be more inclined to sign extended arrange-ments where there is a presumption that they can suppress opposition to the program. Such opposition could potentially be more relevant in the case of extended arrangements which incorporate more structural conditionality.

Institutional factors may also be expected to come into play from time to time. For example, the Fund may be more reluctant to sign extended arrangements if they are perceived as having had a higher failure rate, or if the Fund is concerned about its own liquidity position. A period of heavy usage of extended arrangements and the related increase in the commitment of IMF resources may therefore have built into it a mechanism through which future usage is somewhat truncated. We might, on these grounds, anticipate a cyclical path in the use of extended arrangements.

Can we relate these broad theoretical ideas to the pattern of use reported in the previous section? A potential explanation could run as follows. Stand-bys had been the conventional means through which the IMF sought to assist member countries. The EFF was introduced in 1974 with the intention of assisting developing countries which had been unable, at the time, to secure a link between the allocation of Special Drawing Rights and development assistance (Bird, 1978). However, the relatively low usage of EFFs in the years after their introduction may have reflected a number of things. In particular, many developing countries were using the CFF which had been liberalized and involved low conditionality. By the begin-ning of the 1980s, however, the CFF had become less attractive to them because of increases in its conditionality and poor countries gravitated to the EFF. With the introduction of the Structural Adjustment Facility (and its successors) poor countries were again enticed away from the EFF where the rate of charge was higher and, relative to the SAF, conditionality was tougher. Also, following the spate of EFF arrangements in 1981 and 1982, the Fund's senior management became skeptical of extended lending believing that its record was relatively poor and that the longer term involvement of the Fund could be better achieved by a sequence of short term programs. Although we do not examine it formally in this chapter, it may also be relevant to note that, at the beginning of the 1980s, the World Bank introduced its program of structural adjustment lending. There is therefore the question of the extent to which World Bank structural adjustment loans were viewed as substitutes for or complements to extended lending by the IMF.

In the aftermath of the developing world debt crisis there was also a belief that Latin American economies needed additional liquidity rather than structural adjustment. The debt crisis was initially perceived as a liquidity crisis. In these circumstances, stand-bys were deemed more appropriate than EFFs. However, as the need for structural adjustment in Latin America was recognized, EFFs became more popular as an appropriate modality for Fund support to the region.

Extended arrangements also made something of a comeback in the context of first, Countries in Transition, although this effect was muted by the introduction of the Systemic Transformation Facility, and then South East Asian economies in the aftermath to the East Asian financial crisis in 1997/98. Once this crisis had been overcome, and against the background of a falling demand for IMF resources in general, stand-bys for non-concessionary lending and the PRGF for concessionary lending to poor countries again became the preferred modalities. This was captured by the IMF's own review of its facilities that hesitated as to whether the EFF should be retained at all, but opted to shorten the repayment period on EFF credits from ten to seven years and, to some extent, to re-invent it as a natural progression for countries graduating from eligibility for PRGFs. However, some Executive Directors 'observed that the distinctions between extended and stand-by arrangements had become less clear' with a few of them proposing that 'successive stand-by arrangements could be a more effective way to address balance of payments problems of a longer term nature' (IMF, 2000). Were they right? Had the distinctions become less clear?

Although the above discussion provides an intuitive interpretation of the use of IMF facilities, it is difficult to judge the accuracy of the account in an objective way. In the following section, therefore, we more formally construct an econometric model based on the theoretical framework discussed earlier in this section to see whether regression analysis identifies significant differences in the economic and political circumstances in which various facilities have been used.

3.5　EMPIRICAL RESULTS: METHOD AND FINDINGS

There is a substantial literature that examines the economic circumstances under which countries arrange programs with the IMF (see, for example, Bird and Rowlands, 2002; Conway, 1994; Knight and Santaella, 1997). There are also studies that seek to identify significant differences between different types of user countries. For example, Bird et al. (2004) and the Independent Evaluation Office of the IMF (IEO, 2002) focus on IMF recidivists and prolonged users of IMF resources, and examine how the circumstances in which these countries draw from the Fund differ from those of other users. While we employ this research to inform our own underlying model, our focus is rather different. Our purpose is to see whether there are statistically significant differences between the economic and political circumstances under which countries draw under the three main Fund facilities (SBAs, EFFs, and SAF/ESAF/PRGFs). It may be, of course, that the facilities differ in terms of the conditionalities that are attached to them. We do not examine this directly in this section, although we do discuss it briefly later on. It may seem reasonable to assume that the design of programs and the related conditionality should be linked to the causes of economic distress that lead to IMF support being sought in the first place. In this case differences in the content of conditionality and the propensity to sign different agreements should reflect primarily the differences in the economic factors determining IMF programs. However political factors may also be important, and need to be considered.

The chapter examines SBA, EFF and ESAF/PRGF[4] agreements over the period 1978–2000, a time period selected on the basis of data availability but one that also coincides roughly with the post Bretton Woods period. We only examine cases of signed agreements since our purpose is not to explain whether countries do or do not sign programs, but rather the facility under which the program is signed. We omit from our sample countries that had overlapping programs under different facilities. In total we have complete data observations associated with 324 (231 SBA, 48 EFF, and 55 ESAF/PRGF) agreements out of a total of 577 (379 SBA, 67 EFF, 131 EAF/PRGF). Details relating to data sources and the definitions of the variables included in our model are provided in an Appendix.

We ran the estimations for the full sample period as well as for different sub-periods. The choice of sub-periods does matter. Specifically there is a period from 1984 to 1988 when there are no EFF agreements in our sample, corresponding to a period of near disappearance of them in IMF use (only four agreements were issued in this time period). Therefore we took this period out of the main estimations, looking only at the pre-1984 and post-1988 sub-period estimations. We also attempted to identify structural breaks in the rest of the data using year dummies and simply by running estimations on smaller post-1988 periods. The year dummies only really identified a stark break over the 1984–88 period, and estimations on smaller post-1988 sub-samples either did not converge or were effectively the same as the full post-1988 sub-sample results. We also added the middle 1984–88 period on to the earlier or later sub-samples to see how its inclusion affected the results.

Having created our dataset and identified our sample of countries and different sample periods, we then used Stata to run a robust multinomial logit model on the data when there are multiple agreements (all three are present) and standard probit estimations for the earlier period when there are only SBAs and EFFs.[5] These procedures allow us to identify any significant differences between both EFFs and SBAs, and PRGFs and SBAs in terms of the likely determining factors.[6] Our estimating equation is based on a fairly standard model of the determinants of IMF programs, which we extend to capture the country characteristics that are presented by the IMF as justifying the different facilities. Since EFFs and PRGFs are, in principle, intended to help deal with longer term structural problems as well as problems of short-term stabilization, we include in our basic model proxies for these in the form of long term growth, long term balance of payments current account deficits and reserve levels, as well as long term inflation. We also include a measure of past programs that may be expected to reflect enduring and deep-seated economic difficulties. In the case of ESAF/PRGF arrangements, we incorporate not only measures designed to capture long term supply side weakness but also per capita income, since the concessionary nature of the ESAF/PRGF is claimed to be a key characteristic distinguishing this facility from the Fund's GRA-based ones. The model is therefore designed to capture specifically the country characteristics associated with the need for short-term stabilization and for longer-term structural adjustment. The former characteristics should be expected to drive stand-bys and the latter ones to drive EFFs and ESAF/PRGFs.

We ran various specifications of the model to test the robustness of the results, but only report in detail the results from the one we believe to be the most satisfactory in terms of having as large a sample as possible without losing important results. The results from our preferred model are presented in Tables 3.3 and 3.4.

Table 3.4   *Estimation results for explaining EFF agreements relative to SBA agreements, given that countries signed a conditional IMF agreement*

Explanatory variable	Pre 1984 (probit)		Post 1988 (multinomial logit)	
	Estimated coefficient	Normal test statistic	Estimated coefficient	Normal test statistic
Constant	2.15**	2.17	−5.67****	−2.89
Share of world GDP	1.043*	1.93	−0.0639	−0.08
GNP per capita	0.000105	0.77	0.000310*	1.68
GDP growth	0.0543	1.61	0.153	1.17
Long-term growth	−0.213****	−2.64	−0.119	−0.89
Inflation	0.0110	0.6	−0.00513****	−3.65
Long-term inflation	−0.0277	−1.26	0.00301**	2.12
Reserve-to-import ratio	−3.74****	−2.74	0.820	0.58
Percent change in reserves-to-imports	0.00203***	2.24	−0.00210	−1.55
Current account balance/GDP	8.94	1.27	9.94	1.02
Long-term current account balance	10.5	0.96	−38.3**	−2.1
Percent change in the current account	−0.00166***	−2.55	0.00496****	4.06
Real exchange rate depreciation	0.0126	1.24	−0.0424**	−2.1
Debt service-to-exports ratio	10.5***	2.41	0.670	0.38
Percent change in the debt-service ratio	−0.0134***	−2.45	0.00829	1.51
Public external debt- to-GDP ratio	−2.012***	−2.4	−0.358	−0.29
Current rescheduling	–	–	2.81*	1.96
Reschedulings in past years	–	–	−0.446	−0.94
Rescheduling required next year	–	–	−0.256	−0.38
Past IMF agreements	−1.31****	−3.49	0.116	0.1
Fixed exchange rates	0.0170	0.04	−1.21*	−1.88
Flexible exchange rates	−1.30***	−2.47	1.24	1.09
New government	−0.688	−1.51	−1.16*	−1.74
Civil liberties	−0.00852	−0.07	0.565***	2.34
Change in civil liberties	−0.357	−1.05	1.91**	2.13
Coup	−0.302	−0.64	−84.1***	−2.55
Number of observations	97		175	
Pseudo-R squared	0.29		0.65	
Log pseudo-likelihood	−37.5		−57.6	

Notes:
****, ***, **, * refer, respectively, to statistical significance at the 1, 2, 5, and 10% levels for one-tailed tests.
Note that the rescheduling variables were dropped from the pre 1984 period estimation due to singularities in the data.

Table 3.4 reports our findings for the comparison between EFFs and SBAs. Since we use SBAs as our point of comparison, this table identifies those country characteristics that differ significantly between countries that sign SBAs and those that sign EFF agreements. As the table illustrates, for the early period (pre-1984) there are several statistically significant differences between EFFs and SBAs. First, the positive and statistically significant constant suggests that EFFs were used somewhat more readily than SBAs. More importantly, EFFs were more likely to be used when economic growth performance in recent years was poor, when reserve adequacy was relatively bad but improving, when the current account was deteriorating, when debt service was burdensome but improving and when public debt to GDP ratios were low. In addition, countries with flexible exchange rates were more likely to use SBAs than EFFs, and there is statistically weak evidence that larger countries tended to use EFFs. Finally, recent IMF agreements were more strongly associated with SBAs, suggesting that sequential SBAs might have been seen as a substitute for EFFs. Overall, the results suggest that countries in structurally weaker positions but with recent improvements in performance were more likely to have EFF programs in the pre-1984 period, suggesting that stronger countries facing temporary distress used the SBAs. This result seems consistent with the Fund's initial justification for the EFF.

The post-1988 period reveals many interesting changes. First, the statistically significant estimated coefficient on the constant suggests that there was an overall substitution away from the EFFs relative to the earlier period, possibly because of the availability of the newer concessionary agreements. Countries with EFF programs in the later period tended to be slightly wealthier than those with SBAs (though the estimated coefficient is only marginally significant statistically), and this also implies that poor countries migrated away from EFFs to concessionary windows. Countries with EFFs had a worse record of long term inflation, a prolonged current account deficit that is improving, and less currency depreciation. There is weak statistical evidence that countries that were rescheduling used EFFs more, perhaps as a way of signalling fundamental economic reform and that countries without fixed exchange rates were also more likely to use EFFs than SBAs.

Of more interest is the fact that political factors, unimportant in distinguishing between SBA and EFF users in the previous period, became statistically significant in the post-1988 period. Specifically, countries with good and improving civil liberties, a history of more frequent coups, and new governments, were less likely to use EFF agreements than SBAs. Perhaps as we suggested in our theoretical discussion in Section 3.4 repressive governments were better able or more willing to commit to longer-term structural adjustment, as they had less to fear in terms of provoking civil dissent. Similarly, either the Fund or incumbent governments seem reluctant to sign on to anything other than a short-term SBA when there is a history of recent unscheduled changes in government. Governments recently coming to power also seem somewhat less inclined to arrange long-term programs with the IMF.

By breaking up our sample we can see that the differences between the circumstances under which countries have used SBAs and EFFs have changed rather extensively over time. The mid-1980s in the aftermath of the debt crisis and with the introduction of concessionary structural adjustment seem to be a watershed in terms of the differences between SBAs and EFFs. Including the 1984–88 period in the later sub-sample changes few of the results, suggesting that it is a relatively homogeneous period. In contrast, when the earlier period is expanded up to 1988 most of the coefficient estimates disappear in terms of statistical significance, leaving only imminent rescheduling and past IMF agreements as positively related to the likelihood of SBAs rather than EFFs.

One final variant in our estimations to distinguish between EFFs and SBAs included an indicator of a government's 'leftist' tendencies. Again the difference between sub-periods was stark. In the early period EFFs were strongly associated with 'leftist' governments. In the latter period the associated coefficient estimate is negative, large in magnitude, and very strongly significant statistically, suggesting that more socialist inclined governments were much less likely to adopt EFF agreements after 1988 (and indeed after 1983). More so than governments of a different complexion, they appear to have gravitated away from EFFs and toward SBAs and, indeed, ESAFs/PRGFs. The inclusion of the variable had only minor effects on the other results of the EFF estimations, but since its coding had a strong subjective element and since there was evidence of multicollinearity when it was included in the ESAF/PRGF equation, we have not reported the results here; they are available from the authors.

Table 3.5 reports our findings when we undertake a comparison between ESAF/PRGF programs (i.e., concessionary lending financed by the IMF's Trust Fund) and SBAs financed from the General Resources Account (GRA). This estimation is for the period after 1988 only, when concessionary programs first appeared in our sample. Here we find a number of significant differences between the factors associated with SBAs and concessionary arrangements. First, and as anticipated, countries drawing under the concessionary programs have lower per capita income and also tend to be smaller in absolute economic size. Perhaps more surprisingly, they seem to have a faster rate of economic growth over the five years prior to the program. As anticipated, longer-term inflation is higher for

*Table 3.5 Multinomial logit results for explaining concessional (SAF/
ESAF/PRGF) agreements relative to SBA agreements, given
that countries signed a conditional IMF agreement, post 1988*

Explanatory variable	Estimated coefficient	Normal test statistic
Constant	15.1**	1.96
Share of world GDP	−45.0****	−2.83
GNP per capita	−0.0141**	−2.21
GDP growth	−0.0167	−0.14
Long-term growth	0.692****	2.62
Inflation	−0.00800****	−3.39
Long-term inflation	0.0102***	2.54
Reserve-to-import ratio	−2.42	−0.71
Percent change in reserves-to-imports	0.00544	0.3
Current account balance/GDP	9.50	1.02
Long-term current account balance	−27.6	−1.1
Percent change in the current account	−0.00198	−0.82
Real exchange rate depreciation	−0.0675****	−2.85
Debt service-to-exports ratio	−6.15**	−2.01
Percent change in the debt-service ratio	−0.0000292	−0.05
Public external debt-to-GDP ratio	0.357	0.38
Current rescheduling	2.52	1.32
Reschedulings in past years	0.476	0.59
Rescheduling required next year	−1.04	−1.21
Past IMF agreements	1.15	0.75
Fixed exchange rates	0.620	0.42
Flexible exchange rates	0.203	0.16
New government	−0.335	−0.31
Civil liberties	−1.39	−1.36
Change in civil liberties	3.43*	1.91
Coup	−1.06	−0.84
Number of observations	195	
Pseudo-R squared	0.57	
Log pseudo-likelihood	−77.7	

Note: ****, ***, **, * refer, respectively, to statistical significance at the 1, 2, 5 and 10% levels for one-tailed tests.

programs under concessionary windows, perhaps reflecting in part their structural deficiencies. However, a higher contemporary rate of inflation makes it more likely that countries will have SBAs than ESAF/PRGFs, perhaps reflecting problems of short-term instability which in turn make short-term stabilization under an SBA more appropriate. Interestingly, countries with high debt service-to-exports ratios and rapid real exchange rate depreciation are more likely to sign SBAs rather than concessionary arrangements. This may suggest that the principal need is to stabilize the economy. But it may also suggest that poorer countries with possible debt rescheduling needs prefer to sign on to shorter term programs that still leave them eligible for some form of debt relief under the umbrella of the Paris Club (or London Club). In contrast to EFFs, very few of the political variables had much effect in the case of concessionary arrangements, although, as with EFFs, countries with worsening civil liberties were more likely to sign on to longer term concessionary programs than to SBAs.[7] In the case of concessionary IMF lending, it does appear to be low per capita income, deep seated economic disequilibria as well, no doubt, as the concessionary rate of charge that leads countries to prefer these longer term arrangements over short term SBAs.

The basic message from our findings is that the initial distinction between SBAs and EFFs in terms of the economic circumstances in which they were used largely disappeared after the mid-1980s. In the post mid-1980s period, it appears unsafe to claim that the non-concessionary IMF facilities can be reliably distinguished 'by slow growth and an inherently weak balance of payments position' as the IMF still officially claims that they are. In addition, political factors have become more relevant in explaining whether an SBA or an EFF is signed. Governments facing a less secure political future are more reluctant to commit to a longer term program under an extended arrangement. And the Fund may share in this reluctance.

Since the IMF claims that users of the EFF are expected to have only limited access to private capital, it is also interesting to consider whether EFF arrangements have had a particularly strong catalytic effect on other capital flows as compared with SBAs. The IMF (2000) claimed that in the 1990s countries began to treat EFFs as a 'badge of honor' reflecting their willingness to pursue 'more demanding conditions in the structural realm' (IMF, 2000: 55). Were they trying to send a stronger and more positive signal to markets? Recent empirical analysis reported elsewhere by us (Bird and Rowlands, 2005) suggests that, in fact, across the broad range of private capital flows, the EFF has generally been a less helpful means of encouraging private capital flows than SBAs have been. Indeed, in some circumstances, EFF arrangements have had a negative effect, particularly on FDI.

Turning to the Fund's concessionary lending windows, PRGF countries may indeed have longer term and more deep seated economic problems than those using stand-bys. But political factors do not generally seem to make much difference. As anticipated, it is differences in per capita income that distinguish users of the PRGF from users of SBAs.

3.6   CONCLUDING REMARKS

Two related issues form the basis of this chapter. First, in examining the determinants of IMF arrangements, do different factors exert different degrees of influence on arrangements under different IMF facilities. Second, can the range of IMF facilities be justified in terms of them fulfilling different functions and meeting different needs.

Our findings suggest that the answers to these questions have to be somewhat guarded. Focusing on EFFs and SBAs, our results show that there were significant differences in the economic circumstances in which the facilities were used in the initial period following the introduction of extended arrangements. However, this situation changed in the mid-1980s. After this time, a stronger difference appears to have existed in terms of political factors. Political instability and the ability of governments to suppress opposition to reform exercised a significant influence, while economic differences largely disappeared. Unsurprisingly, we find that low-income countries tend to favor the Fund's concessionary facility and also that the PRGF may be used more heavily than SBAs by poor countries that face deep-seated economic problems.

From a policy point of view our findings suggest that there is a reasonably strong case for retaining the PRGF as a separate and distinct facility, or at least retaining its essential properties in some form. There is a much less compelling economic justification for retaining both SBAs and EFFs in their current form. In this regard, Executive Directors who argued that they now perceived little difference between EFF arrangements and a sequence of SBAs will find supporting evidence from our results. However, this observation raises another question which we do not answer in this chapter. The question is whether the original spirit of the EFF should be retained for countries other than for poor countries under the umbrella of the PRGF. If SBAs and the PRGF are to be retained, should the EFF be abandoned, or should it be re-invigorated to meet the objectives originally laid out in its rubric? Or should SBAs be reformed in order to better accommodate longer-term structural adjustment when deemed necessary? At a time when much attention is being paid to IMF governance and organizational structure, the portfolio and design of the Fund's lending windows deserves closer attention than it has received up until now. Hopefully this chapter offers a useful contribution to such a debate.

ACKNOWLEDGMENTS

We are grateful to a number of anonymous referees, as well as to Axel Dreher for their comments on an earlier draft of this chapter. The usual disclaimer applies.

NOTES

1. This section draws heavily on Bird (2003).
2. A critique of the early changes may be found in Dell (1985) who argues that they largely eliminated the distinctive features of the CFF.
3. IMF (1999) quotes James Boughton's assessment of the contingency window as 'a hydra-headed facility of mind-numbing and self-defeating complexity'.
4. There are only two SAF agreements present in the estimated sample, as missing data on country characteristics meant that other SAF recipients were excluded from the estimation. These two agreements were signed in1988 and were replaced by ESAF agreements the following year.
5. When run as a multinomial logit estimation the results effectively collapsed to a standard logit procedure, which were essentially the same as those produced by the probit procedure.
6. See Greene (2003) for a fuller discussion. The model is generally deemed superior to running separate dichotomous estimations because of the cross-equation constraints that an IMF program has. The estimations process uses the Huber/White/sandwich variance calculation and corrects for possible within-group (or country specific) variance dependence.
7. In the estimation with the indicator for socialism, it was again the case that governments further to the 'left' were less likely to sign on to concessionary programs than the shorter term SBA programs.

REFERENCES

Anderson, T., Harr, T., and Tarp, F. (2006). On US politics and IMF lending. *European Economic Review*, 50(7), 1843–1862.

Barro, R.J. and Lee, J-W. (2005). IMF programs: Who is chosen and what are the effects? *Journal of Monetary Economics*, 52, 1245–1269.

Bird, G. (1978). *The International Monetary System and the Less Developed Countries*. London: Macmillan.

Bird, G. (1995). *IMF Lending to Developing Countries: Issues and Evidence*. London: Routledge.

Bird, G. (2003). Restructuring the IMF's lending facilities. *The World Economy*, 26(2), 229–245.

Bird, G. (2007). The IMF: A bird's eye view of its role and operations. *Journal of Economic Surveys*, 21(4), 683–745.

Bird, G., Hussain, M., and Joyce, J. (2004). Many happy returns? Recidivism and the IMF. *Journal of International Money and Finance*, 23, 231–271.

Bird, G. and Rowlands, D. (2001). IMF lending: How is it affected by economic, political and institutional factors? *Journal of Policy Reform*, 4(3), 243–270.

Bird, G. and Rowlands, D. (2002). IMF lending: An analysis of prediction failures. *Journal of Policy Reform*, 5(3), 173–186.

Bird, G. and Rowlands, D. (2005). The analysis of catalysis: The IMF and private capital flows. mimeographed. *SCIES Working Paper*.

Bird, G. and Rowlands, D. (2006). The demand for IMF assistance: What factors influence the decision to turn to the Fund? In G. Ranis, J.R. Vreeland, and S. Kosack (eds), *Globalization and the Nation State: The Impact of the IMF and World Bank*: 231–262. London: Routledge.

Conway, P. (1994). IMF lending programs: Participation and impact. *Journal of Development Economics*, 45, 355–391.

Dell, S. (1985). The fifth credit tranche. *World Development*, 13(2), 245–249.

Greene, W. (2003). *Econometric Analysis* (5th edn). Upper Saddle River, NJ: Prentice Hall.

Independent Evaluation Office, IMF (2002). *Evaluation of the Prolonged use of IMF Resources*. Washington, DC: International Monetary Fund.

International Monetary Fund (IMF) (1999). Review of the Compensatory and Contingency Financing Facility (CCFF) and Buffer Stock Financing Facility (BSFF). Preliminary Considerations, Paper prepared by the Policy Development and Review Department, mimeographed, Washington, DC: IMF.

IMF (2000). Review of Fund facilities: Preliminary considerations, paper prepared by the Policy Development and Review Department, mimeographed, Washington, DC: IMF.

Knight, M. and Santaella, J.A. (1997). Economic determinants of IMF financial arrangements. *Journal of Development Economics*, 54, 405–436.

Reinhart, C. and Rogoff, K. (2004). The modern history of exchange rate arrangements: A reinterpretation. *Quarterly Journal of Economics*, 119(1), 1–48.

Stone, R.W. (2002). *Lending Credibility: The International Monetary Fund and the Post-communist Transition*, Princeton, NJ: Princeton University Press.

Thacker, S.C. (1999). The high politics of IMF lending. *World Politics*, 52(1), 38–75.

APPENDIX

Data Definitions and Sources

'Signing of an IMF agreement in the following year.' An indicator variable with the values '1', '2' and '3' if a country signed, respectively, a stand-by, EFF, or SAF/ESAF/PRGF agreement in the following year. Source: IMF, Annual Report, various years.

'GNP per capita.' GNI per capita in thousands of US$, Atlas method (World Bank, World Development Indicator) deflated by US consumer price index (IMF: IMF Financial Statistics).

'GDP growth.' Percentage change in GDP from the previous year (annual percent). Source: World Bank, World Development Indicators.

'Long-term growth.' Average annual GDP growth rate for the previous five years. Source: World Bank, World Development Indicators.

'Inflation.' Average annual percentage increase in the consumer price index. Source: World Bank, World Development Indicators.

'Long-term inflation.' Average annual inflation rate for the previous five years. Source: World Bank, World Development Indicators.

'Reserves-to-imports.' Total foreign reserves divided by total imports of goods and services (both in current US$). Source: World Bank, Global Development Indicators.

'Percent change in reserves-to-imports.' The percentage change in the reserves-to-import ratio from the previous year to the current year, as a proportion of the previous year.

'Current Account Balance/GDP.' The current account balance divided by total GDP (both in current US$). Source: World Bank, Global Development Indicators.

'Long-term current account balance.' The average annual current account balance-to-GDP ratio for the previous five years.

'Percent change in the current account.' The percentage change in the current account balance from the previous year to the current year, expressed as a percentage of the previous year. Source: World Bank, Global Development Indicators.

'Real exchange rate depreciation.' The official number of domestic currency units per US$ multiplied by the ratio of the US consumer price index to the country's consumer price index. This number is calculated for the current year and for three years previously (adjusting for changes in base years) and the difference between the two is expressed as a proportion of the value from three years before. Source: World Bank, World Development Indicators.

'Debt–service ratio.' Total long-term debt service payments divided by total exports of goods and services (all in US dollars). Source: World Bank, World Development Indicators.

'Percent change in the debt–service ratio.' The percentage change in the total debt service payments-to-exports ratio from the previous year to the current year, expressed as a percentage of the previous year.

'Public external debt-to-GDP ratio.' The ratio of public and publicly guaranteed long-term debt expressed as a ratio of total GDP. Source: World Bank, World Development Indicators.

'Current rescheduling.' A binary indicator of whether or not the country had to reschedule some portion of its debt (principal or interest, official or private) in the current year, which requires by convention an IMF agreement to be in place. Source: World Bank, Global Development Finance.

'Reschedulings in past years.' The number of years out of the previous two years in which a country rescheduled some portion of its official or private interest or principal repayments. Source: World Bank, Global Development Finance.

'Rescheduling required next year.' A binary indicator of whether or not the country is about to reschedule some portion of its debt (principal or interest, official or private) in the following year, which requires by convention an IMF agreement to be in place. Source: World Bank, Global Development Finance.

'Past IMF agreements.' A binary variable indicating whether an IMF arrangement has been in place for the country in either of the previous two years. Source: IMF, IMF Annual Report various years.

'Fixed exchange rates.' An indicator that the country had a fixed exchange rate regime. Source: Reinhart and Rogoff (2004).

'Flexible exchange rates.' An indicator that the country had a flexible (floating or falling) exchange rate regime. Source: Reinhart and Rogoff (2004).

'New government.' An indicator of whether the government that year was newly formed. Source: Authors' coding from Europa World Yearbook.

'Civil liberties.' A measure of the level of civil liberties in a country, on a scale from 1 to 7 where 1 means very free and 7 means fewer civil liberties. Source: Freedom House.

'Change in civil liberties.' A measure of the level of change in civil liberties in a country, where negative means more freedom and positive means less freedom (this year's level minus last year's level). Source: Freedom House.

'Coup.' An indicator of whether there was a coup in the country in a given year. Source: Authors' coding from Europa World Yearbook.

4.   Aggregate IMF lending

4.1   INTRODUCTION

The global financial crisis of late 2008 and beyond has had numerous and far-reaching implications for a large range of micro, macro and international economic issues. One of them has involved a reassessment of the world's premier international financial institution, the International Monetary Fund (IMF). Although the Fund had previously claimed that the challenges of globalization made it indispensable, by the beginning of 2008 some were arguing that it had in fact lost its importance. To them the IMF seemed to be increasingly irrelevant, as illustrated by its apparent inability to exert a discernible impact on global economic imbalances through its multilateral surveillance and consultations. Even its bilateral surveillance of emerging and low-income countries was losing significance, as some of these traditional users of IMF resources emigrated away from it.

The largely benign global economic environment had allowed many of the IMF's former client countries to build up their own holdings of international reserves and thereby to self-insure against future economic crises. By early 2008, the Fund had only a limited portfolio of outstanding loans. Even amongst poor countries there was a shift away from the IMF's provision of direct financial assistance. At the beginning of 2008, the Fund's outstanding credit was only about SDR 9 billion, in comparison to more than SDR 70 billion at the beginning of 2004. Consequently, the Fund's adjustment role was also reduced, as it lacked the leverage to compel members to follow its advice on economic policy. On top of this, the reduced demand for IMF loans was causing significant problems for its own income stream. Compounding these operational restrictions were governance problems, with accusations that its management and voting structure were unrepresentative of its membership and hence lacked legitimacy. The IMF was by many accounts an ailing institution.

By the end of 2008, however, the global economic situation had changed dramatically in ways that seemed to offer the Fund a new lease of life. The economic crisis was global and the IMF is a global institution. The crisis was financial and the IMF is a financial institution. The crisis brought with it balance of payments problems and deteriorating overall economic performance, problems that the IMF was initially established and designed to deal with. The crisis required an internationally coordinated response and the IMF provides a forum for policy coordination. Although there are ample grounds to doubt its current capacity to offer the degree of multilateral surveillance and coordination that are needed (Bird and Willett, 2007), it is premature to judge the Fund's efficacy in meeting the challenges created by the global economic crisis that emerged at the end of 2008.

With the sharp rise in IMF lending and the anticipated effects of the global economic crisis on the future demand for IMF credits, the most pressing concern appeared to be the adequacy of the Fund's own resource base. One of the main actions at the April meeting of the G20 in London in 2009 was to endorse a tripling of the Fund's lending capacity by agreeing to additional borrowing under the New Arrangements to Borrow and by making new allocations of SDRs. One of us has elsewhere provided a brief description and assessment of what the G20 meeting achieved and we therefore do not replicate that analysis here (see Bird, 2009a).

The rapid turnaround in global economic conditions and in the IMF's lending activity raises two connected questions that form the focus of this chapter. First, is it possible to explain and predict aggregate IMF lending? Can we identify the variables that influence it and, furthermore, can we forecast future values of these variables so that we can also predict the future demand for IMF resources? Second, are the mechanisms via which the Fund attempts to ensure that it has adequate resources to meet the demands of its members satisfactory, and, if not, how might they be improved? The latter question has important implications for global economic performance, as the Fund is generally perceived as a global quasi lender of last resort. If it is unable to meet the demand for its resources, illiquid member countries will generally have to place more emphasis on short-run adjustment-intensive balance of payments strategies involving the compression of domestic aggregate demand, with all its attendant economic and political consequences.

The chapter is organized in the following way. Section 4.2 provides a brief empirical picture of the overall nature of IMF lending, which is revealed as being episodic. Section 4.3 attempts to explain the picture painted in Section 4.2. It offers a conceptual framework within which IMF lending may be analysed, and then provides a few simple bivariate and multivariate tests of the ideas that emerge from this framework. Section 4.4 builds on this analysis to discuss the policy implications for financing the Fund's activities. It is critical of current modalities and proposes alternative arrangements to deal with the episodic nature of the demand for IMF resources. A concluding section places the analysis and policy proposals in the context of current debates about reforming the Fund and the global financial system. This study complements earlier work of ours (Bird and Rowlands, 2001a, 2002, 2006b, 2009) by analysing the aggregate amount of IMF lending rather than the pattern of lending to individual countries or groups of countries and the probability that individual countries will have programs with the IMF. However, as will be explained later, the two dimensions of IMF lending are interrelated.

4.2   THE NATURE OF IMF LENDING

There are various measures of the amount of IMF lending; outstanding credit to member countries associated with contemporary programs, the value of new credit extended or committed in any given year, and the value of net flows in and out of the IMF. With less emphasis on the amount of lending, another measure of IMF lending activity examines the number of programs in operation, and the number signed in any given year. It can also be useful to distinguish between loans made to better-off emerging and developing economies under stand-by and Extended Fund Facility (EFF) arrangements financed from the General Resources Account, and those made to low-income countries on a concessionary basis under the Poverty Reduction and Growth Facility (PRGF).[1] There are also other lending mechanisms through specialized programs, as well as through automatic non-program drawings from the reserve tranche.

Multiple portraits of Fund lending can be painted by using these various measures. The amount of credit used by, for example, Russia or Turkey or Mexico will dwarf the amount used by, for example, a small sub-Saharan African economy. The overall amount of IMF lending, either in the form of new loans, loan commitments or outstanding credit, will depend importantly on whether large emerging economies have Fund programs in place, even though such programs may be few in number.

Figures 4.1 and 4.2 illustrate respectively the number of agreements in effect and the annual use of Fund resources. Over the period 1987–2009, the average number of stand-by and EFF arrangements in operation, arrangements for which all IMF members are eligible, is significantly fewer than the number of SAF/ESAF/PRGF arrangements for which only low-income countries are eligible (20 versus 29). For the same period, however, average annual purchases under stand-by and EFF arrangements are more than 13 times higher than the amount borrowed under the concessional facilities (9.6 billion SDRs as against 0.7 billion SDRs). In addition, the volatilities (measured by the coefficients of variation) in financing levels per year, in the number of new agreements, and in the number of agreements in operation are approximately twice as high for

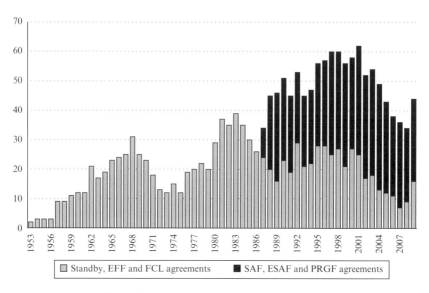

Figure 4.1   Number of IMF agreements in operation (1953–2009)

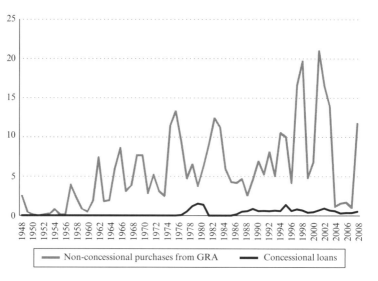

Figure 4.2   Annual purchases and loans from the IMF, 1948–2009 (billion constant 1983 US dollars)

the non-concessional agreements as for concessional ones. The evidence, therefore, clearly depicts non-concessional IMF lending as much more volatile and episodic than concessional lending.

Not surprisingly, therefore, recent episodes of increased lending are generally associated with crises involving larger emerging economies. Lending peaks are apparent prior to the collapse of the Bretton Woods system, after the oil shock in the 1970s, and following the debt crisis of 1982, the Mexican peso crisis of the mid-1990s, the Asian crisis of 1997 / 98 and the economic turmoil surrounding Argentina and Turkey in 2002 / 03. The number of arrangements shows a similar pattern but in more muted form.

Focusing on the period since the late 1990s, the amount of new IMF financing has ranged from a peak of about SDR 30 billion in 2002 to a trough of about SDR 1.5 billion in 2008. The number of arrangements in operation was at its maximum in 2001 when there were 62 arrangements in effect, and was at its minimum in 2008 when there were only 34 arrangements in place; the clear majority of these (25) were with low-income countries under the PRGF (see Figure 4.1). Indeed, 2008 saw the fewest number of new agreements signed since 1957, and the fewest number of concessional agreements. While the number of PRGF programs in operation ranges from 37 (2001) to 25 (2008), the number of stand-bys in operation ranges from 17 (2001) to 6 (2007), and, in the case of EFFs, from 13 (1998) to only 1 (2006, 2007 and 2009).

These data illustrate the large swings in IMF lending throughout its history, volatility that has also been identified in earlier research (Bird, 1995). Can these swings in IMF lending be explained other than in terms of whether or not large emerging economies have programs with the Fund? What are the underlying determinants of overall IMF lending?

4.3   FACTORS INFLUENCING IMF LENDING

4.3.1   A Conceptual Framework

There are two approaches to trying to explain the aggregate amount of IMF lending. The first takes aggregate lending as the dependent variable and attempts to explain it directly in terms of global determinants. Early attempts to explain aggregate IMF lending adopted this first approach and were largely informal and descriptive (for example, Bird, 1995). Alternatively, explaining participation in IMF programs can be attempted at the level of individual countries. Bird and Rowlands (2001a), Bird (2007), Ghosh et al. (2007) and Steinwand and Stone (2008) provide recent reviews of this literature, so we do not examine it in detail here. The second approach would then calculate indirectly the aggregate level of IMF lending by summing the drawings made by individual members.

Potential influences on aggregate IMF lending are, in principle, to be found on both the demand side, affecting countries' propensities to turn to the IMF for financial assistance, and on the supply side, affecting the willingness of the IMF to respond positively to requests for help within institutional constraints on the amount of lending. However, the classification of demand- and supply-side factors is complex and varies over time, as changes within the Fund on the supply side may in turn influence or facilitate the demand for IMF resources. For example, the Fund may reform the range, nature and lending limits of the facilities under which member countries may borrow. Thus, Bird (1995) points out how reforms to the Compensatory Financing Facility in the mid-1970s, making access to it easier and more appealing, contributed to the sharp increase in IMF lending soon afterwards, much of which took place under this particular facility. However, as many of these supply-side changes themselves reflect the prevailing economic conditions and have been made in response to the latent demand for IMF resources, and as they are sporadic and difficult to measure systematically, we focus here primarily on demand-side factors.[2]

More generally, the aggregate demand for IMF resources may be influenced by the size and distribution of current account balance of payments deficits, the size and distribution of holdings of international reserves, the access to private international capital markets, levels of external debt and the cost of borrowing from the IMF. The cost of borrowing comprises both the rate of charge on IMF credit, and, perhaps more significantly, the perceived cost in terms of the conditionality associated with IMF programs. This latter cost will depend on the size of the gap between a country's preferred economic policies and those that have to be accepted in order to gain access to IMF finance.

It might be anticipated that the demand for IMF resources will increase as the size of balance of payments deficits in countries with a fairly recent history of IMF programs increases. For this reason, an increase in the size of the US balance of payments deficit would not by itself be expected to be associated with an increase in aggregate IMF lending, as wealthy economies generally have access to international capital which, experience shows, they prefer to IMF financing. Indeed, given the zero-sum nature of the global balance of payments, an increase in balance of payments deficits in advanced economies might be expected to go together with an increase in balance of payments surpluses in emerging economies, reducing the need for IMF lending.

If borrowing from international capital markets is a preferred alternative to borrowing from the IMF then, more generally, aggregate IMF lending would be expected to depend negatively on the access that emerging or developing countries have to such markets. As the scarcity of international capital may be expected to be reflected positively by global interest rates, it follows that aggregate IMF lending should tend to rise alongside a rise in global interest rates. Similarly, countries with large amounts of external debt may find it more difficult to borrow and may therefore be pushed toward the Fund in circumstances where they would otherwise have built up their indebtedness to private capital markets.

One composite factor may help to explain aspects of balance of payments performance, capital market characteristics and economic sustainability. Global economic growth provides for expanding export markets and improved prospects for domestic growth, as well as being correlated with financial market aggregates. This simple indicator may help to capture changes in the demand for IMF lending.

Countries with balance of payments deficits may also finance them by running down their own international reserves. This implies that aggregate IMF lending will go down as holdings of international reserves in the Fund's potential client countries go up. Furthermore, the demand for IMF resources may be expected to fall when the perceived cost of IMF conditionality rises. A rise in this cost may also help to explain an observed increase in holdings of international reserves.

Some caution needs to be exercised when considering the exact nature of the relationship between IMF lending and the explanatory variables discussed above. As our interest is in forecasting IMF resource use, these variables are only useful if they are consistently connected with IMF lending as leading variables. If the relationship is contemporaneous then we must be able to forecast them with reasonable confidence.

Finally, in studies of participation in IMF programs at the level of individual countries, previous near-term programs are shown to be a significant positive determinant of current programs. This result would seem to imply that, at the aggregate level, IMF lending in any one period will depend on the recent past. Such a conclusion, however, seems to be somewhat at odds with the episodic nature of IMF lending revealed in the previous section.

In summary, rudimentary theorizing would suggest that aggregate IMF lending is a complex phenomenon but will probably depend on a contingent combination of the above demand factors. But is this conjecture confirmed by the empirical evidence and have the underlying relationships changed over time?

4.3.2 Existing Empirical Evidence

Recent research undertaken by the IMF (Ghosh et al., 2007) sets out to model aggregate IMF lending in the form of outstanding credit. Similar to Rowlands (1998), Ghosh et al. use both of the approaches to estimate IMF activity. The first approach involves time series estimation, with the use of IMF resources as the dependent variable, while the second approach uses a two-stage 'program selection and access' model which provides a 'bottom-up' estimation of aggregate IMF lending. Focusing on drawings under GRA facilities, their aggregate econometric model includes measures of the balance of payments in the form of changes in the current account, international reserves in the form of changes in reserve cover for imports, previous IMF programs and the relative cost of IMF borrowing relative to the cost of borrowing international capital.

In terms of this aggregate model they distinguish between long-run coefficients and short-run dynamics that may explain deviations from their long-run model. The long-run determinants included in their model are total debt as a percent of output, short-term debt as a percent of reserve assets, IMF quotas as a percent of output, and the difference between the rate of charge on IMF resources and US bond rates. They attempt to capture short-term dynamics by including the change in IMF credit, the change in the terms of trade, the change in the current account as a percent of previous period output and the change in reserves as a percent of previous period imports. Their estimation results over the period 1980–2005 suggest a long-run positive relationship between the aggregate use of IMF resources and countries' external debt, short-term debt and IMF quota (which they claim may be a proxy for openness). Over the short run, the change in the current account and the import coverage of reserves are also significant.

Their bottom-up analysis reaches broadly similar conclusions, with the decision to seek IMF support depending on the existence of previous programs, oil prices, external debt, international reserve levels, changes in the current account balance of payments, the government balance and the rate of inflation. They also find that access levels depend on total debt in relation to GDP and changes in the current account of the balance of payments. Ghosh et al. claim that their models perform reasonably well in explaining aggregate IMF lending in terms of both 'out-of-sample' forecasting and 'in-sample' estimation, where nearly 70 percent of the variation in IMF credit outstanding is explained.

While adding to our understanding of the use of Fund resources, the relevance of this study for our purposes comes more when the authors turn to using their econometric models to predict the future. While they acknowledge that the predictive power of their models depends on the accuracy with which it is possible to forecast the determinants, and while allowing for over-optimism in IMF macroeconomic forecasts, they predict with some confidence the future path of IMF lending, claiming that 'the use of IMF resources over the next few years is likely to be considerably lower than in the recent past' (Ghosh et al., 2007: 29). They do not anticipate the sharp rise in the use of IMF resources that occurred between early 2008 and 2009.

A fundamental problem is that drawings from emerging economies are affected by the incidence of economic crises. If these crises are difficult to predict accurately then it follows that it will also be difficult to predict accurately the demand for IMF resources. If, beyond this, there are significant elements of interdependence and contagion between emerging economies, the volatility of aggregate IMF lending will be exacerbated.

The remainder of this chapter therefore addresses two issues. First, can further empirical analysis offer greater insights into the determination of aggregate IMF lending? Are there basic empirical regularities that can be identified and, if so, have these changed over time? And second, if it remains difficult to explain past claims on IMF resources, let alone to predict future ones, what implications does this uncertainty have for the design of policy regarding the Fund's lending capacity?

4.3.3 Further Empirical Analysis[3]

In this section of the chapter we undertake three things. First, we examine in more detail the episodic nature of aggregate IMF lending by focusing on variance, cycles and large changes in lending. Second, we calculate bivariate correlations between various measures of IMF lending and some of the variables that our conceptual framework and existing empirical evidence suggest could be relevant. Third, we undertake a simple multivariate regression analysis to examine how the nature of IMF lending has changed over time. As pointed out in Section 1, this contrasts with our previous work that examines the pattern of IMF lending and the probability that individual countries will borrow from the Fund (see, for example, Bird and Rowlands, 2001a, 2002, 2006b, 2009).

IMF lending volatility
We start with two different measures of volatility: the coefficient of variation, and the absolute difference of total new lending from trend expressed as a ratio of the trend level. The results for the full period between 1948 and 2008 as well as 10-year intervals are shown in Table

4.1. Both of the measures indicate that after declining steadily from the early years of operation, the variance in IMF new lending has begun to increase again from the relatively stable period between 1979 and 1988. Over the full sample period the coefficient of variation is 1.24, reflecting the highly volatile early period of IMF operations, including the years in which there were no regularized lending facilities. The coefficient of variation for the period 1998–2008 is nearly twice what it was for the period 1987–97. For this more recent period the deviation from trend measure has also risen above the post-1958 average for the first time since the period 1959–68.

Next we examine the peaks and troughs of annual new IMF lending under stand-by, EFF and PRGF facilities. A peak (trough) is defined as a year in which lending exceeds (is lower than) that of the previous two years and the following two years.[4] Using this definition, peaks occur in 1954, 1957, 1962, 1966, 1970, 1976, 1984, 1999 and 2002, while troughs occur in 1951, 1956, 1960, 1967, 1971, 1974, 1978, 1989, 1997, 2000, 2005 and 2008. On average there are six years between peaks, with a minimum of three years and a maximum of 15. The average number of years between troughs is just over five years, with a minimum of three and a maximum of 11. There is often only one year from a peak to the next trough, though the average is two years and the maximum is five years. The number of years from a trough to the next peak is somewhat higher, with a maximum of six years. A regular cycle is difficult to identify within this pattern. Finally, the profile of peaks and troughs reinforces the results shown in Table 4.1. The volatility of IMF lending is relatively high in the early period, declining from the late 1970s to early 1990s, and then increasing again after the late 1990s.

As the biggest difficulty for resource management within the Fund is in anticipating large increases in lending, we also examine instances where year-on-year increases in lending were more than 75 percent of the previous year's level.[5] These jumps occurred in 1954, 1957, 1961, 1962, 1965, 1969, 1975, 1995, 1998 and 2002. The first six of these significant increases occur in the period building up to, and in the immediate aftermath of, the collapse of the Bretton Woods system, and often involved lending to large industrial countries. There is then a lapse of 20 years before we observe a return to equivalently large jumps, starting in 1995. Once again it is apparent that the volatility of IMF lending appears to be rising back toward the levels last seen during the Bretton Woods period.

It is tempting to surmise that the emerging pattern of increasing volatility is associated with the large expansion in capital markets that has taken place in conjunction with the rapid growth of emerging market economies. By the mid-1990s, there was an increasing number of relatively

Table 4.1   Measures of variation of total new IMF lending

Years	Number of Observations	Coefficient of Variation	Average Absolute Deviation from Trend
1948–2008	61	1.24	0.51
1959–2008	50	1.06	0.44
1948–58	11	1.32	0.87
1959–68	10	0.78	0.73
1969–78	10	0.62	0.41
1979–88	10	0.48	0.22
1989–98	10	0.59	0.37
1999–2008	10	0.88	0.47

Note: The absolute deviation from trend is computed as the absolute difference between actual new lending and the average of the previous and subsequent years' new lending, expressed as a ratio to the average of the previous and subsequent years' new lending.

large economies that were exposed to pronounced capital instability and sudden stops in capital flows that could drive them toward the IMF for financial assistance. If this explanation is accurate then the observed trend toward more volatile lending is not likely to be one that dies away quickly. More countries are expected to join the middle-income emerging market category over time, and even some established wealthier countries have become increasingly vulnerable to financial market turmoil. Indeed, the global economic crisis of late 2008 and early 2009 has shown how quickly nations that were thought to be creditworthy can come under severe economic stress. Borrowing from the Fund by Iceland, Hungary and Latvia may be a harbinger of a new period in the IMF's history during which some wealthier countries return to the group of potential borrowers alongside low-income countries.

Bivariate analysis of IMF lending
In this section we use simple bivariate analysis to examine the extent to which IMF lending is associated with key economic variables at the aggregate level. These variables are selected to reflect the conceptual framework discussed earlier in this section, and include various measures of the balance of payments, debt, interest rates, economic growth and international reserves.

We start by investigating the association between current account balance of payments deficits and IMF lending (all expressed in SDRs). To do this we examine several measures of the current account balance, including the sum of all deficits, the sum of all deficits representing more than 3 percent of GDP of a given country, and the sum of all deficits exceeding 5 percent of GDP. As there will probably be a delay following a balance of payments crisis before a country can reach an agreement with the IMF, we test various lag structures in our estimations. We then repeat this exercise for low-income countries (the 108 poorest countries classified by the World Bank as low-income or low-middle income), for middle-income countries (the 42 countries classified by the Bank as high-middle income) and for low- and middle-income countries (LMIC) combined.

From our conceptual discussion we concluded that increasing global imbalances as reflected by larger current account deficits would not necessarily be associated with larger drawings on the IMF but that it might be reasonable to assume that larger deficits in countries that have traditionally used IMF resources would lead to greater IMF lending. Indeed, correlations with the aggregated current account deficits of all countries reveal no compelling relationship with IMF lending. As deficits in large wealthy countries dominate these totals, the lack of a systematic relationship is reasonably consistent with the conceptual framework. The correlations for the middle-income and low-income groups seem the most coherent and consistent when examined as one combined group, and some of the representative results are presented in Table 4.2.

Three observations may be made based on this table. First, after declining for several years, current account deficits for the low- and middle-income countries appear to be increasing in volatility; forecasting these deficits may prove harder in the future. Second, the generally positive correlation between IMF lending and the different current account measures seems fairly reasonable on a priori grounds, even for the contemporaneous correlation. These results suggest that larger deficits are indeed associated

Table 4.2   Correlations between new IMF lending and LMIC current account (CA) balances

Period	CA Deficit Coefficient of Variation	Contemporaneous		Lagged One Year	
		All	Deficits > 3%	All	Deficits > 3%
1970–2006	1.42	−0.121	−0.328	−0.301	−0.495
1970–78	1.36	−0.313	−0.510	−0.488	−0.543
1979–88	0.43	−0.127	−0.219	−0.634	−0.725
1989–98	0.35	−0.605	−0.704	−0.382	−0.628
1999–2006	0.54	−0.479	+0.747	−0.515	+0.172

with larger IMF lending. In addition, there is no evidence that this correlation is getting consistently weaker over time. Third, and of some interest, the correlation between IMF lending and the sum of larger current
account deficits becomes unexpectedly positive in the 1999–2006 period.
The positive contemporaneous correlation may reflect a process in which
countries are simultaneously borrowing from the IMF and adjusting to
reduce their current account deficits. However, the positive lagged correlation is somewhat less easily explained. It may be that countries are less
inclined to turn to the Fund early on in the adjustment process, but may
be persuaded to draw resources from the IMF when the costs of balance
of payments correction without the Fund's assistance become apparent. In
short, the relationship between Fund activity and current account deficits
appears to be changing.

Finally, as some of the correlation between current account deficits and
IMF lending may reflect upward trends in both, we repeated the analysis using first differences. Apart from the period 1979–88, when there is
some suggestion that large current account deficits drive countries to the
IMF and have a lagged effect on IMF lending, the results for subsequent
periods reveal no clear pattern between current account deficits and IMF
lending.

Countries may sustain a current account deficit without going to the
IMF by borrowing from other official or private sources. To finance substantial deficits, however, a country may have to accumulate debt at an
unsustainable rate that ultimately ends in crisis when lenders seek to limit
their exposure. Thus it is possible that rapid expansions in LMIC debt may
foreshadow crises that require IMF engagement. Accordingly, accumula-
tions of debt should eventually lead to financial difficulties, generating
a positive correlation with IMF lending. We expect that the contemporaneous correlation will be weaker or negative. To test this proposition
we examine the profile of debt accumulation (both public and publicly
guaranteed long-term debt and short-term debt) in this group of countries
to see if it is correlated with IMF lending, and whether the relationship, if
any, has changed over time.

Our results fail to find a clear and stable relationship between debt and
IMF lending. For long-term debt the correlations are mostly positive,
although the period 1979–89 exhibits only a small positive contemporaneous correlation and a negative lagged correlation. Generally the correlations strengthened over the 1989–2007 period to levels of around 0.7, with
correlations for the contemporaneous relationship generally exceeding
slightly those for the lagged one. Of some note is the dramatic decline in
the two-year lagged correlation between IMF lending and long-term debt
in the 1999–2007 period to 0.06, down from 0.75 in the previous 10-year

period. For short-term debt correlations the results are more striking, as these are all positive, fairly high and rise consistently to values of 0.6, 0.7 and 0.75 for the contemporaneous, one-year lagged and two-year lagged (respectively) debt levels for the years 1989–98. Over this period, debt accumulation did appear to be positively associated with IMF lending. After 1998, these correlations change dramatically and become negative at around −0.6. Countries may have been opting to accumulate debt rather than borrow from the Fund. The basic point, however, is that the empirical relationship between debt accumulation and IMF lending does not provide a firm basis upon which to predict either contemporary or future claims on the Fund.

If borrowing from international capital markets is a preferred alternative to borrowing from the IMF then it might be expected that aggregate IMF lending will tend to rise in step with global interest rates. While this pattern is apparent in the overall correlation with real interest rates,[6] which is highest (0.11) for the two-year lag on interest rates, the relationship only holds for the 1979–88 period. For these years there is a strong contemporaneous correlation of 0.71, which declines as lags are introduced. For the period 1989–98 the correlations decline further and become negative for the two-year lag. Finally, in the period 1999–2008 there is a weakly negative (−0.06) contemporaneous correlation that becomes weakly positive (0.02) and then strongly positive (0.43) for the one- and two-year lagged values, respectively. Once more the absence of a stable pattern calls into question any simple story of IMF lending based on access to capital markets and the cost of borrowing from them.

Of course swings in IMF lending may simply follow the global business cycle. The recession of 1982 was a key factor in the subsequent debt crisis and expansion of IMF activity, just as the crisis in 2008–09 might be expected to generate a similar episode of Fund lending. Business cycles are notoriously difficult to predict as well, but in the absence of unusual shocks they do seem to display some stability in frequency from one cycle to the next. Table 4.3 examines how well the actual pattern of IMF lending fits that of business cycles.

Most of the correlations are negative, as expected, with one-year lagged correlations generally exceeding in magnitude their contemporaneous counterparts. While the correlation values are quite high when lagged, the relationship is rather unstable, with the direction of the lagged correlation becoming positive in the 1961–68 and 1989–98 periods.

Finally, we examine the relationship between reserve holdings and IMF lending; it is likely to be complicated and also subject to lags. Countries might finance balance of payments deficits by running down their own international reserves rather than by borrowing from the IMF. But such

Table 4.3   Correlations between new IMF lending and growth rates

Period	Average Growth		Coefficient of Variation		Correlation (No Lag)		Correlation (One-year Lag)	
	World	Low and Middle Income	World	Low and Middle Income	World	Low and Middle Income	World	Low and Middle Income
1961–2006	3.66	4.48	0.42	0.37	−0.43	−0.26	−0.56	−0.36
1961–68	5.39	4.69	0.14	0.38	0.03	−0.35	0.23	0.65
1969–78	4.24	5.66	0.42	0.18	−0.17	−0.29	−0.74	−0.53
1979–88	3.06	3.59	0.46	0.39	−0.05	−0.48	−0.72	−0.85
1989–98	2.78	3.36	0.28	0.37	−0.30	0.10	0.08	0.47
1999–2006	3.10	5.29	0.32	0.34	−0.43	−0.52	−0.90	−0.74

a strategy may not prevent eventual recourse to the Fund. Therefore, low contemporary levels of reserves for low- and middle-income countries should be related to higher levels of IMF lending. Comparisons across time may be complicated by endogeneity, however, as countries may build up their levels of reserves during periods of economic uncertainty and volatility in part to avoid the policy restrictions associated with future IMF borrowing. Given the potentially large swings in capital movements, the pattern may well be that reserves begin to decline sharply in vulnerable countries, but also in aggregate, in the months prior to increased Fund lending.

Our examination of the data suggests that there is no stable relationship between reserves and IMF lending. During the 1969–78 and 1989–98 sub-periods, the full sample correlations are positive for contemporaneous, one-year and two-year lags using total middle- and low-income country international reserves. This group of countries was both accumulating reserves and borrowing from the IMF during these times. For the 1999–2006 period, however, the correlations are all negative and large (roughly −0.55) compared to values of approximately 0.7 for the previous period. The negative correlation observed in recent years reflects the simultaneous increase in reserves and the relatively low use of IMF resources. As with current account deficits, our results find no consistent relationship between decreases in aggregate reserves and increases in IMF lending.

For completeness we re-examined the correlations reported above using first differences. No strong patterns emerged; indeed the correlations generally displayed even greater instability across different periods and with different lags. Similarly there was no apparent pattern by which the peaks or troughs of these different potential determinants aligned with those of IMF lending.

In summary, our bivariate analysis suggests that there is no clear, simple and stable relationship between IMF lending and the factors that theory might suggest would exert an influence on it. Consequently, IMF lending will remain difficult to explain, let alone predict.

Regression analysis of IMF lending

While useful in understanding the basic relationships between new IMF lending and key characteristics of the global economy, bivariate correlations may not reveal true relationships in the presence of multiple contributing factors. Therefore we supplemented our analysis by undertaking some simple multivariate regressions to generate a more comprehensive picture.

Our dependent variable remains new IMF lending in a given year. We first confirmed that this variable did not possess a unit root, using the Phillips–Perron test. We then ran estimations (correcting for first-order autocorrelation using the Prais–Winsten transformed data). As we are primarily interested in forecasting IMF lending, we lagged all the explanatory variables by one year (when two-year lags are used there are no significant coefficient estimates for any of the explanatory variables).

The results shown in Table 4.4 suggest that, while the bivariate correlations reported earlier exhibit considerable instability, these mask some apparently stable and significant relationships. In fact, the adjusted R-squares for both sample periods are reasonably high for the sample sizes (between 0.66 and 0.71). Over both the early and later periods global economic growth has a significant and lagged association with new IMF lending. For the period 1971–89, a 1 percent fall in global growth is associated with an SDR 1.3 billion increase in IMF lending, while for the 1990–2007 period the increase in lending is SDR 6.3 billion. Similarly real interest rates are positively (though weakly) associated with IMF lending. For the period 1971–89, a 1 percent increase in real interest rates is associated with an increase in IMF lending in the following year of SDR 0.96 billion, while for the period 1990–2007 the increase is SDR 2.52 billion. Finally, in the latter period, an increase in short-term debt of SDR 1 billion is associated with an SDR 0.52 billion increase in the following year's level of IMF lending. The regressions provide further evidence that the relationship of IMF lending with other variables (international reserves, long-term debt and current account deficits) is not significant. Our regression results provide some limited support for those reported

Table 4.4   Estimations for new IMF lending, 1971–2007 (million SDRs)

Variable (One-year Lag)	Pre-1990 Estimation Results		Post-1989 Sample Results	
	Estimated Coefficient	t-Statistic	Estimated Coefficient	t-Statistic
Constant	7,457***	4.14	−29,531**	−2.66
Global growth	−1,331***	−3.50	−6,296***	−3.43
Real interest rates	962*	2.06	2,521*	2.17
LMIC reserves	0.580	1.47	−0.106	−0.98
LMIC long-term PPG debt	−0.478	−0.77	0.792	1.11
LMIC short-term debt	−4.83	−0.83	0.518***	4.36
LMIC CA deficits >3% of GDP	−0.20	−0.23	0.0103	1.37
Sample size		19		18
Adjusted *R*-squared		0.66		0.71

Note: Growth and interest rates are expressed in percentages, while reserves, debts and deficits are in billions of SDRs. ***, **, * indicate different from zero at the 1 percent, 2.5 percent and 7.5 percent levels of statistical significance, respectively.

by Ghosh et al. (2007), particularly in being able to identify a reasonable *ex post* explanation of aggregate IMF lending.

While there are too few observations to conduct a satisfactory out-of-sample analysis, we do examine the within-sample accuracy of our underlying econometric model. Specifically, we compare the predictions of the equations with actual lending to see if large increases in IMF lending (an increase of over 50 percent from the previous year) are predicted. While the equation does reasonably well by identifying the big increase in 2002, and does moderately well by predicting the jump in 1990, it does poorly in anticipating the large increases in 1993, 1995 and 1998.

Overall, the conclusion we draw from our empirical investigation is that, while it is possible to isolate a number of factors that seem to exert an influence over aggregate IMF lending, there is substantial evidence that the relationships identified are rather unstable over time. Structural breaks are difficult to anticipate, and new relationships may emerge quickly in an integrated and rapidly changing global financial system. Predicting future IMF lending with any degree of accuracy is extremely difficult and quite possibly too unreliable to be useful.

4.4   POLICIES TO DEAL WITH THE EPISODIC NATURE OF IMF LENDING

While the principal purpose of this chapter is to examine empirically the nature of IMF lending, it would seem appropriate to offer a few observations on the policy implications of our findings. If it is impossible to forecast with reasonable accuracy future claims on the IMF, attention needs to focus on designing a flexible approach to the lending capacity of the Fund in order to meet varying levels of demand for financial assistance. In an earlier article (Bird and Rowlands, 2001b), we discussed this issue in detail, so we discuss it only briefly here.

How has the Fund dealt with variations in the demand for its resources in the past? When initially established the Fund was seen as a credit union. Members paid in their subscriptions based on their quotas and had access to IMF resources when needs arose, again based on their quotas. With both the demand for and supply of IMF resources linked to quotas, there appeared to be an assumption that the demand for Fund assistance would not outstrip the ability of the Fund to meet it. However, over time it became evident that large simultaneous claims on the Fund could lead to a shortage of IMF liquidity and the Fund negotiated the General Arrangements to Borrow (GAB) as a way of augmenting it when needed, borrowing from large, wealthy and financially sound member countries.

After the Mexican 'Peso Crisis' in 1994 / 95, the IMF and its members created the New Arrangements to Borrow to supplement the GAB. Before it came into effect in 1998, however, the East Asian financial crisis had sparked renewed demand for Fund resources. In the aftermath of this new crisis, it became evident that the then current level of quota-based access did not provide the affected emerging economies with adequate amounts of support, given the size of capital outflows they were experiencing. As a result, the Fund invoked its new Supplemental Reserve Facility to allow 'exceptional access' significantly above conventional quota limits. While most Fund arrangements continued to fall within normal access limits, the relatively few that did not in fact often accounted for the clear majority of the IMF's total financial commitments. For example, at the end of 2002, 85 percent of the Fund's commitments were concentrated in five arrangements involving exceptional access, with Turkey borrowing an amount 15 times more than its quota. By this time, in practice, quotas no longer provided much of a constraint on aggregate IMF lending and could not be relied upon to generate an adequate amount of resources for the Fund.

Increasing quotas as a way of dealing with a shortage of IMF liquidity is a double-edged sword, as it increases the potential demand for IMF resources as well as providing additional resources. Moreover, the increased demand associated with quota increases will be for internationally acceptable currencies while the increased supply will, to a large extent, be in currencies that are not 'usable'. On top of this, quota increases are likely to take a long time to negotiate. Using an automatic formula to increase quotas might overcome the problem of delay but it encounters problems of its own. The precise nature of the formula would need to be addressed in such a way that it proxies the need for IMF resources and, as the empirical findings reported above show, it would be difficult to design such a formula. Moreover, given that quota changes would probably be asymmetrical, having the capacity to increase but not diminish, there would be a real possibility that for protracted periods the Fund could have substantial unused lending capacity. Finally, quota changes would also probably affect the balance of voting within the Fund and the distribution of institutional management control, introducing contentious political debates into an already difficult economic problem. Quota reform by itself, therefore, seems an inadequate tool for addressing problems at the IMF (see Bird and Rowlands, 2006a, for a further discussion).

Borrowing by the IMF from wealthy and financially secure member countries, as is incorporated in the GAB and NAB, and as endorsed by the G20 in early 2009, also has undesirable characteristics. It may again involve delay. Certainly it carries with it the additional politicization of IMF lending. Those countries providing the resources may take the opportunity to argue for concessions; there may be a *quid pro quo*. Finally, the 2008 / 09 crisis highlighted the degree to which the demand for IMF resources by emerging market countries may coincide with (or be caused by) financial and economic problems in wealthy countries. Domestic problems may limit the willingness or ability of some countries to provide the necessary resources.

An alternative is for the IMF to borrow from private international capital markets when it faces short-term problems of illiquidity. While the quota system could be retained—albeit on a reformed basis (see Bird and Rowlands, 2006a)—the Fund could substitute borrowing from private capital markets for borrowing from wealthy and financially sound member countries as a way of augmenting its lending capacity when the need arises.

The advantage of this method of financing the IMF is that it would be quick-acting and would avoid the political aspects of borrowing from member countries. It would be an option that would only be activated in circumstances of IMF illiquidity, so it would not involve the Fund holding excess lending capacity. It would also expose the portfolio of IMF loans to market judgment and this would constrain the possibility that the Fund might be tempted to engage in excessive lending. As the Fund would only be activating the option in circumstances where large emerging economies were turning to it for financial support, and as there is a reasonable presumption that such countries would only be coming to the Fund where they had lost direct access to private capital markets, there is little danger that borrowing by the IMF would crowd out direct lending by capital markets to the affected countries. The Fund could use its holdings of gold as collateral and the evidence on arrears suggests that it is highly unlikely that the Fund would face a serious problem of default on its own loans; the costs of defaulting on IMF debt in terms of future access to international capital would be perceived by borrowing countries as exceeding the short-term benefits.

The idea of the Fund borrowing from private capital markets is not a new one and it has been rejected in the past. The reasons for rejection have been, first, that it is out of character for the Fund and inconsistent with the credit union idea, and, second, that it would crowd out direct lending to member countries and possibly the World Bank as well. There has also been, one suspects, the feeling amongst important shareholding countries that quota-based resources impose a constraint on IMF lending and that using quotas and borrowing from powerful members keeps the Fund on a 'short leash'. Finally, there is the suggestion that the Fund would become too dependent on private capital markets and would become an agent of the markets, with this exerting an adverse effect on other aspects of the Fund's operations, such as the design of conditionality. While certainly worthy of serious scrutiny these counter-arguments are not compelling. As noted above, the character of the Fund has been, and is, changing and the IMF needs to look to the future and not the past. The important point is to ensure that the Fund has sufficient flexibility in terms of its own resources to perform its global functions properly, including lending to member countries in appropriate circumstances. Also as noted above, the Fund would not be borrowing while emerging economies retained direct access to international capital markets. Once more as noted earlier, quotas have not imposed an effective constraint on IMF lending, and borrowing under the GAB and NAB arrangements carries political implications. The danger of 'unleashing' an expansionist IMF by allowing it uncontrolled access to international capital markets, as some public choice theorists fear, can also be seriously overstated. The markets themselves would impose discipline. And, even if the IMF were to be granted a greater degree of independence such that political constraints via the Executive Board were to be reduced, the Independent

Evaluation Office could be used to audit the Fund's borrowing operations. The danger of allowing private markets to exert excessive influence over IMF policy because of their creditor role may also be less than some might assume. The IMF would be an attractive borrower given the low risk of it defaulting, and the relative attraction of lending to the IMF would be particularly strong in circumstances where direct lending to individual countries had become unattractive. Combined with the fact that the behavior of individual private lenders would be difficult to coordinate, the threat of withholding financial support for the IMF by international capital markets would lack credibility. It therefore seems unlikely that the Fund would merely be swapping one group of 'principals' in the form of those member countries providing additional financial support under the NAB or GAB, for another group in the form of private international capital markets.

In the aftermath of the global financial crisis, many national governments borrowed in order to provide resources to companies to which the banks were not prepared to lend. Moreover, a strong argument has been made that these activities need to be internationally coordinated. There may be a logical consistency between this policy and the idea that the Fund should be prepared to borrow from international capital markets in order to finance loans to countries to which the markets are no longer prepared to lend directly. In the former case, the rationale is to help avoid prolonged economic recession and to stimulate economic growth. A similar rationale can be applied to the proposal for an expansion in IMF lending financed by direct borrowing from private international capital markets.

A more ambitious solution to meet the Fund's need for resources would be to expand the role of the SDR, allowing SDR creation to be used as a means of financing the Fund's lending operations. This is not a new idea either. However, the chances of it happening depend on the political acceptability of significantly enhancing the functions of SDRs in the international monetary system. For reasons examined in Bird (2010), these chances appear to be rather low and considerably lower than the chances of activating a scheme for borrowing from private international capital markets.

4.5   CONCLUDING REMARKS

One legacy of the global financial crisis that engulfed the world at the end of 2008 has been to refocus attention on the IMF. In early 2008, the Fund's profile had been fairly low. It had a limited portfolio of outstanding loans and some influential observers were claiming that it was becoming irrelevant to the world economy. But, by the end of the year, the Fund was being seen as a potentially pivotal institution for helping to deal with the global crisis. Some notable affected countries were turning to the Fund for financial assistance and the concern was that the IMF might run out of resources. Attempting to explain the often dramatic swings in IMF lending has been the main purpose of this chapter.

Empirical investigation reveals that IMF lending is episodic and unpredictable. Unforeseen crises in important emerging economies can have a dramatic effect on aggregate IMF lending. This implies that a method for financing the Fund's lending operations needs to be found that allows a quick and large response. Flexibility needs to be built into the resource capacity of the IMF. This is not satisfactorily achieved by the current quota system or by the current borrowing arrangements based on the GAB and NAB. Nor would it be achieved by having an automatic system based on a revised quota formula as the underlying determinants of the demand for IMF resources are unclear and unstable. An alternative that is worthy of close inspection is to encourage the Fund to borrow directly from private international capital markets when its own liquidity is threatened. Such reform could be one element of a broader reform of the international monetary system that incorporates occasional allocations of SDRs and enhanced regional monetary arrangements.

ACKNOWLEDGMENTS

The authors acknowledge the helpful comments of Jeff Chwieroth on an earlier version of this chapter as well as an anonymous referee.

NOTES

1. These concessional arrangements for low-income countries became a constant feature of IMF lending after 1987 following the introduction of the Structural Adjustment Facility (SAF) and the immediate predecessor to the PRGF, the Enhanced Structural Adjustment Facility (ESAF). For a brief description and discussion of recent changes to the range of IMF facilities, see Bird (2009b).
2. Supply-side factors are certainly deserving of their own analysis, especially if we wished to determine how anticipated policy changes might affect resource claims on the IMF. The analysis would be complex, however. For example, if policy conditionality became more stringent we might expect a decline in the demand for IMF loans. In truth, the period of the 1980s is associated with both increasingly intrusive conditionality and high lending, in part because the high demand for its resources gave the IMF leverage over its clients. Similarly, an expansion in quotas and relaxation of access limits would be likely to lead to larger loans, but would themselves probably be lagged reflections of high demand.

3.　All data on IMF lending and programs were collected from the IMF Annual Reports. All other data are taken from the World Bank's World Development Indicators 2008 CD-ROM.
4.　It should be noted that the measure of a trough is independent of the measure of a peak, and hence there can be two peak years without an intervening trough year. Consequently these peaks and troughs do not define true cycles, but rather provide an alternative means of examining variability.
5.　In fact all of these cases, with the exception of 1995, represented more than a doubling of the previous year's new lending.
6.　The real interest rate was calculated as the secondary market LIBOR on six-month US Treasury bills, less the US rate of consumer inflation.

REFERENCES

Bird, G. (1995). *IMF Lending to Developing Countries: Issues and Evidence*. London: Routledge.

Bird, G. (2007). The IMF: A bird's eye view of its role and operations. *Journal of Economic Surveys*, 21(4), 683–745.

Bird, G. (2009a). So far so good, but still some missing links: A report card on the G20 London summit. *World Economics*, 10(2), 1–10.

Bird, G. (2009b). Reforming IMF conditionality: from streamlining to major overhaul. *World Economics*, 10(3), 81–104.

Bird, G. (2010). Special drawing rights: How fashions change. *World Economics*, 11(1), 83–98.

Bird, G. and Rowlands, D. (2001a). IMF lending: How is it affected by economic, political and institutional factors? *Journal of Policy Reform*, 4(3), 243–270.

Bird, G. and Rowlands, D. (2001b). Catalysis or direct borrowing: The role of the IMF in mobilizing private capital. *World Economy*, 24(1), 81–98.

Bird, G. and Rowlands, D. (2002). The pattern of IMF lending: An analysis of prediction failures. *Journal of Policy Reform*, 5(3), 173–186.

Bird, G. and Rowlands, D. (2006a). The political economy of IMF quotas: Construction with inferior building blocks. *Review of International Organizations*, 1(2), 153–171.

Bird, G. and Rowlands, D. (2006b). The demand for IMF assistance: What factors influence the decision to turn to the Fund?, in J. Vreeland, G. Ranis and S. Kosack (eds), *Globalisation and the Nation State: The Impact of the IMF and the World Bank*: 231–262. London: Routledge.

Bird, G. and Rowlands, D. (2009). A disaggregated empirical analysis of the determinants of IMF arrangements: Does one model fit all? *Journal of International Development*, 21, 915–931.

Bird, G. and Willett, T.D. (2007). Multilateral surveillance: Is the IMF shooting for the stars? *World Economics*, 8(4), 167–189.

Ghosh, A., Goretti, M., Joshi, B., Thomas, A., and Zalduendo, J. (2007). Modeling aggregate use of Fund resources: Analytical approaches and medium term projections. *IMF Working Paper* No. WP / 07 / 70, Washington, DC: International Monetary Fund.

Rowlands, D. (1998). Quantitative approaches to sovereign risk assessment: Implications for IMF response, in S. Schmeidl and H. Adelman (eds), *Early*

Warning and Early Response, Columbia International Affairs Online. New York: Columbia University Press. Retrieved on January 20, 2010 from http://www. ciaonet.org/book/schmeidi/index.html.

Steinwand, M. and Stone, R. (2008). The International Monetary Fund: A review of the recent evidence. *Review of International Organizations*, 3(2), 123–149.

5. Participation in IMF programs

5.1 INTRODUCTION

As shown in Chapters 1 and 4 the use of IMF credits is episodic. IMF lending was low in the mid-2000s but rose sharply toward the end of the decade and in the aftermath of the global financial and economic crisis in 2008–09. Some relatively rich Eurozone countries with balance of payments problems entered into programs with the Fund. In contrast and following the East Asian crisis in 1997–98 some emerging economies may have sought to run balance of payments surpluses in order to accumulate large reserves and avoid the need to participate in IMF programs. Unfortunately the factors that shape the pattern of participation remain unclear.

Many contend that participation reflects the political influence of the Fund's most powerful members. More specifically allies of the United States are suspected of receiving programs more easily, and on better terms. Others argue that while political factors may be important in some cases, it is invalid to claim that IMF lending is purely political in nature. Their argument is instead that there are a number of economic factors that lie at the heart of participation. Our purpose in this chapter is to investigate the range of economic and political factors that may in principle be associated with participation in IMF programs.

We begin the chapter by outlining an analytical framework within which the determination of participation may be conceptualized. We then examine what the existing literature tells us about the potential determinants. Next, we present and estimate our own base model, but extend this by disaggregating it in various ways. In a concluding section we summarize our most important findings and explore some of their policy implications.

5.2 PARTICIPATION IN IMF PROGRAMS: A SIMPLE ANALYTICAL FRAMEWORK

A brief and informal model to explain the pattern of IMF arrangements begins with the assumption that a country will be more likely to contemplate turning to the Fund when its balance of payments becomes unsustainable.[1] While the specific causes may vary, unsustainability generally reflects a combination of domestic economic imbalances and external shocks. Economic imbalances typically arise from economic mismanagement including excessive fiscal deficits financed either by the accumulation of large foreign debts or by inflationary monetary expansion. Shocks may emanate from the current account (such as terms of trade shocks) or the capital account (such as capital reversals, or sudden stops or capital flight). These underlying problems will sometimes be structural, deep seated and difficult to correct in the short to medium term. On other occasions they may be temporary and self-correcting. Consequently we should expect that some countries will have an enduring relationship with the IMF while others will be infrequent clients.

Responding to an unsustainable balance of payments situation requires a blend of financing (including the running down of international reserves) and adjustment (including exchange rate devaluation or aggregate demand compression). Some governments may quickly seek IMF assistance to supplement short term financing capacity. But even governments that are initially disinclined to turn to the Fund may ultimately be forced to do so if their international reserves and borrowing options are depleted before adjustment policies bring about a sustainable balance of payments. Foreign creditors may also place considerable pressure on a country to follow an IMF program in order to improve their chances of getting repaid. Participation may then be a precondition of debt rescheduling.

Domestic politics seem likely to play a role in determining whether or not governments seek IMF assistance. When facing powerful special interests that are adversely affected by IMF policy requirements, and especially if elections are approaching, they may be disinclined to refer to the Fund. This may be in spite of the fact that, in principle, a program provides resources that can accommodate a slower (and politically more acceptable) speed of adjustment or can be used to compensate those who lose from participation in an IMF program and therefore oppose its adoption. Having the IMF as a scapegoat for politically unpopular policies (Vreeland, 1999) may be insufficient to overcome a government's desire to retain national control over economic policy.

When a combination of these demand side factors ultimately compels a government to request its assistance, the IMF has to determine its response. In principle, politics may also play a significant role on the supply side as well. A principal–agent model suggests that the IMF will seek to promote (at least in part) the interests of its principals, variously identified as international financiers (Gould, 2003), the richer shareholders of the IMF (Copelovitch, 2005), or just the US (Thacker, 1999).

There is little doubt that the US has the ability to exert considerable influence within the IMF. It retains an effective veto over key decisions affecting quota increases, SDR allocations, and reforms to conditionality and IMF lending facilities. The tradition of consensus for important decisions also gives it considerable influence, which may be supplemented by the use of 'soft power' to affect outcomes indirectly. The US Congress provides clear guidelines on how US Executive Directors (USED) are to act at the IMF in order to promote US interests, as documented in the annual reports produced by the Treasury Department for Congress.[2] Of the fourteen provisions circumscribing the USED's actions, only five deal with technical economic guidance. The remaining ones address democratic governance, social stability, corruption and bribery, social equity, labor standards, ethnic strife, the environment, and heavily indebted poor countries.

But how might it be expected that the US (and other important stakeholders) would use their influence? When their interests are not at stake, they may opt not to interfere with the IMF's routine decisions and endorse the views of the Fund's senior management. However, when they are at stake, they may either apply direct pressure or use their voting power to bring about a particular outcome. Alternatively, they may rely on the discretion of IMF staff and management to accommodate their interests. In addition, there may be considerable self-selection on the demand side for IMF programs; governments on good terms with powerful countries may quickly turn to the Fund, while other less favored ones may not bother to approach the IMF anticipating that an agreement will be opposed.

The simple framework outlined above suggests that there is likely to be a fairly standard list of economic and political factors that will be closely associated with participation in IMF programs. Agreements will be quite probable when there are severe economic problems and where the political circumstances are conducive. However the analysis also suggests that, in many cases, participation will be contingent on the presence of certain combinations of economic and political factors. Their relative significance and the required combinations are also likely to differ across time periods, regions, and income groups, as well as across individual countries. The causes of balance of payments difficulties may, for example, differ between low-income and emerging economies. Domestic politics may or may not create a barrier to an agreement. Finally the influence of international politics may sometimes be crucial.

This theoretical discussion implies that standard large sample estimations may fail to identify a single universal model of IMF participation with strong explanatory powers. Instead, the results of statistical models are likely to be sensitive to the characteristics of the sample, such as country wealth, program type, time, and regional location.

5.3   EXISTING STUDIES OF IMF PARTICIPATION

There is an extensive literature that looks either directly or indirectly at participation in IMF programs. Useful reviews of the literature may be found in Bird (2007), Steinwand and Stone (2008) and Moser and Sturm (2011).

Most studies involve large sample regression analysis. However, there are also small-scale investigations. With respect to international politics, for example, Swedberg (1986), Finch (1989), Stiles (1991), and Meltzer (2000) cite instances of US influence on Fund operations. However these accounts are anecdotal, and do not in themselves constitute strong evidence of systematic bias.

Early quantitative studies typically focused on the country-level economic conditions associated with IMF programs. Bird and Orme (1981) provided the first examination and concluded that a more nuanced approach that incorporated political and institutional factors was needed. However, the studies that followed continued to focus primarily on economic determinants (Cornelius, 1987; Joyce, 1992; Conway, 1994; Rowlands, 1995; Santaella, 1996; and Knight and Santaella, 1997). These papers highlighted factors such as balance-of-payments performance, international reserve cover, gross domestic product (GDP) growth, external debt and debt service, inflation, the fiscal balance, and a country's domestic credit to the government. Though a degree of consensus began to form around some of the economic dimensions of the basic model, for others, such as reserve depletion, a rather ambiguous and complex relationship with IMF programs emerged (Bird and Rowlands, 2002).

A consistent finding was that a history of frequent engagement with the IMF did much to explain future involvement. This variable was in turn interpreted as incorporating unobserved phenomena such as institutional learning or inertia. There was also the notion that there is a fixed political cost associated with turning to the Fund which, once incurred, makes subsequent agreements less daunting. More frequent interactions between the country officials negotiating programs and IMF staff may also facilitate future programs.

Unfortunately these studies failed to identify a single uniform model that explains well the pattern of IMF programs. For example, in a typical sample an unconditional guess of 'no agreement' would itself be correct 80–85 percent of the time given the overall incidence of IMF programs. The prediction rates of participation models were only marginally superior.

The challenge of finding a better model encouraged further investigation. Several researchers pursued the path of developing more sophisticated economic models. Elekdag (2006) for example emphasizes global economic conditions such as oil prices, world interest rates, and GDP, while Bal Gunduz (2009) emphasizes the link between economic shocks and the more specific use of individual IMF facilities. Others opted to explore the domestic political dimensions of participation in more depth (Vreeland, 1999, and Przeworski and Vreeland, 2000, 2002). Generally these studies reinforced previous results in terms of the significant economic variables, but they also found that countries were more likely to seek an IMF program reasonably shortly after elections had taken place.

While Rowlands (1995) had found a weak connection between US military and economic assistance and IMF agreements, it was not until Thacker (1999) that the perspective of international relations and geostrategic interests became a critical component in the analysis of participation. Researchers had become interested in the use of UN voting similarities as a measure of foreign policy alignment (Voeten, 2000). Thacker operationalized this idea by examining whether a country voted the same way as the US on United Nations (UN) resolutions deemed to be of importance to the US. More specifically, he examined whether a country's votes were becoming increasingly aligned with US votes over time, and whether the change in alignment affected its access to IMF resources and the probability of there being an IMF program. He concluded that US foreign policy interests had a statistically significant effect that was robust over both the Cold War and post-Cold War periods of his sample that covered the period 1985–94. Although Thacker was somewhat cautious about how his results should be interpreted, and others were concerned about the lack of underlying theory (Woods, 2003), his paper made a strategically important contribution to our understanding of participation.

There were several studies that followed up on Thacker's results. Bird and Rowlands (2001) concluded that some of the results were sample-specific, and that many basic political economy variables failed to improve the explanatory power of a well-designed economic model of IMF agreements. Oatley and Yackee (2000, 2004) found that countries to which US banks were heavily exposed were treated more favorably by the IMF. However, the coefficient estimate on UN voting proximity was only marginally significant. In their probit regression of 24 developing countries, Eichengreen et al. (2004) found that while UN voting affinity with the United States had a statistically significant relationship with participation in IMF programs, the coefficient's sign implied that a country voting differently than the US on key UN votes was *more* likely to receive IMF financing. Stone (2008) sought to capture US interests by using foreign aid allocations, and found that countries that received relatively large amounts of US foreign aid were significantly more likely to have an IMF program; by contrast he found that UN voting had no apparent influence.[3]

In an attempt to test for more general political influence, Barro and Lee (2005) examined not only UN voting coincidence with the US but also similar UN voting proximity variables and trade variables for the UK, Germany, France and Europe as a whole. Of these, only the UN voting affinity with Europe, and the US trade variables, had statistically significant coefficient estimates in their fully specified model. Copelovitch (2005) also extended the focus beyond US influence, finding that Group of Five (G5) bank exposure increased the amount of financial support offered. These findings were supported by Broz and Hawes (2006) who found that US and German bank exposure were linked to higher IMF participation rates; though again they discovered no connection to UN voting affinity with US or European interests. Breen (2010) also emphasized G5 banking exposure with results that were consistent with those of Copelovitch (2005). While Sturm et al. (2005) could not replicate Copelovitch's results for bank exposure, they did find that IMF participation was affected by executive elections, legislative elections, the percentage of veto players who drop from the government, and the presence of ethnic tensions. Ghosh et al. (2007) did not find any significant relationship between US or Western European foreign policy variables and IMF lending. More recently, however, Presbitero and Zazzaro (2012) have found that political similarity with G7 countries is positively correlated with the probability of entering a loan agreement with the Fund.

The pattern of inconsistent results encouraged additional attempts to incorporate political influence in more complex ways. For example, Anderson et al. (2006) argue that a country's true preferences, or 'bliss point', are reflected in its voting patterns on non-key UN resolutions. Their empirical analysis supported the hypothesis that countries which subordinated their preferences and voted with the US more often on key votes than non-key votes were rewarded with IMF resources. Dreher, Sturm, and Vreeland (2006, 2009) and Dreher and Vreeland (2011) extended the literature by examining whether temporary United Nations Security Council (UNSC) membership affected a country's relationship with organizations such as the Fund. Their results indicated that UNSC membership led to a greater likelihood that an IMF member would receive a Fund arrangement during their period of tenure; this effect was less important after the period of the Cold War.

Contrasting results were, however, found by Reynaud and Vauday (2009) who constructed a 'geopolitical potential' variable to measure a country's geopolitical importance. The variable's components included energy resources, nuclear energy endowment, military power, and geographic size. Their geopolitical potential variable was found to be statistically significant in all specifications, while the UN voting variable was significant in only one specification, and the UNSC membership indicator was never significant. Disaggregating a part of their study by program type also revealed that geopolitical factors seemed to be most important when non-concessional loans were being disbursed.

Insights from disaggregation were also provided by Pop-Eleches (2008, 2009) who estimated participation equations for different regions and time periods. In terms of political influence, he found that voting alignment with the United States at the UN only seemed to matter for post-Soviet countries following the collapse of the Communist bloc, whereas American foreign assistance was important only for Latin American countries from 1990 to 2001. Similarly, Bird and Rowlands (2009) disaggregated their sample by per capita income and concluded that even the economic factors driving participation in IMF programs differed significantly between low-income and middle-income countries.[4]

Finally, Moser and Sturm (2011) made an important contribution to our understanding of the post-Cold War participation of countries in IMF programs by using a variety of techniques to identify the variables that exert a statistically significant and robust effect on IMF agreements. They emphasize the need to distinguish between concessional and non-concessional arrangements, and show that political variables exert greater influence over program conditions than participation. Their results are, however, somewhat at odds with Steinwand and Stone's (2008: 129) overall conclusion that 'one of the most robust findings that emerges from the new focus on political determinants of IMF lending is that program initiation is significantly shaped by the geopolitical preferences of the countries that contribute the most resources, particularly the United States.'

Given the conflicting evidence cited above, the objective of this chapter is to provide a systematic examination of the evidence relating to participation in IMF programs. Our base probit model incorporates both economic and political variables and we investigate almost all the variables that have been found to be significant in earlier studies. Given the simple analytical framework that we introduced in the previous section, we test to see whether the determinants of participation vary across countries and regions, across IMF facilities, and over time. We also test to evaluate the extent of political influence over participation.

5.4   LARGE SAMPLE EVIDENCE ON IMF PARTICIPATION

The empirical analysis uses probit estimations to explain the signing of IMF agreements. The dependent variable is coded as 0 for a country in a calendar year where it did not sign a conditional Fund program, and 1 when it did. We exclude from the sample those cases where for most of a given calendar year a country was either already operating under an agreement or suspended from its borrowing rights at the IMF (usually for being in prolonged arrears to the Fund). By failing to exclude these cases, our focus on the signing of an agreement as opposed to having an IMF agreement in place would result in countries being expected to sign but not doing so because they already have an agreement in place. Our work here and elsewhere confirms that not adjusting the sample accordingly severely affects the performance of the model. The 'preliminary model' is estimated using an unbalanced panel of 1622 observations for 113 countries covering agreements signed during the period 1984–2008. The start date in 1984 is determined by the availability of one of the core political influence variables based on UN voting affinity with the United States, which is first reported in 1983. We chose to end the data in 2008 in order to avoid the noise that might be connected to the global economic and financial crisis that erupted in that year.

A second model, the 'base' model, adds current and future rescheduling indicators to the preliminary model, and is consequently estimated on a smaller sample of 1546 observations from 1984 to 2007. The forward looking element of the base model can be seen as somewhat controversial, though in our view it is critical to include these additional variables because institutional arrangements surrounding debt rescheduling essentially require an accompanying IMF agreement. Therefore if a country does need to reschedule its debt, it will be important to receive an IMF program before or contemporaneously with the rescheduling agreement.

The choice of explanatory variables follows from our earlier conceptual discussion and the results of previous studies. Variables that do not generate statistically significant coefficient estimates in the preliminary model are dropped from the estimation in order to maximize the sample size. This preliminary model reflects our best attempt to incorporate all of those variables identified by previous studies as being important, either in terms of magnitude or statistical significance. In many cases an explanatory variable has been represented by many different versions, and we choose the one which worked best in our estimation. For example, a country's foreign reserves have been used in participation equations in several forms such as: reserves with or without gold; reserves scaled to GDP, imports, debt–service obligations, short-term debt, or some combination of these; and levels of reserves as well as changes in levels. For the most part the results are broadly comparable for similar representations of the same variable, and where there are significant differences in the theory underlying a variable, we test each one separately. The Appendix provides the summary statistics and formal definition of the basic variables, and the associated hypotheses that typically link them to IMF program participation. For the most part the results are largely robust to variations in the variables and models as estimated for the full sample.

A key dimension of this study and of related previous work, however, is the frequent absence of robustness and consistency of the results when examining different samples. While perhaps not surprising, this inconsistency suggests that there is no uniform general model of explaining participation, and that to get a more accurate understanding of the processes that explain the IMF's relations with its member countries it is necessary to use more disaggregated models and samples. The absence of a general model also makes it more difficult to evaluate the effects of IMF programs, as we discuss in Chapter 7.

Our first test examines the importance of a country's past participation in IMF programs, which most studies find to be of significance both statistically and in terms of the magnitude of its effect. Running the estimation using a model that has only an indicator of past IMF agreements in the previous three years yields a pseudo R^2 value of 0.1415 on a sample of 3200 observations.[5] Further tests indicate that this effect is not due solely to the need to refinance past debts to the IMF, so this variable may well be reflecting the fostering of institutional linkages between a government and the Fund, or the presence of a political predisposition on the part of the government to return to the IMF.

To get a sense of how well our model performs relative to others, we eliminated some explanatory variables that had many missing observations so as to expand our sample. One version of the model can be estimated on a sample of 2508 observations, with the resulting pseudo R^2 of 0.21. By this basic but standard measure of model performance our model compares quite favorably to that reported in Moser and Sturm (2011) who obtain a pseudo R^2 of 0.11 using a sample of 2753 observations. We conclude from this that our modeling approach performs quite well relative to competing versions in the literature. When we examine our base model we obtain a pseudo R^2 of 0.27 on a much reduced, but still large, sample of 1546 observations. In this model the percentage of countries in the sample signing an agreement is 24.64, meaning that if we made an uninformed guess of 'no agreement' for each case we would be correct 75.36 percent of the time. Our model has a correct prediction rate of 81.18 percent, suggesting that our model improves our predictive capacity by a modest, but still important, 5.82 percent. Of course this crude calculation does not indicate how confident we could be in our model, and so later we examine the sensitivity of our results.

The results of the preliminary and base models appear in Table 5.1, where we report the marginal effects of each variable (as calculated conditionally for all other variables being at their mean) as well as their associated z-scores. Here we focus on explaining the main results that arise from the base model only, and subsequently examine how the results change for the other estimation versions we examine. The first two variables examine the importance of IMF-related variables. Having had an IMF program in any of the past three years increases the probability of signing a new agreement by about 20 percent. Similarly, a one standard deviation increase (about 4 percent) in outstanding debts to the Fund as a share of GDP raises the likelihood of signing an agreement by about 2 percent.

The global economic variables, which have a statistically significant effect in the preliminary model, perform less well in the base model. The impact of these variables appears to be displaced by the importance of rescheduling, though there is some diminution in their influence attributable to the sample change as well.[6] We conclude from these results that the global economic effects are probably mostly felt through capital market conditions and rescheduling opportunities, rather than through trade relationships. The only global economic factor that does seem to have a significant, but statistically marginal, effect is that of exports to G5 countries. This variable is often used to measure the commercial interests of the wealthier states, though in our results the sign of the effect is negative, suggesting that countries with G5 commercial links are less likely to sign an IMF agreement. Therefore this relationship seems more likely to reflect the impact of economic conditions rather than political ones, and hence we include it here rather than in the political variables section.

In constructing the base model, several political variables were tried before arriving at the final specification used.[7] The variables included US economic aid, USAID aid, US State Department aid, US military aid, total G5 aid (including testing each G5 country individually), total G5 exports (including testing each G5 country individually), total G5 imports (including testing each G5 country individually), G5 bank exposure (including testing each G5 country individually), numerous variations of UN voting patterns on key votes for the US, membership on the UN Security Council, presence of coups, democracy and autocracy measures, the timing of elections, and various levels and changes in levels of Freedom House measures of civil and political freedom. While many of these variables have been found to have statistically significant coefficient estimates in models presented by other researchers, there was often no such finding when the variables were added individually or in combination to our model. Consequently we suspect that previous conclusions regarding the importance of these political variables may not be very robust. While

Table 5.1   Non-rescheduling and base models: probit of IMF program signing

Explanatory Variable (all lagged one year)	Preliminary Model		Base Model	
	Marginal effects	Z-score	Marginal effects	Z-score
IMF variables				
Past IMF program	0.189***	8.52	0.201***	8.46
IMF debt/GDP	0.496*	2.07	0.477†	1.87
Global Economic Variables				
Crude oil prices	−0.114**	−2.27	−0.134	−1.47
Agricultural prices	0.00175**	2.56	0.000790	0.99
Exports to G5 countries	−0.244*	−2.04	−0.210†	−1.83
Political Variables				
UN voting proximity	0.146***	3.64	0.164***	3.83
US economic aid	0.443***	4.86	0.441***	4.48
Legislative election	0.0599*	2.23	0.0521†	1.84
Executive elections	0.0766**	2.31	0.0879**	2.49
Domestic Economic Variables				
Debt service to exports ratio	0.389***	6.51	0.339***	4.86
Current account/GDP< −0.03	0.0745***	3.56	0.0758***	3.37
Reserves to months of imports	−0.0136***	−3.02	−0.00777†	−1.78
Currency depreciation	−0.00000194†	−1.93	−0.00000260**	−2.27
Real per capita GDP growth	−0.369***	−3.21	−0.392***	−3.27
Real per capita GDP	−0.0111***	−2.78	−0.00773†	−1.89
Official arrears	−0.00460**	−2.27	−0.00595**	−2.56
Private arrears	0.00253**	2.53	0.000903	0.85
Debt Rescheduling Variables				
Past private rescheduling	0.0218	0.49	−0.0990**	−2.39
Past official rescheduling	0.0139	0.36	−0.0605	−1.43
Current private rescheduling	–	–	0.228***	3.91
Current official rescheduling	–	–	0.0318	0.73
Future private rescheduling	–	–	0.0690	1.45
Future official rescheduling	–	–	0.124***	2.77
Sample size	1622		1546	
Pseudo R^2	0.217		0.268	
Percentage with an agreement	24.17		24.64	
Percentage correctly classified	79.41		81.18	
Improvement over 'no' guess	3.58		5.82	

Note: Reported marginal effects significant at the 1, 2.5, 5 and 10 percent levels (one-tailed test) are identified with ***, **, * and † respectively.

we cannot definitively reject their potential influence, the statistical insignificance of these variables' coefficient estimates in our model, which has more observations and higher overall R^2 values, suggests that the influence of these factors is far less systematic than has sometimes been suggested.

From the above list, political variables were included in the base model where they generated statistically significant coefficient estimates. These were the one-year lagged versions of UN voting similarities with the US, US economic aid, elections (both legislative and executive) and trade links with G5 countries. The first two of these corroborate the idea that there is a higher likelihood of IMF agreements for countries with favorable links to the US. The magnitude of this effect seems rather small, however, at least relative to other claims in the literature. In Table 5.1 we also report for the base model the marginal effects of each variable, as calculated for a country with explanatory variables at the mean of their distribution. For example, a 10 percent movement in its UN voting pattern toward the United States would increase such a country's probability of entering into an IMF program by about 1.5 percent (10×0.146). A recent election is also associated with a higher propensity (of around 6 to 7 percent) for a country to sign an IMF agreement.

In terms of the more conventional economic variables, a reasonably typical story emerges from the base model. Higher propensities to enter a Fund agreement are linked to high debt service burdens (a 10 percent increase in the debt–service to exports ratio increases signing probability by over 3 percent),[8] current account deficits in excess of 3 percent of GDP (a serious current account deficit increases the signing probability by over 7 percent), and lower levels of reserves (if the number of months of imports covered by reserves increases by one, the signing propensity declines at the margin by under 1 percent). Exchange rate depreciation is linked to a lower signing propensity, though the effect is very small. By contrast a 1 percent increase in the average growth rate reduces the signing probability by nearly 40 percent in the base model, though having a higher per-capita income level of $1000 reduces the probability of signing by less than 1 percent. High levels of arrears to private creditors increases signing propensities.[9] Unexpectedly, arrears to official creditors are linked to lower propensities to enter into IMF agreements. This result may reflect the tolerance of official arrears by bilateral donors and less pressure to sign an IMF agreement or seek rescheduling. In a sense, official arrears may serve as a substitute for alternative official help via the IMF. In any case, the magnitude of the effects of arrears are quite small.

Finally, the base model includes an expanded examination of rescheduling behavior. As discussed already, the inclusion of rescheduling activity is critical for understanding the need for a Fund agreement, as the London

Club and Paris Club processes effectively require the IMF's participation and imprimatur. In general, having rescheduled debt already in the previous year is associated with a lower propensity to sign an agreement again, presumably since the immediate rescheduling needs have been met. The results here indicate that IMF agreements occur in the same year as London Club rescheduling, suggesting that they seem to be negotiated in close conjunction with one another. This temporal proximity is not observed for Paris Club agreements, however, with IMF agreements associated with future (following year) official reschedulings. The marginal effects for these rescheduling agreements are significant as well, with a current London Club agreement associated with a 23 percent higher probability of signing an IMF agreement, and a future Paris Club rescheduling associated with a 12 percent increase in this probability.

We examine the base equation for problems of multicollinearity by examining the variance inflation factors (vif) from an OLS regression with the same variables, and concluded that there was no evidence that it was a problem. Specifically, none of the vif values exceed three, thus falling well below even the more strict cutoff of five as an indicator of multicollinearity. Further tests on other samples also do not indicate any multicollinearity problems. The results of the base model are very similar when using robust standard errors, and when using panel estimation techniques (random effects and population averaged effects). So overall the base model appears to perform reasonably well for the full sample; our next step examines its performance for variations in program type and sample.

5.4.1 Model Specification: Disaggregation by Country Income and Program Type

Our first exploration of our model's sensitivity to different samples examines whether participation is linked to the income levels of member states. Table 5.2 presents the results of the base model estimated using the low-income, low-middle income, and high-middle income country groups. Overall the coefficient estimates tend to be less statistically significant than those in the full sample. All three groups indicate that higher income levels are generally associated with lower proclivities to turn to the IMF, at least weakly, which is consistent with the full sample results. The same is true for the importance of past IMF programs, which remains a key variable in terms of magnitude and statistical significance across all income groupings. It is also the case that the correlation between past US economic assistance and program signings is important across all three groups, though the magnitude of the effect diminishes as income increases. In general, however, the effects of the different variables are much more muted for

Table 5.2 Base model by income group: probit of IMF program signing

Explanatory Variable (all lagged one year)	Low income countries		Low-middle income countries		High-middle income countries	
	Marginal effects	Z-score	Marginal effects	Z-score	Marginal effects	Z-score
IMF variables						
Past IMF programme	0.140***	2.76	0.132***	3.82	0.160***	3.58
IMF debt/GDP	0.489	1.20	0.757	1.57	2.65**	2.48
Global Economic Variables						
Crude oil prices	-0.199	-0.99	-0.204†	-1.84	-0.466**	-2.35
Agricultural prices	0.00415†	1.90	0.00419***	3.41	0.000802	0.44
Exports to G5 countries	-0.444	-0.62	-0.166	-0.87	-0.269*	-2.03
Political Variables						
UN voting proximity	-0.00881	-0.10	0.0804	1.40	0.148	1.61
US economic aid	2.09**	2.33	0.697**	2.42	0.543***	3.28
Legislative election	0.0727	1.11	0.0286	0.77	0.0563	1.19
Executive elections	0.149†	1.84	0.0185	0.40	0.121*	1.98
Domestic Economic Variables						
Debt service to exports ratio	0.246	1.61	0.490***	4.12	0.424***	3.91
Current account/GDP < -0.03	0.115**	2.36	0.0373	1.26	0.0577	1.61
Reserves to months of imports	0.0114	0.88	-0.0128†	-1.91	-0.0169**	-2.34
Currency depreciation	0.00334	0.15	-0.000000351***	-3.15	0.000140	0.42
Real per capita GDP growth	-0.0333	-0.14	-0.319†	-1.85	-0.304	-1.51

	(1)		(2)		(3)	
Real per capita GDP	−0.0845*	−1.96	−0.0203**	−2.30	−0.00934	−1.12
Official arrears	0.00245	0.32	−0.00400	−1.58	−0.0121*	−2.17
Private arrears	−0.0181	−0.68	0.000299	0.16	0.00107	0.93
Debt Rescheduling Variables						
Past private rescheduling	−0.186†	−1.87	−0.221***	−3.45	0.100	1.18
Past official rescheduling	−0.111	−1.18	0.0816	1.25	−0.127**	−2.26
Current private rescheduling	0.320***	3.21	0.0653	1.07	0.131	1.39
Current official rescheduling	0.0294	0.34	0.0507	0.91	0.0381	0.48
Future private rescheduling	0.00813	0.09	0.0285	0.49	0.122	1.44
Future official rescheduling	0.211***	2.63	0.188***	3.10	0.0192	0.28
Sample size	450		702		394	
Pseudo R^2	0.203		0.333		0.396	
Percentage with an agreement	29.56		21.79		24.11	
Percentage correctly classified	78.44		85.47		82.74	
Improvement over 'no' guess	8.00		7.26		6.85	

Note: See notes from Table 5.1.

the smaller income-based samples. For the poorest countries there is often only a weak association between signing an agreement with the Fund and other characteristics such as global economic factors (only agricultural prices are weakly associated with an agreement), political variables (US economic aid flows are strongly correlated with signing, with executive elections weakly related) and domestic economic variables (primarily the presence of current account problems). For these poorest countries only the immediate need to reschedule private debt, or the impending intention to reschedule official debt, have strong and statistically reliable effects.

Global economic variables show considerable variation across income groups in terms of their effects. The negative relationship between IMF program signings and higher oil prices seems most important for middle-income countries, while the same connection to exports to G5 countries is apparent only for high-middle income countries. In terms of political variables other than US economic assistance, the effects of UN voting patterns are never statistically significant, though they seem increasingly important as per capita income levels increase. Legislative elections never seem to affect IMF programs, while executive elections have a weak and inconsistent effect across income groups. With higher levels of income the debt–service ratio begins to have a larger and statistically significant effect, and the relationship between signing and debt rescheduling variables changes as well. For low-middle income countries future official rescheduling remains important, as does past private rescheduling; for higher income countries only past official rescheduling seems to have any relationship to IMF agreements.

The other economic variables exhibit some potentially interesting patterns, though often only weak conclusions can be drawn from them. The presence of current account problems, important for low-income countries using the IMF, diminishes in magnitude and statistical significance for the higher income countries. Currency depreciation has a weak but statistically strong connection to lower signing propensities, but only for the lower-middle income sample. A similar but less significant pattern arises for country growth.

The base model's overall performance also varies widely across the sub-samples, with a pseudo R^2 ranging from almost 0.4 for the higher-middle income group, to 0.33 for the lower-middle income group, and 0.2 for the low-income group. Thus the biggest challenge remains the explanation of the pattern of IMF program signing by low-income countries (Bird and Rowlands, 2009) (see Table 5.3).

As an alternative approach to dealing with differences in income levels, many researchers have also differentiated between concessional (SAF, ESAF and PRGF) and non-concessional (SBA and EFF) arrangements.

Table 5.3   Base model by program type: probit of IMF program signing

Explanatory Variable (all lagged one year)	Concessional programmes		Non-concessional programmes	
	Marginal effects	Z-score	Marginal effects	Z-score
IMF Variables				
Past IMF programme	0.00102***	4.09	0.130***	7.23
IMF debt/GDP	0.00105	0.66	0.169	0.97
Global Economic Variables				
Crude oil prices	−0.00177**	−2.36	−0.163**	−2.55
Agricultural prices	0.0000369***	5.13	0.00210***	3.20
Exports to G5 countries	−0.0172*	−2.10	−0.120†	−1.83
Political Variables				
UN voting proximity	−0.000654†	−1.86	0.125***	4.00
US economic aid	−0.00275	−0.84	0.287***	4.28
Legislative election	0.000650*	2.14	0.0170	0.85
Executive elections	0.000261	0.85	0.0688**	2.49
Domestic Economic Variables				
Debt service to exports ratio	0.000757	1.123	0.261***	5.46
Current account/GDP < −0.03	0.000523***	2.72	0.0335*	2.11
Reserves to months of imports	−0.0000135	−0.34	−0.00684*	−2.22
Currency depreciation	−0.00000618	−0.44	−0.00000164	−1.21
Real per capita GDP growth	0.000740	0.80	−0.400***	−4.51
Real per capita GDP	−0.000281***	−3.37	0.00968***	3.59
Official arrears	−0.0000467***	−2.68	−0.00235	−1.41
Private arrears	−0.0000400	−0.84	0.00111†	1.79
Debt Rescheduling Variables				
Past private rescheduling	−0.000861***	−2.67	−0.0436	−1.32
Past official rescheduling	−0.000382	−1.20	−0.0335	−0.95
Current private rescheduling	0.00327***	3.46	0.121***	3.30
Current official rescheduling	0.000292	0.82	−0.0293	−1.02
Future private rescheduling	−0.000250	−0.93	0.144***	4.16
Future official rescheduling	0.00323***	4.79	0.000454	0.02
Sample size	1295		1392	
Pseudo R^2	0.381		0.301	
Percentage with an agreement	10.04		16.31	
Percentage correctly classified	91.89		86.28	
Improvement over 'no' guess	1.93		2.59	

Note: See notes from Table 5.1.

Estimating our base model for these different agreements generally yields stronger statistical results, at least in part because of the presence of more observations. In addition, we are careful to exclude from the concessional signing estimation those observations where a country instead signed a non-concessional program, and vice versa.

There should be some similarities between the results for program specific estimations and those from the income-based samples, since concessional programs are available only to low-income countries. The base model does reasonably well overall in estimating both types of programs, with the concessional program estimation having a high pseudo R^2 of 0.38, and the non-concessional estimation having a pseudo R^2 of 0.30. As noted in Bird and Rowlands (2007), however, the explanatory variables that are important differ across the two agreement types. There are only a few variables that influence concessional and non-concessional agreements in the same way and with statistical significance; past IMF programs are positively related to new signings for both estimations (though the effect is much smaller at the margin for concessional programs, possibly because these programs are longer in duration). The effects of the global economic variables are also similar in direction, though quite different in magnitude. The same applies to current private rescheduling. For the other explanatory variables, if the coefficient estimate is statistically significant for one type of agreement, it is usually statistically insignificant for the other. Four explanatory variables (the country's indebtedness to the IMF, currency depreciation, and past and current official reschedulings) are not statistically important for either program equation, while only the presence of current account difficulties increases the signing propensity for the two types of agreement. Interestingly, UN voting proximity is weakly related (both statistically and in terms of magnitude) for concessional programs, but with a negative sign that contradicts the political influence hypothesis. By contrast its effect for non-concessional programs is positive and large in both magnitude and statistical significance; this differentiated result aligns with the results reported by Anderson et al. (2006). Similarly, for income per capita, the estimated coefficients are statistically significant for the estimations on both types of program, but also of opposite sign; higher income levels are associated with lower signing probabilities for concessional programs, and higher signing probabilities for non-concessional agreements. This effect is probably just a reflection of eligibility requirements for concessional programs, and the opportunity for poorer countries to substitute toward them.

While the examination of signing propensities by income group and program type provides some interesting insights, overall, the variations reinforce the idea that participation equation results are generally quite sensitive to the sample or the type of agreement. This sensitivity suggests that it is very difficult to identify a 'general' model that explains participation in IMF programs well across a range of sub-samples. We examine other potential sources of sensitivity in the next sub-section.

5.4.2   Model Specification: Stability Over Time and Across Regions

The absence of a strong general model that applies well to different income groups and different programs suggests that there may be other important sources of model variation. Here we examine the sensitivity of our results across time and across different regions.

To examine the sensitivity to time we estimate our base model for different decade periods in the sample, the 1980s, 1990s, and post-2000. Using the decades we chose is convenient in part to provide some balance in tracing the evolution of participation, but, more importantly, because the selected decades were associated with varying political circumstances. The 1980s represents a period dominated by the developing country debt crisis, the Cold War and a Republican President in the United States. The 1990s represents the immediate post-Cold War period with the White House occupied by a Democrat for eight years. The new millennium is dominated by a Republican presidency in the United States and the associated 'War on Terror'. The time-differentiated estimation results are presented in Table 5.4.

The results in Table 5.4 exhibit considerable volatility. Only past IMF programs and the debt service-to-exports ratio have comparable results (in terms of magnitude and statistical significance) across time. The coefficient estimates and statistical significance suggests that the effects of some variables fade away over time (indebtedness to the Fund, agricultural prices, US economic assistance, current account problems, and arrears to private creditors). For other variables the effect appears to emerge slowly with time (exports to G5 countries, the effects of economic growth and income levels, past private debt rescheduling, and current and future official rescheduling). In some cases (oil prices, reserves, currency depreciation, past official and future private reschedulings) the marginal effects of the explanatory variable never attain statistical significance. There are a few interesting cases where a variable seems important only briefly. UN voting patterns suddenly appear as very important in the 1990s, but then begin to fade afterwards. The effects of elections appear highly volatile, with legislative elections having a significant effect only during the 1990s, the only period executive elections seem to be unimportant. So overall each decade seems to have its own peculiarities in terms of the characteristics that appear related to IMF program signing, while the importance of other

Table 5.4 Base model by decade: probit of IMF program signing

Explanatory Variable (all lagged one year)	1980s		1990s		2000s	
	Marginal effects	Z-score	Marginal effects	Z-score	Marginal effects	Z-score
IMF variables						
Past IMF programme	0.191***	3.28	0.218***	5.1	0.131***	4.54
IMF debt/GDP	1.03†	1.94	0.546	0.88	0.0255	0.08
Global Economic Variables						
Crude oil prices	0.0106	0.04	0.160	0.32	-0.0312	-0.12
Agricultural prices	0.00822**	2.56	0.00358†	1.82	-0.00587	-0.82
Exports to G5 countries	0.427	0.92	-0.117	-0.69	-0.339*	-2.06
Political Variables						
UN voting proximity	0.136	1.46	0.246***	2.57	0.0958†	1.71
US economic aid	1.71***	2.66	0.912***	2.62	0.117	0.94
Legislative election	-0.0141	-0.20	0.106*	2.04	0.00773	0.29
Executive elections	0.260***	2.69	-0.00313	-0.05	0.0872**	2.28
Domestic Economic Variables						
Debt service to exports ratio	0.543***	3.53	0.354**	2.34	0.213***	3.25
Current account/GDP < -0.03	0.169***	3.29	0.0693†	1.84	0.0192	0.74
Reserves to months of imports	-0.0200	-1.60	-0.0103193	-1.46	0.00125	0.35
Currency depreciation	0.000124	1.14	-0.00000253	-1.52	-0.00901	-1.32
Real per capita GDP growth	0.111	0.38	-0.311	-1.44	-0.335*	-2.01
Real per capita GDP	-0.0187	-1.34	-0.00220	-0.3	-0.00746†	-1.8
Official arrears	-0.00150	-0.22	-0.0115***	-3.19	-0.00218	-1.1
Private arrears	0.0169**	2.28	0.000665	0.41	-0.000272	-0.22

Debt Rescheduling Variables						
Past private rescheduling	–	–	–0.118†	–1.82	–0.0733**	–2.24
Past official rescheduling	–	–	–0.0532	–0.75	–0.0423	–1.19
Current private rescheduling	0.204†	1.71	0.290***	3.48	0.0601	0.97
Current official rescheduling	–0.200	–0.95	–0.0355	–0.53	0.0865†	1.92
Future private rescheduling	0.199	1.49	0.0981	1.33	0.0539	0.87
Future official rescheduling	–0.0711	–0.41	0.193***	2.67	0.116*	2.18
Sample size	383		619		544	
Pseudo R^2	0.288		0.280		0.311	
Percentage with an agreement	28.98		27.46		18.38	
Percentage correctly classified	78.33		78.51		86.58	
Improvement over 'no' guess	7.31		5.97		4.96	

Note: See notes from Table 5.1. Missing marginal effects are for independent variables that are dropped due to collinearity.

associated variables fades away or appears gradually. Our conclusion is that the factors driving IMF participation evolve over time. Despite the fact that pseudo R^2 values appear quite good for each period, predicting the pattern of agreements using older models is unlikely to yield very satisfactory results. In fact, only the importance of past IMF programs and a high debt service burden seem to have sufficiently consistent statistical effects to be useful in predicting IMF program signings over time.

The instability of model results exhibited over time is repeated when the estimations are run for the different regions. The pseudo R^2 values for the regional estimations (all years) vary widely (0.274 to 0.568) suggesting that the model 'fits' better these smaller regional samples. In other ways, however, the results are less encouraging, as in several cases there are only a few statistically important associations between program signing and the explanatory variables, and little similarity across regional results. Tables 5.5a and 5.5b present the results of the base model estimations for six different regions.

Over the full sample period, the different regions exhibit noteworthy differences in terms of the explanatory variables that appear to be statistically significant. The link between past IMF engagement and subsequent signing propensity, a dominant and robust relationship in most program estimations, is only present in two regions: Latin America and the Caribbean, and Africa. Indebtedness to the IMF has a large (but only weakly significant) and positive association with program signing in Europe and Central Asia, but a negative connection for countries in South Asia.

Latin America appears as the most sensitive to global economic variables, though program signing in Africa appears to be strongly linked to higher agricultural prices. Political variables exhibit no statistical link to program signing when examined by region, except for a large (but statistically only weak) connection between US economic aid and signing in Latin America, and a weak positive link between legislative elections in Africa and entering into an agreement with the Fund. Economic variables also generally perform relatively poorly, though debt–service burdens appear important (with at least weak statistical significance) in all regions except Europe and Central Asia. For the other economic variables Latin America exhibits the most overall sensitivity to economic forces, since the effects of currency depreciation and growth also appear to have statistically significant effects on program signing. By contrast current account difficulties appear to be an important factor associated with program signing only in sub-Saharan Africa. Other economic variables that appear as statistically linked to program signing are reserves and real per-capita income (for the Middle East and North Africa), reserves and currency depreciation (South Asia), and currency depreciation (East Asia and the Pacific,

Table 5.5a Base model by region: probit of IMF program signing

Explanatory Variable (all lagged one year)	Latin America		Sub-Saharan Africa		Middle East and North Africa	
	Marginal effects	Z-score	Marginal effects	Z-score	Marginal effects	Z-score
IMF variables						
Past IMF programme	0.226***	4.47	0.230***	5.54	0.00871	0.67
IMF debt/GDP	0.544	0.98	0.197	0.63	0.0885	0.26
Global Economic Variables						
Crude oil prices	−0.422*	−2.17	−0.07654	−0.46	−0.178*	−2.19
Agricultural prices	0.00641***	3.24	0.00461***	2.77	0.000598	1.33
Exports to G5 countries	−0.307†	−1.72	−0.580	−0.93	−0.183	−0.41
Political Variables						
UN voting proximity	0.0195	0.19	0.116	1.53	−0.0143	−0.46
US economic aid	0.966*	2.19	0.791	1.08	−0.456	−1.54
Legislative election	0.0578	0.93	0.0958†	1.66	0.00627	0.52
Executive elections	0.0979	1.37	0.0276	0.44	−0.00327	−0.21
Domestic Economic Variables						
Debt service to exports ratio	0.535***	3.50	0.241†	1.82	0.0899†	1.87
Current account/GDP< −0.03	0.0479	1.03	0.0875*	2.18	0.000465	0.04
Reserves to months of imports	−0.00348	−0.44	−0.00117	−0.19	−0.00804**	−2.31
Currency depreciation	−0.00000322**	−2.27	−0.00570	−1.34	0.0178	0.89
Real per capita GDP growth	−0.718***	−2.65	−0.121	−0.63	−0.112	−1.02
Real per capita GDP	−0.000504	−0.04	−0.00934	−1.02	−0.0189*	−2.06
Official arrears	−0.00605	−0.81	−0.00182	−0.58	−0.00303**	−2.51
Private arrears	0.00240†	1.72	−0.0158†	−1.70	0.0146	1.54

Table 5.5a (continued)

Explanatory Variable (all lagged one year)	Latin America		Sub-Saharan Africa		Middle East and North Africa	
	Marginal effects	Z-score	Marginal effects	Z-score	Marginal effects	Z-score
Debt Rescheduling Variables						
*Past private rescheduling	−0.0925	−1.06	−0.198**	−2.55	0.689***	4.70
*Past official rescheduling	−0.0408	−0.44	−0.08154	−1.07	−0.575***	−5.37
Current private rescheduling	0.0783	0.95	0.268***	3.10	(0.907)	–
*Current official rescheduling	−0.00402	−0.05	0.0270	0.37	−0.426***	−4.78
Future private rescheduling	0.135	1.48	0.0559	0.75	0.0290	0.76
Future official rescheduling	0.116	1.16	0.243***	3.75	−0.0180	−0.57
Sample size	408		540		114	
Pseudo R^2	0.274		0.305		0.568	
Percentage with an agreement	25.49		29.07		19.30	
Percentage correctly classified	83.33		80.74		92.11	
Improvement over 'no' guess	8.82		9.81		11.41	

Note: See notes from Tables 5.1 and 5.4. Marginal effects in parentheses indicate that there were too few observations to compute a reliable standard error.

Table 5.5b *Base model by region: probit of IMF program signing*

Explanatory Variable (all lagged one year)	Europe and Central Asia		South Asia		East Asia and the Pacific	
	Marginal effects	Z-score	Marginal effects	Z-score	Marginal effects	Z-score
IMF variables						
Past IMF programme	0.0434	0.27	-0.0205	-1.27	0.0106	0.32
IMF debt/GDP	3.99†	1.67	-1.78*	-2.21	0.971	0.90
Global Economic Variables						
Crude oil prices	-0.426	-0.97	-0.0902	-1.08	-0.0466	-0.80
Agricultural prices	-0.00395	-0.65	0.000873	1.31	0.00172	1.83
Exports to G5 countries	0.339	0.38	-0.665**	-2.46	0.00874	0.32
Political Variables						
UN voting proximity	0.313	1.25	-0.0376	-1.06	-0.00684	-0.21
US economic aid	0.232	0.82	0.411	1.07	0.433	1.50
Legislative election	0.110	0.98	-0.0147	-1.35	–	–
Executive elections	0.117	0.85	-0.0128	-0.83	0.00700	0.32
Domestic Economic Variables						
Debt service to exports ratio	-0.147	-0.28	0.304***	2.95	0.150†	1.92
Current account/GDP < -0.03	0.0916	0.76	0.0181	1.05	0.0283	1.37
Reserves to months of imports	0.0212	0.65	-0.0130**	-2.4	-0.0101	-1.38
Currency depreciation	0.00392	1.46	0.205*	2.08	0.0211†	1.81
Real per capita GDP growth	-0.638	-1.25	-0.122	-0.62	0.1041	0.67
Real per capita GDP	-0.0223	-0.83	-0.0102	-1.11	-0.0105	-1.57
Official arrears	-0.00985	-1.14	0.0421	0.34	-0.00176	-0.46
Private arrears	0.0168	1.42	0.0302	1.19	-0.000348	-0.32

Table 5.5b (continued)

Explanatory Variable (all lagged one year)	Europe and Central Asia		South Asia		East Asia and the Pacific	
	Marginal effects	Z-score	Marginal effects	Z-score	Marginal effects	Z-score
Debt Rescheduling Variables						
Past private rescheduling	−0.228	−1.26	−0.0588***	−3.06	0.918***	6.20
Past official rescheduling	−0.0640	−0.43	(−0.0628)	–	(−0.225)	–
Current private rescheduling	0.583***	2.89	(0.967)	–	0.773***	3.84
Current official rescheduling	−0.187	−1.09	–	–	(−0.118)	–
Future private rescheduling	−0.150	−0.79	0.0147	0.44	0.995***	8.61
Future official rescheduling	−0.126	−0.75	–	–	(−0.103)	–
Sample size	140		107		228	
Pseudo R^2	0.306		0.426		0.396	
Percentage with an agreement	40.00		18.69		9.65	
Percentage correctly classified	74.29		85.98		93.42	
Improvement over 'no' guess	14.29		4.67		3.07	

Note: See notes from Table 5.1, 5.4 and 5.5a.

112

but only very weakly). The Eastern Europe and Central Asia estimation yields no economic variable of importance.

Finally, debt rescheduling requirements appear to be important for several regions, but in a variety of patterns. Unexpectedly none of the rescheduling variables have a statistically significant coefficient estimate in estimations for Latin America, with the debt connection seemingly captured in the debt–service burden variable alone. For sub-Saharan Africa, past private reschedulings seem to negate the need for future IMF programs, though current private and future official debt reschedulings are strongly linked to signing new agreements. The Middle East and North Africa results indicate almost the opposite, with past private rescheduling associated with future new ones, and past and current official reschedulings being negatively associated with agreements. These largely unexpected results are strong in terms of magnitude and statistical significance. Current private debt rescheduling is linked to the current signing of an agreement in Europe and Central Asia, while for South Asia the estimations can only generate coefficient estimates and standard errors for past and future private rescheduling, and only the former exhibits statistical significance. A similar problem affects the estimations for East Asia and the Pacific, where the influence of official debt reschedulings cannot be determined, though all versions (past, current and future) of the private rescheduling variables have strong and statistically very significant positive associations with IMF programs.

While it is possible to tell some interesting and plausible stories about what affects IMF program signings across different country groups and time periods, what stands out as most apparent is the high degree of inconsistency across the different estimations. Although by standard goodness of fit measures the results appear quite useful, the disparate results suggest a high degree of idiosyncrasy and instability. Therefore it may simply be impossible to identify a single estimation model that does well across a wide range of important samples. Finding a general model of IMF program signing remains elusive. While the equation we present here appears to perform extremely well in comparison with other models in the literature, it too has some severe restrictions in terms of how well it applies across a variety of sub-samples. Are we therefore condemned to have to make do with highly imperfect estimating models? The next section examines some of the prediction failures to see if there might be some ways of improving our ability to explain, and hopefully predict, IMF program participation.

5.5   EXAMINING THE DETAILS OF PREDICTION ERRORS

Following Bird and Rowlands (2002), we examine the prediction failures of our model in more detail. We examine cases where the model predicts that a country will sign an agreement, but does not ('false positives') and where an agreement is signed which the model fails to predict ('false negatives'). We also examine the extent to which these prediction errors are repeated across the different models and samples that we have investigated earlier in this chapter.

Given the nature of IMF agreements it is tempting to consider the matter of false positives to be more problematic. If a country is in serious economic circumstances and has run out of alternative financing options, turning to the Fund should be unavoidable. It may also be desirable if the IMF is playing the salutary and beneficial role for which it was intended. At the same time, the intrusion of the IMF into a government's policymaking might simultaneously be seen by some as undesirable from a political perspective. If countries are avoiding the IMF despite being in a situation where their balance of payments is unsustainable, then arguably the IMF is failing to execute its mandate for global economic supervision and management; or it is being constrained from performing this useful systemic function. In addition, false positives may identify specific cases where politics within the IMF or within the member state are impeding Fund agreements from being reached. False positive cases, therefore, draw attention to potential impediments to the IMF's ability to pursue successfully its stated institutional objectives. How many cases of false positives are there and what is going on?[10]

Examining false positives for the base model highlights some interesting insights into its capacity to predict agreements accurately. In some ways the analysis is encouraging. In the period covered by our analysis the model predicts 237 agreements, of which 166 are actually signed ('true positives') and 71 are not (the 'false positives'). This gives a false positive rate of 30 percent. However, looking at these false positive cases in detail indicates that the model actually performs better than initially appears. First, false positives occur mostly for cases where the predicted signing probability is fairly low, as shown in Table 5.6. In addition, of the 71 false positives there are 41 in which an agreement is signed the following year, and another 18 in which it is signed the year after that. So for 59 of the 71 false positives the model is generally reasonable, but is unable to incorporate delays in signing which may be associated with the calendar-year basis of the data or the ability that some countries have to postpone turning to the IMF as a result of factors not captured adequately by the model. While delays in signing

Table 5.6 False positives from the base model estimations

Predicted probability of signing	Number of cases	True +	False +	Signing delayed by		Exceptions
				1 year	2 years	
> 90 %	22	20	2	2	0	0
80%–90%	34	29	5	4	0	Zambia (1987)
70%–80%	38	31	7	4	3	0
60%–70%	70	48	22	11	6	Belarus (1986) Dominican Republic (1987) Guinea Bissau (1992) Indonesia (2005) Paraguay (1989)
50%–60%	73	38	35	20	9	Burundi (1997) Dominican Republic (1988) Ecuador (1997) Honduras (1986) Papua New Guinea (1992) Tunisia (1995)
Total	237	166	71	41	18	12

may also be important in terms of understanding both the economics and politics of IMF agreements, they constitute a different analytical problem than is our focus here. There are only 12 cases that appear significantly inconsistent with the model in as much as participation was predicted but did not occur even in the following two years. For only one of them is the estimated probability of signing above 70 percent.

A brief review of these cases (the 'exceptions' in Table 5.6) points to some issues that the large sample model is not capturing. Such case-specific explanations need to be viewed with caution, since they may simply be *ex post* explanations that lack a strong basis for generalization or predictive capacity. Many of the 12 cases exhibit a pattern in which the prediction of a high probability of signing for a given year is a temporary departure from previous and subsequent predicted signing probabilities that are often significantly lower. These cases include Belarus (1996), which completed an agreement in September 1996. While it could have signed another agreement at the end of the year, its predicted probability of signing fell from 65 percent in 1996 to 35 percent in 1997. Indonesia had a similar experience in 2005, as did Papua New Guinea in 1992. Both countries had completed programs just before the years in question. Paraguay (1989), Burundi (1997), Honduras (1986), Tunisia (1995) and Ecuador (1997) also had dramatic declines in the estimated probability of signing in the year after that of the predicted program. There are interesting circumstances associated with some of these cases. For example, Indonesia received large aid inflows in 2005 related to the tsunami. There are also unusual political situations, such as the end of Paraguay's long-standing Stroessner dictatorship in 1989, and the serious constitutional and political instability affecting Ecuador in 1997.

The remaining four cases also highlight some serious problems not just for estimating models, but for the IMF as well. Two of these cases are the Dominican Republic in 1987 and 1988, which had just finished two unsuccessful and highly unpopular Fund programs. The new government under President Balaguer was very critical of the IMF and World Bank, and resisted pressure to sign a new agreement during his term in office. Guinea-Bissau in 1992 had a predicted signing probability of 0.64, yet did not enter into an agreement with the IMF. However, the government had reached an impasse with the IMF after missing fiscal targets that were part of previous arrangements; the Fund was consequently unwilling to offer a new program. The final case is that of Zambia in 1987, the year in which Zambia's President Kaunda cancelled an existing IMF agreement. The cancellation started a nine year period during which relations between Zambia and the IMF were difficult. For many of these years, Zambia was precluded from borrowing from the Fund due to accumulated arrears.

These cases suggest that in order to achieve a full understanding of participation in IMF programs large-sample quantitative models have to be augmented by reference to the nuances of members' domestic politics, as well as the details of the IMF's administrative rules.

If we leave aside those cases in which the model's predictive accuracy was out by one year, the false positive rate drops from 31 percent to 13 percent. Removing agreements signed one or two years after the predicted year brings the false positive rate to only just over 5 percent. It emerges that one clear problem for model accuracy is timing. Why are some countries able and willing to delay signing a Fund agreement? Allowing for the timing dimension would dramatically improve the model's accuracy, at least in terms of false positives.

Analysing false negatives is more challenging (see Table 5.7). Not only are there more of them (215 cases of unpredicted programs), but the case specifics are more idiosyncratic. The 215 false negatives represent just over 16 percent of the 1305 cases where the model inaccurately predicts

Table 5.7   False negatives from the base model estimations

Predicted probability of signing	Number of Cases	True	False	A	B	C	D	E	F
40%–50%	118	69	49	5	24	6	5	7	2
30%–40%	152	98	54	4	16	9	2	9	14
20%–30%	175	129	46	1	18	4	4	9	10
10%–20%	283	244	39	0	6	6	3	4	20
0%–10%	577	550	27	0	3	5	0	0	19
Total	1305	1090	215	10	67	30	14	29	65

Notes:
Column A: The predicted signing probabilities exceed 50% for both the previous and following year.
Column B: The predicted signing probability exceeds 50% either the previous or following year.
Column C: Cases where there were debt reschedulings.
Column D: The predicted probability is elevated (above 45% or more than double the previous year's probability).
Column E: Cases where there is a pattern of recent IMF agreements preceding the signing.
Column F: Other cases not previously assigned to categories A–E.

no program. Again it is perhaps reassuring that the false negative rate falls steadily from 42 percent of the cases where the predicted signing probability is between 40 and 50 percent, to less than 5 percent for the cases with signing probabilities between 0 and 10 percent. Therefore, false negatives are occurring disproportionately for cases where the predicted signing probability is closer to the 50 percent threshold.

As with false positives, false negatives seem likely to reflect economic and political characteristics for which we do not have adequate large sample data. First, there is the state of the government's own finances, which if perilous may lead to an approach to the IMF for temporary resources to meet expenditures in circumstances in which a program would otherwise not have been expected. Unfortunately high quality and comparable budget data are not available for a large enough set of countries over a long enough time period to include it in our estimations. Second, the theory underlying the signing of IMF agreements needs to be strengthened to permit more complex interactions amongst the conventional explanatory variables. While individually these variables may help to explain some component of a country's signing propensity, it may be that specific combinations of contingent variables are required to identify more complex conditions that drive a country to the Fund. An example would be to design an estimating model that reflects more deterministically the requirement for IMF agreements in instances of debt rescheduling. Third, timing is another issue, as it is with false positives. In many cases agreements are entered into during a period of years when on average there is a high signing propensity, but the actual program signing coincides with a particular year when the probability was relatively low. For example, whereas the program in Cameroon in 1988 was not predicted, the predicted probability of a program in the following year was over 96 percent. Fourth, according to its Articles of Agreement IMF lending is appropriate when there is a contemporary or a potential balance of payments need. The data may not be capturing the potential need adequately. Finally, it may be that particular governments have a predisposition to engage with the IMF under the umbrella of a program. This could be consistent with the idea of the Fund fulfilling a scapegoat role in these cases or that experience with previous programs has led the incumbent government to perceive advantages, such as a catalytic effect on the willingness of private markets to lend, to be associated with IMF programs.

Our final analysis of the prediction failures examines them in the context of different models. We compared our most general base model case to three more specific versions of it. First, we examine the importance of including UN voting and the US economic aid in the model, the two variables that could reflect the political influence of key IMF members. Second, we examine the changes in prediction failures when estimating IMF program signing by income group. Finally, we examine how the prediction failures of the base model compare to those of models that estimate concessional and non-concessional programs separately.

For the model that excludes the political influence variables, the rate of false positives increases slightly from 29.5 percent to 30 percent, and the rate of false negatives increases slightly from 16.5 percent to 17.1 percent. So adding the political influence variables marginally improves the prediction capacity of the base model. However the improvement is slight, and it is only in about 5 percent of cases that the models make different predictions. Of these, the difference between the predicted probabilities exceeds10 percent for 27 of the 60 cases. So political influence seems to be important in some cases, but does not appear to be the driving factor in determining IMF program allocations as a whole.[11]

For the sub-sample estimations on income, the false positive rate falls to under 27 percent, while the false negative rate falls to 15 percent. In this case the model predicts different outcomes from the base model for a total of 113 cases of the 1165 observations, or almost 10 percent of the sample. This represents a significant improvement on the base model's performance. By contrast, when merging the estimations that distinguish between concessional and non-concessional programs, the false positive and false negative rates are very similar to those of the base model, despite the fact that it reclassifies 105 cases.

5.6 CONCLUDING REMARKS

The objective of this chapter has been to examine the determinants of participation in IMF programs by undertaking a detailed and disaggregated empirical investigation based on an informal analytical framework. It is important to understand why some countries turn to the IMF for assistance while others do not. One of the purposes of the IMF is to pool international reserves and thereby avoid the need for countries to self-insure against economic crises by accumulating their own reserves. An unwillingness to borrow from the IMF may lead countries to design economic policies with a view to running balance of payments surpluses. However the zero-sum nature of the global balance of payments means that this objective is unattainable for all countries taken together. Its pursuit may widen global economic imbalances, lead to the adoption of beggar thy neighbor policies and impart a contractionary bias to the world economy. The IMF was established to help overcome just such problems but it will only be successful if countries are willing to borrow from it and participate in its programs when they encounter severe balance of payments difficulties. We therefore need to know what factors influence participation.

Knowledge of why individual countries opt to participate in IMF programs also helps in estimating the overall demand for credits from the IMF and the adequacy of its resources. Total IMF lending is after all merely the sum of the Fund's lending to individual countries.

On top of this, a better understanding of participation permits us to make an informed judgment about claims that IMF lending is driven by international politics rather than economics and that the Fund is used by rich and powerful countries as a way of furthering their commercial and political interests. This potential bias has important implications for the governance of the IMF.

Finally, we need to be able to evaluate the effects of IMF programs. Such evaluations are crucial when thinking about ways in which the Fund should be reformed, but they may suffer from the underlying problem of selection bias. Comparing the performance of countries with and without IMF programs does not allow for other differences between them that affect performance. The propensity score matching approach to dealing with the selection problem that we use later in this book, or indeed other approaches, such as one based on instrumental variables, require a sound knowledge of what determines participation. In the case of the propensity score matching (PSM) approach, understanding participation allows us to identify countries with similar propensities to adopt IMF programs, and then proceed to compare what happens in those of them that do have programs with what happens in those that do not.

The following conclusions may be drawn from the empirical analysis in this chapter. First, while we are able to draw up a reasonable list of factors that may in principle influence participation, the significance of these variables depends importantly on the particular sample that is being examined; there is no individual model of participation that fits well all cases. However, there are some discernible patterns. For example, poor countries drawing on the IMF under concessional facilities participate in programs in circumstances that are discernibly different from those that influence the participation of better-off developing and emerging economies that use non-concessional facilities.

Second, while the goodness of fit of the models we estimate in this chapter compares favorably with the models estimated elsewhere in the literature, there is still much that we cannot explain by using large sample models. It does not appear to be the case that there is just one key variable (or a small number of them) that is being omitted. Indeed, our findings suggest that apart from previous engagement with the Fund, there is no one particular variable whose omission substantially reduces our ability to explain the incidence of IMF programs. Even previous programs seem to be more significant in affecting participation in concessional programs in poor countries than they are in affecting participation in non-concessional programs in better-off countries. It seems to be that participation in IMF programs involves a degree of idiosyncrasy that large sample models are insufficiently subtle to pick up.

The initial response to the inadequacies of models that relied exclusively on economic variables was to suggest that there was a key omitted factor and that this omission related to the politics of IMF lending. Out of this emerged the influential idea that IMF lending reflected the interests of the IMF's powerful advanced economies in general and the US in particular. In this chapter we reach a different conclusion. Adding political variables to models that seek to explain participation does relatively little to improve the overall goodness of fit and, in some samples, does nothing to improve our ability to explain participation. However, just as in the case of the economic variables, certain political variables seem to be more significant in some circumstances than in others. For example, they seem to be more significant in explaining participation in non-concessional programs than they are in explaining concessional ones. Moreover, there is the possibility that our measures of political influence are not capturing it effectively, or that the influence is felt more strongly on the design of the programs and the size of loans rather than whether or not a program is initiated.

An analysis of prediction failures suggests that they may be more apparent than real with, for example, false positives often becoming true ones after a relatively short delay. Where prediction errors cannot be explained in this way it appears that there are other idiosyncratic factors that are at work that can be used to explain the 'failure' of the general participation model.

Recognizing that participation in IMF programs is complex carries important messages for the design and evaluation of IMF programs. These are issues to which we return in Chapter 7.

ACKNOWLEDGMENTS

The authors would like to thank the participants at the Political Economy of International Organizations conference at Villanova University, Philadelphia, January 2012 and at a seminar at the Stanford Center for International Development, May, 2013, and Yelda Gulderen for research assistance.

NOTES

1. Bird and Rowlands (2006) and Bird (2007) present expanded versions of the conceptual framework.
2. The Secretary of the Treasury is required by Section 610(a) and 613(a) of the *Foreign Operations, Export Financing and Related Programs Appropriations Act, 1999*, to report the USED's actions in relation to policies described in Section 610 of the Act (United States Department of the Treasury, 1999 and 2008).
3. Of course the end conclusion is much the same: countries close to the US are treated better. The question is which variable best measures this closeness.
4. Bird and Rowlands (2006) also make the case for disaggregation, particularly by income group. Boughton (2001) describes the institutional evolution of Fund agreements, suggesting that the factors associated with signing a Fund agreement are likely to change significantly over time. In Chapter 4 we provided an analysis of aggregate IMF lending, presenting it as episodic and unpredictable.
5. Various pseudo R-squared goodness-of-fit measures have been used and criticized in the econometric literature (see Windmeijer, 1995, for a good investigation into the various methods). To avoid being drawn into this debate the conventional pseudo R-squared measure is used throughout this study. While not ideal, the Pseudo-R^2 is one of the few means of comparing basic model performance in terms of explanatory power. We have also included in the tables the percentage of correct predictions.
6. Specifically, when the preliminary model is estimated on the same, smaller, sample as the base model, the results are closer, but not identical. The difference in the relationship between IMF programs and agricultural prices is particularly sensitive to the sample.

7. This same iterative process was used to narrow down the categories and precise form of the other economic and institutional variables as well.

8. Other debt variables were used as well, but ultimately dropped as they had statistically insignificant coefficient estimates in the final model. Two variations of the external debt stock and service variables were tested: public and publicly guaranteed (PPG) long- and short-term debt; and private nonguaranteed long- and short-term debt (PNG).

9. Of five studies that examined how a country's arrears influences its propensity to initiate an arrangement, however, only Rowlands (1995) finds any statistically significant results, a finding consistent with political economy arguments such as those offered by Gould (2003).

10. The existence of false positives seems at face value to be inconsistent with the idea of governments swiftly turning to the IMF to find a scapegoat for their preferred policies. It also seems to be at odds with the moral hazard critique of IMF lending that again suggests that the low financial cost of borrowing from the IMF will entice countries to borrow from it as soon as they can.

11. This finding coincides with other research where we specifically examine the extent to which US influence helps to explain prediction errors. In the theory the idea is that friends and allies of the US will receive IMF loans where they would not otherwise have been expected, while countries opposed to the US will fail to receive loans even where they would have been expected on the basis of other factors (Bird, Mylonas and Rowlands, 2015). In this study we discovered that there were a large number of departures from such a pattern. Many countries that had severe economic circumstances and had voted with the US at the UN did not have IMF programs, while countries with less severe problems and a record of not having voted with the US had them.

REFERENCES

Anderson, T.B., Harr, T., and Tarp, F. (2006). On US politics and IMF lending. *European Economic Review*, 50(7), 1843–1862.

Barro, R., and Lee, J.W. (2005). IMF programs: Who is chosen and what are the effects? *Journal of Monetary Economics*, 52(7), 1245–1269.

Bird, G. (2007). The IMF: A bird's eye view of its role and operations. *Journal of Economic Surveys*, 21(4), 683–745.

Bird, G., and Orme, T. (1981). An analysis of drawings on the International Monetary Fund by developing countries. *World Development*, 9(6), 563–568.

Bird, G., and Rowlands, D. (2001). IMF lending: How is it affected by economic, political and institutional factors. *Policy Reform*, 4(6), 243–270.

Bird, G., and Rowlands, D. (2002). The pattern of IMF lending: An analysis of prediction failures. *Policy Reform*, 5(3), 173–186.

Bird, G., and Rowlands, D. (2006). The demand for IMF assistance: What factors influence the decision to turn to the Fund, in S. Kosack, J.R. Vreeland, and G. Ranis (eds), *Globalization and the Nation State: The Impact of the IMF and the World Bank*: 231–262. New York: Routledge.

Bird, G., and Rowlands, D. (2007). Should it be curtains for some of the IMF's lending windows? *Review of International Organizations*, 2(3), 281–299.

Bird, G., and Rowlands, D. (2009). A disaggregated empirical analysis of the determinants of IMF arrangements: Does one model fit all? *Journal of International Development*, 21(7), 915–931.

Bird, G. Mylonas, J., and Rowlands, D. (2015). The political economy of participation in IMF programs: A disaggregated empirical analysis. *Journal of Economic Policy Reform*, 18(3), 221–243.

Boughton, J.M. (2001). *Silent Revolution: The International Monetary Fund, 1979–1989*. Washington, DC: International Monetary Fund.

Breen, M. (2010). Domestic interests, international bargaining, and IMF lending. *Working Paper in International Studies*. Centre for International Studies—Dublin City University. No. 7.

Broz, J.L., and Hawes, M.B. (2006). US domestic politics and International Monetary Fund policy, in D. Hawkins, D.A. Lake, D. Nielson, and M.J. Tierney (eds), *Delegation and Agency in International Organizations*: 77–107. Cambridge, MA: Cambridge University Press.

Conway, P. (1994). IMF lending programs: Participation and impact. *Journal of Development Economics*, 45(2), 365–391.

Copelovitch, M.S. (2005). *Governing global markets: Private debt and the politics of International Monetary Fund lending*. PhD Dissertation, Harvard University.

Cornelius, P. (1987). The demand for IMF credits by sub-Saharan African countries. *Economic Letters*, 23(1), 99–102.

Dreher, A., and Vreeland, J.R. (2011). Buying votes and international organizations. *CEGE Working Paper*, No. 123.

Dreher, A., Sturm, J.E., and Vreeland, J.R. (2006). Does membership on the UN Security Council influence IMF decisions? *KOF Working Paper*, No. 151.

Dreher, A., Sturm, J.E., and Vreeland, J.R. (2009). Global horse trading: IMF loans for votes in the United Nations Security Council. *European Economic Review*, 53(7), 742–757.

Eichengreen, B., Gupta, P., and Mody, A. (2004). Sudden stops and IMF-supported programs. *NBER Working Paper*, No. 12235.

Elekdag, S. (2006). How does the global economic environment influence the demand for IMF resources. *IMF Working Paper*, WP/06/239.

Finch, C.D. (1989). *The IMF: The Record and the Prospect, Essays in International Finance, No.175*. Princeton, NJ: Princeton University Press.

Ghosh, A., Goretti, M., Joshi, B., Thomas, A., and Zalduendo, J. (2007). Modeling aggregate use of Fund resources: Analytical approaches and medium-term projections. *IMF Working Paper*, WP/07/70.

Gould, E.R. (2003). Money talks: Supplementary financiers and International Monetary Fund conditionality. *International Organization*, 57(3), 551–586.

Gunduz, Y.B. (2009). Estimating demand for IMF financing by low-income countries in response to shocks. *IMF Working Paper*, WP/09/263.

Joyce, J.P. (1992). The economic characteristics of IMF program countries. *Economic Letters*, 38(2), 237–242.

Knight, M., and Santaella, J.A. (1997). Economic determinants of IMF financial arrangements. *Journal of Development Economics*, 54(2), 405–436.

Meltzer, A.H. (2000). *International Financial Institution Advisory Commission*. Washington, DC: United States House of Representatives.

Moser, C., and Sturm, J-E. (2011). Explaining IMF lending decisions after the Cold War. *The Review of International Organizations*, 6(3/4), 307–340.

Oatley, T., and Yackee, J. (2000). Political determinants of IMF balance of payments lending: The curse of Carabosse. *IMF Working Paper*.

Oatley, T., and Yackee, J. (2004). American interests and IMF lending. *International Politics*, 41(3), 415–429.

Pop-Eleches, G. (2008). Crisis in the eye of the beholder: Economic crisis and partisan politics in Latin American and Eastern European International Monetary Fund Programs. *Comparative Political Studies*, 41(9), 1179–1211.

Pop-Eleches, G. (2009). Public goods and political pandering: Evidence from IMF programs in Latin American and Eastern Europe. *International Studies Quarterly*, 53(3), 787–816.

Presbitero, A., and Zazzaro, A. (2012). IMF lending in times of crisis: Political influences and crisis prevention, *World Development*, 40(10), 1944–1969.

Przeworski, A., and Vreeland, J.R. (2000). The effect of IMF programs on economic growth. *Journal of Development Economics*, 62(2), 385–421.

Przeworski, A., and Vreeland, J.R. (2002). A statistical model of bilateral cooperation. *Political Analysis*, 10(2), 101–112.

Reynaud, J., and Vauday, J. (2009). Geopolitics and international organizations: An empirical study on IMF facilities. *Journal of Development Economics*, 89(1), 139–162.

Rowlands, D. (1995). *International Monetary Fund conditional credit allocations*. PhD Dissertation, University of Toronto.

Santaella, J. (1996). Stylized facts before IMF-supported macroeconomic adjustment. *Staff Papers, International Monetary Fund*, 43(3), 502–544.

Steinwand, M.C., and Stone, R.W. (2008). The International Monetary Fund: A review of the recent literature. *Review of International Organizations*, 3(2), 123–149.

Stiles, K.W. (1991). *Negotiating Debt: The IMF's Lending Process*. Boulder, CO: Westview Press.

Stone, R.W. (2008). The scope of IMF conditionality. *International Organization*, 62(4), 589–620.

Sturm, J., Berger, H., and Haan, J. (2005). Which variables explain decisions on IMF credit? An extreme bounds analysis. *Economics and Politics*, 17(2), 177–213.

Swedberg, R. (1986). The doctrine of economic neutrality of the IMF and the World Bank. *Journal of Peace Research*, 23(4), 377–390.

Thacker, S.C. (1999). The high politics of IMF lending. *World Politics*, 52(1), 38–75.

United States Department of the Treasury. (1999). *Report on IMF reforms: Report to Congress in accordance with Sections 610(a) and 613(a) of the Foreign Operations, Export Financing, and Related Programs Appropriations Act, 1999*.

United States Department of the Treasury. (2008). *Quarterly Report to Congress on International Monetary Fund Lending*.

Voeten, E. (2000). Clashes in the Assembly. *International Organization*, 54(2), 185–215.

Vreeland, J.R. (1999). The IMF: Lender of last resort or scapegoat? Prepared for the Midwest Political Science Association Annual Meeting, Chicago, April 15–17.

Windmeijer, F.A.G. (1995). Goodness-of-fit measures in binary choice models. *Econometric Review*, 14(1), 101–116.

Woods, N. (2003). The United States and the international financial institutions: Power and influence within the World Bank and the IMF, in R. Foot, N. MacFarlane, and M. Mastanduno (eds), *US Hegemony and International Organizations*: 92–114. Oxford: Oxford University Press.

APPENDIX: KEY EXPLANATORY VARIABLES (MEAN, STANDARD DEVIATION, MINIMUM, MAXIMUM FOR THE FULL SAMPLE OF 1546 OBSERVATIONS USED IN THE BASE ESTIMATION), AND THE SPECIFIC HYPOTHESIS BEING TESTED REGARDING THEIR EFFECT ON IMF PROGRAM SIGNING. NOTE THAT THERE ARE, IN SOME INSTANCES, ALTERNATIVE HYPOTHESES

IMF-related Variables

Past IMF program (0.512, 0.500, 0, 1). An indicator variable taking the value of 1 if the country had been under an IMF program in any of the previous three years. If a country has a history of recent IMF programs, then it should have a higher propensity to sign a new agreement.

IMF debt/GDP (0.0235, 0.0453, 0, 0.522). The ratio of IMF credit (outstanding and disbursed) used by a country as a proportion of its GDP. If a country has a high outstanding IMF debt use, then the IMF may be inclined to continue to support it with new agreements.

Global Economic Variables

Crude oil prices (0.329, 0.129, 0.162, 0.656). The spot price market for oil in dollars per barrel, deflated by the US GDP deflator. If oil prices are high, global economic conditions are likely strong and the demand for IMF credit will be lower.

Agricultural prices (95.6, 15.3, 61.3, 120.3). The world agricultural price index. If the world agricultural price index is high, then the high price of critical food imports will increase demand for IMF support.

Exports to G5 countries (0.0810, 0.309, 0.00000823, 5.38). The sum of the country's exports to the G5 countries, in thousands of real $US. If exports to G5 countries are rising, then demand for hard currency from the IMF will decline and the propensity to sign an agreement will decline.

Political Variables

UN voting proximity (0.465, 0.259, 0, 1). The number of key resolutions at the United Nations in which a country voted the same as the United States as a share of total votes (not including abstentions or absences). If a country votes in a similar manner to the United States, then it will receive more IMF programs.

US economic aid (0.0303, 0.136, 0, 2.69). The share of US economic aid to a country as a share of total US foreign aid. If the share of US aid to the country increases then the country will be more likely to receive an IMF agreement.

Legislative election (0.221, 0.415, 0, 1). An indicator of whether a country has had a recent legislative election. If a country has had a recent election, then the country is more likely to be willing to sign an IMF agreement.

Executive elections (0.128, 0.334, 0, 1). An indicator of whether a country has had a recent executive election. If a country has had a recent election, then the country is more likely to be willing to sign an IMF agreement.

Domestic Economic Variables

Debt service to exports ratio (0.193, 0.154, 0.00119, 1.10). The ratio of the country's total external debt service payments to exports. If the debt service ratio increases, then there is a higher likelihood of an IMF program being signed.

Current account/GDP < −0.03 (0.521, 0.500, 0, 1). An indicator of whether a country has a current account deficit in excess of 3 percent of GDP. If a country has a large current account deficit then it is more likely to sign an IMF program agreement.

Reserves to months of imports (3.58, 3.10, −0.0919, 27.1). The total number of months of imports that a country can finance using its total reserves. If a country has higher reserve levels, it will be less likely to sign an IMF agreement. (The one negative value for reserves to imports refers to an unusual case of Guinea-Bissau in 1986, where reserves are recorded as a negative number. The results presented in the chapter are not affected noticeably by removing this observation.)

Real per capita GDP growth (2.12, 6.50, −45.4, 66.1). The rate of growth of real per capita GDP. If a country has a higher growth rate, then there is a lower probability that it will need an IMF program.

Currency depreciation (108, 3885, −0.387, 152726). The rate of nominal exchange rate depreciation relative to the US dollar, calculated as the difference between the previous year's exchange rate and the exchange rate from three years before, as a share of the exchange rate three years before. For example, the value 1 implies a doubling of the nominal exchange rate. The mean is highly skewed by a few outliers with exceptionally large depreciations.

Real per capita GDP (3.85, 2.96, 0.287, 14.3). The level of real per capita GDP as calculated using the Penn World Tables chain method. If a country's population has a higher income level on average, then it will be less likely to need an IMF program.

Official arrears (1.97, 7.88, 0, 64.86). The amount of interest arrears a country owes to official creditors, in $US millions. If a country owes interest to official creditors then it will be less likely to sign an IMF program since it will be excluded by official creditors or will receive financial support directly from creditors.

Private arrears (1.60, 8.78, 0, 137). The amount of interest arrears a country owes to private creditors, in $US millions. If a country owes interest to private creditors then it will be more likely to sign an IMF program since it will need IMF support for rescheduling its private debt.

Past private rescheduling (0.132, 0.339, 0, 1). A binary indicator of whether or not a country rescheduled any principle or interest owed to private creditors, in the previous year.

Past official rescheduling (0.174, 0.379, 0, 1). A binary indicator of whether or not a country rescheduled any principle or interest owed to private creditors, in the previous year.

Current private rescheduling (0.132, 0.339, 0, 1). A binary indicator of whether or not a country rescheduled any principle or interest owed to private creditors, in the current year.

Current official rescheduling (0.173, 0.379, 0, 1). A binary indicator of whether or not a country rescheduled any principle or interest owed to private creditors, in the current year.

Future private rescheduling (0.152, 0.359, 0, 1). A binary indicator of whether or not a country rescheduled any principle or interest owed to private creditors, in the next year.

Future official rescheduling (0.193, 0.395, 0, 1). A binary indicator of whether or not a country rescheduled any principle or interest owed to private creditors, in the next year.

6. The implementation of IMF programs

6.1 INTRODUCTION

Although much has been written about IMF conditionality, for a long time research into the effects of IMF programs failed to distinguish between those that were implemented and those that were not. Recently, more attention has been paid to implementation. In principle the IMF's Executive Board only approves programs that it is confident will be implemented. But what is the scientific basis for this judgment? What determines the implementation of IMF programs? This is the central question that this chapter seeks to answer.

Since the late 1990s advances have been made in our understanding of implementation on three fronts; theory, empirical estimation and policy. It is therefore an appropriate time to take stock of what we know and to offer new analysis based on the advances made.

What can reasonably be expected from such an exercise? Expectations should not be set unrealistically high. Just as studies of the determinants of IMF lending have been able to identify a range of variables that seem to be important in influencing the pattern of IMF arrangements, but have been less successful in explaining them in detail, so it may be that an investigation into the determinants of implementation will provide a list of factors that influence it, but will be less efficient at estimating the probability of implementation in individual cases (Conway, 1994; Bird and Rowlands, 2001, 2002).

Our objective in this chapter is to assemble a list of factors that theory suggests may be important and to see which of them are shown to be statistically significant based on large sample regression analysis. Although our ambitions are modest, the endeavor is far from easy. Many of the independent variables that we would like to test are only imperfectly captured by the available data. Moreover, the dependent variable—the implementation of IMF programs—can be measured in various ways. The results we report should therefore be viewed as suggestive and indicative rather than definitive.

The layout of this chapter is as follows. Section 6.2 examines the existing evidence on implementation. Section 6.3 discusses its measurement, while Section 6.4 summarizes the record on the implementation of IMF programs. Section 6.5 provides a conceptual framework that builds on recent theoretical work and allows us to identify, in principle, a range of economic and political factors that may be expected to exert an impact on implementation. Section 6.6 undertakes new large sample regression analysis of implementation based on a political economy model. This section is divided into sub-sections that explain the econometric methodology adopted, the data used and the results found. It also interprets the results, drawing on the theory of implementation and examines cases where the model was relatively poor at explaining the interruption of IMF programs. Finally, Section 6.7 offers some concluding remarks and discusses some of the policy implications of the empirical results.

6.2 EXISTING EVIDENCE ON IMPLEMENTATION

The existing literature on the implementation of IMF programs is summarized briefly in Table 6.1. Various measures of implementation, as well as various methodologies and time periods have been used. Areas of consensus have emerged, but there are also disagreements. Most studies concur that political factors are important in influencing implementation, although there is disagreement about the precise nature of the political influence.

Building on earlier research into the implementation of World Bank programs by Dollar and Svensson (2000), Ivanova et al. (2003) combine three measures of implementation using the 'Multiple Indicators and Multiple Causes' (MIMIC) model. They set out to discover whether implementation is affected by political conditions, initial economic conditions, and IMF conditionality and effort. They find that the political factors used in their study and listed in Table 6.1 are significant but that other factors are not. In related research, Nsouli et al. (2004) find further evidence of the importance of political factors, and discover that there is better implementation where ethnic tensions are low, governments are stable and less corrupt and where the military are less involved in politics. They find that more time spent in previous IMF programs, and larger amounts of financing (relative to a country's IMF quota) aid implementation. They also find that superior implementation contributes to superior macroeconomic performance in terms of inflation and ultimately balance of payments and fiscal outcomes.

Studies by Dreher (2003) and Joyce (2006) emphasize the importance of the timing of elections and the openness of economies respectively.

Table 6.1 Empirical evidence on implementation

	Programs	Span	Countries	Proxy	Method	Results
Edwards (1989)	34	1983–85	34	Conditionality	Case	Negative shocks
Polak (1991)	22	1988–99	–	Conditionality	Case	Negative shocks
Killick (1995)	305	1979–93	–	Disbursement Rate	Probit	Export base, Debt, Size of IMF loan
Mecagni (1999)	36	1986–99	28	Interruption	Case	External shocks, domestic political economy factors
Ivanova et al. (2003)	170	1992–98	95	Combination of Interruption, Disbursement, MONA	MIMIC	Special interests, political cohesion, inefficient bureaucracy, ethnic fractionalization
Nsouli et al. (2004)	195	1992–2002	95	Interruption, Disbursement, MONA	Tobit, Probit	Political stability, military involvement, corruption, ethnic tensions, growth, size of IMF loan
Joyce (2006)	384	1975–99	77	Disbursement Rate	Tobit	Democracy, trade volume, length of tenure, ethnic fractionalization
Dreher (2003)	104	1975–98	67	Disbursement Rate	Probit	Democracy, elections, government consumption, short-term debt, GDP pc, budget deficit
Current Study	218	1992–2004	95	Interruption, Disbursement	Tobit, Probit, Ordered Probit	Volume of Trade, Number of Veto Players, IMF Loans relative to Quota

However, their studies fail to confirm some of the key results of earlier research, for example, finding no support for the claim that special interest groups play a central role. Further differences in the existing literature relate to the importance of initial conditions in general, as well as specific initial conditions in particular, and to the importance of democracy. For example, Edwards (1989) and Polak (1991) attribute poor implementation to adverse initial conditions and negative shocks. Dreher (2003) also finds certain initial conditions to be relevant and Mecagni (1999) supports the idea that negative shocks impede implementation. Ivanova et al. (2003) discover some supportive evidence for the importance of adverse initial conditions, but this fails to pass tests of statistical significance. Whereas Ivanova et al. (2003) find that the degree of democracy is statistically insignificant, Joyce (2006) suggests that it is, and Dreher (2003) finds that democracy helps implementation at election times. Political cohesion is found to be significant by Ivanova et al. (2003) but not by Joyce (2006), although he does find that regimes that have been in power for longer are less likely to complete programs.

The existing literature leaves enough ambiguities to justify further empirical research. Questions still remain to be answered. To what extent do the different results found in the existing literature reflect the different ways in which implementation has been measured? If there are different ways of measuring implementation, is one of them better than the rest? How well have the estimations been related to the theory of implementation? And how well have the determinants derived from the theory been captured by empirical measures? The research reported in this chapter contributes by studying more recent evidence and better data, by drawing on ideas that have evolved from the literature, and by extending the methodologies adopted. Our underlying purpose, however, remains to achieve a sound understanding of the implementation of IMF programs, on the basis of which policy can be formulated better to reduce the incidence of interruption.

6.3 MEASURING IMPLEMENTATION

There is no straightforward way of measuring the extent to which IMF conditionality is implemented; approximation is needed. Various proxies have been developed.

6.3.1 The Rate of Loan Disbursement

The most common proxy used is the extent to which loans are disbursed (Killick, 1995; Mussa and Savastano, 2000; Joyce, 2006). The disbursement of IMF loans is tied to the completion of program reviews, and thus to the fulfillment of conditionality. The IMF stops disbursing a credit if there is insufficient implementation.

The advantages of this proxy are that it provides continuous data and it is easy to measure. However, it also has disadvantages. Policy actions may be taken, but few or no resources drawn. Some countries choose not to draw down the full amount of an IMF loan. Programs may be precautionary. 'Failure' to complete a program as measured by the disbursement of Fund resources may reflect economic 'success' in as much as Fund financing is no longer needed.

However, and in contrast, a program may be completed in the sense that all the resources are used, while some of the conditions agreed at the initiation of the program may be left unimplemented. Waivers may be granted or conditionality may be modified.

6.3.2   Interruption Index

An alternative approach to implementation is to see whether the program is interrupted. Mecagni (1999) defines interruption as either an interval of more than six months between IMF arrangements, or a delay of more than six months in completing a program review. Schadler et al. (1995) examine the quarterly reviews of IMF programs, and define non-compliance as situations where performance criteria are not met and loans are suspended.

Ivanova et al. (2003) offer two binary variables measuring reversible and irreversible program interruption. Reversible interruption is where the review of a program is delayed, but the program is revived subsequently. Irreversible interruption is where the arrangement is eventually terminated. Although termination may be followed by a replacement program such that a relationship with the Fund is restored, even in these circumstances interruption does provide a signal of the poor implementation of conditionality.

6.3.3   Implementation Index

A third measure of implementation uses the Fund's Monitoring of Fund Arrangements (MONA) database, which contains detailed information about program countries, and has been compiled since 1992 by the IMF's Policy Development and Review Department. Although this measure uses actual conditions, it relies on the subjective judgment of the Fund and weights individual conditions equally.

Furthermore, the MONA database only covers programs coming up for review by the Fund's Executive Board, and thereby excludes cancelled or

Table 6.2   Correlations of implementation measures

	Overall Implementation Index	Share of Committed Funds Disbursed	Programs Having Irreversible Interruptions
Overall Implementation Index	1		
Share of Committed Funds Disbursed	0.413	1	
Programs Having Irreversible Interruptions	−0.403	−0.745	1

Note: Based on programs approved between 1992 and 2004. Each cell contains Pearson Correlation Coefficient.

Source: Authors' own calculations based on IMF data.

interrupted programs. Excluded programs are likely to exhibit poor implementation, and, therefore, the MONA index overstates implementation. For these reasons we deem the MONA based measure of implementation to be largely unsatisfactory; an opinion shared by the IMF's Independent Evaluation Office (IEO, 2002).

The three measures of implementation described above are correlated with one another. But as shown in Table 6.2, the correlation coefficients suggest that the measures are picking up different dimensions of implementation. They also show that there is a closer correlation between disbursement and interruption than between the MONA implementation index and either of the other two measures.

In light of the above discussion, in the empirical investigation that follows we focus on irreversible interruption since this appears to be the best single measure of severe implementation problems. Given our focus on irreversible interruption, it may be sensible to explain briefly the institutional process by which this comes about.

A financial arrangement with the Fund involves setting test dates for performance criteria on the basis of which progress with the program is assessed. Access to successive tranches of Fund finance depends on meeting these conditions. If performance criteria are not met, the Fund may grant a waiver on the grounds that either the deviation is minor or temporary or that corrective action is being taken to meet the program's overall objectives. The program may also need to be modified at this stage to accommodate the reasons for failing to comply with the original performance criteria. However, if the country's authorities and the IMF cannot agree on actions that will bring the program back on track, it will be interrupted and Fund financing will stop. Regular program reviews involve a similar process in which waivers may be granted and modifications made to the program and performance criteria. Difficulties in completing a review that result from disagreement between the country's authorities and the IMF will mean that the review is uncompleted, and this will again lead to the program being interrupted until agreement can be reached. However, if the review is not completed during the remaining life of the program the interruption becomes irreversible and financing never resumes.

As noted above, from the various measures discussed in this section and used in the literature, irreversible interruption is the strictest test of implementation. The MONA data excludes cases where a country's authorities and IMF staff cannot agree on corrective actions, with the consequence that a proposal never comes to the Fund's Board, and the disbursement ratio could, in principle, include as non-implementers countries that have in fact implemented the agreed program but have opted not to draw on the available IMF resources. The latter would, however, appear as having implemented the program according to the irreversible interruption measure. Information provided to us by the IMF points out that 'even if a country no longer needs the money, there is little cost to keeping the program afloat on a "precautionary" basis, and the Fund typically encourages this' (private communication with Fund staff). The irreversible interruption measure of implementation therefore captures cases where the conditionality incorporated in the original program has not been met, where the deviation is neither minor nor temporary, and where agreement on corrective action cannot be reached between the country's authorities and the IMF staff.

6.4   THE RECORD ON IMPLEMENTATION

The record on the implementation of IMF programs has been explored in a number of studies. These are summarized in Table 6.3. Overall they span a period running from 1969 to 2002. Early studies focused on the implementation of fiscal conditionality or, in some cases, other components of conditionality. Killick (1995) was the first to examine the disbursement rate, using an 80 percent cut off point (20 percent or more undrawn) for judging whether a program had been fully implemented. He examined a large number of programs relative to earlier studies and discovered that only 47 percent of them were fully implemented. He also argued that case study research implied that his measure of compliance was a good proxy

Table 6.3   Record on implementation of IMF programs

	Programs	Span	Countries	Implementation (%)	Proxy
Beveridge and Kelly (1980)	105	1969–78	105	60	Fiscal Conditionality
Haggard (1985)	30	1974–84	30	20	Interruption and Conditionality
Zulu and Nsouli (1985)	35	1980–81	35	61	Objectives and Instruments
Edwards (1989)	34	1983–85	34	31	Fiscal Conditionality
Polak (1991)	22	1988–99	22	50	Fiscal Conditionality
Killick (1995)	305	1979–93	–	47	Disbursement Rate (80%)
Mecagni (1999)	36	1986–99	28	28	Non-interruption
Mercer-Blackman and Unigovskaya (2000)	33	1993–97	33	51	Structural Conditionality by MONA
Edwards (2001)	347	1979–97	–	60	Non-interruption
Ivanova et al. (2003)	170	1992–98	95	57/71/73	Non-interruption, Disbursement Rate, Conditionality by MONA
Nsouli et al. (2004)	197	1992–2002	95	60/75/75	Non-interruption, Disbursement Rate, Conditionality by MONA
Current Research	218	1992–2004	95	60/74/75	Non-Interruption, Disbursement Rate, Conditionality by MONA

for judging the 'success' of programs. More recent studies have continued to use the disbursement rate but have also examined program interruption as well as the implementation index based on the MONA database. As anticipated in the previous section, interruption appears to be the most demanding test for implementation, with Ivanova et al. (2003) and Nsouli et al. (2004) reporting that only about 60 percent of programs passed this test. Implementation measured by the disbursement rate and by the MONA-based index occurred in over 70 percent of programs; although, as Ivanova et al. show, the implementation of macro conditions in the MONA-based index is superior to that of structural conditions.

Our own calculations, based on 218 programs over 1992 to 2004, confirm the results found by both Ivanova et al. (2003) and Nsouli et al. (2004). Forty percent of the programs over this period were irreversibly interrupted. In our econometric estimations some observations were excluded because of missing data, and, in our final sample, 61 of the 145 programs, or 42 percent, were irreversibly interrupted. Not only do our results show that irreversible interruption is the most demanding test of implementation, but they also suggest that, according to this measure, implementation has not improved since 2002, even though the Fund's policy of 'streamlining' conditionality, launched in the early 2000s, was in part intended to improve the rate of implementation (IMF, 2001). Although we would not claim that this provides definitive evidence of the failure of streamlining, it is perhaps suggestive that our estimated rate of implementation (using data including 23 more programs than they did and incorporating the 2002–2004 streamlining period) is so close to that reported by Nsouli et al. (2004).

6.5 A CONCEPTUAL FRAMEWORK

With the kind of exercise to be undertaken in this chapter the temptation is to embark on a data-mining approach with little theoretical motivation. The problem is that such an approach frequently reveals results that vary significantly along with the specification of the equations estimated and the details of the sample. It is then difficult to draw firm conclusions. Unfortunately, formal theoretical modeling of implementation does not lend itself to specifying one particular and unique model that can be conveniently tested. Either models tend to be excessively narrow, or the data needed to test them are unavailable.

A more detailed discussion of a conceptual framework within which implementation may be analysed has been provided by Bird (2007). This focuses on the marginal benefits and costs of implementation as perceived by a country's authorities. The benefits are largely associated with the additional resources coming either directly from the IMF or indirectly via any catalytic effect IMF programs have on other financial flows. The costs are associated with the economic and political sacrifices related to implementation as perceived by the authorities.

Other theoretical work has emphasized the importance of special interest groups (SIGs) opposed to the economic reforms embedded in programs. The more powerful are these opposition groups, the less likely it becomes that the authorities will be able to fully implement the program. These approaches are related since, with more external financing, the authorities may be in a stronger position to compensate those opposed to reform. On this basis, implementation may be expected to vary positively with the amount of financing and negatively with the strength of SIGs opposed to reform.

However, as noted above, in our empirical investigation we do not set out to test a rigorously specified model. Instead we attempt to estimate a broader and more inclusive model that is informed by political economy considerations, and incorporates variables that are likely, in principle, to exert an impact. In some cases a priori reasoning may lead to a clear expectation of the sign of the relationships. In others, there may be opposing forces at work such that it is unsafe to form a particular a priori view.

A first component of our model relates to *initial economic conditions* at the outset of programs, with these covering performance variables such as inflation, economic growth, the current account, and international reserve levels (which reflect the degree of currency misalignment), as well as policy variables such as fiscal deficits and monetary expansion. The most straightforward assumption is that the worse are the initial conditions, the less will be the degree of implementation. However, this need not necessarily be the case. It may be, for example, that the design of programs is modified to take initial conditions into account. Targets may be less ambitious where initial conditions are weak. Or it may be that where economic performance and policy have deteriorated to a low level, a government's commitment to reform becomes stronger. As a consequence, there may be less disharmony between the government and the IMF, and implementation may be better.

A second component of our model captures a country's *vulnerability to exogenous shocks*. For low-income countries, shocks may emanate from the current account and be the consequence of their heavy reliance on export revenue from producing primary products whose prices are unstable, while for emerging economies they may also come from the capital account. It is tempting to assume that shocks will have a negative impact on implementation and will blow programs off course. At the very least they may create additional problems for economic management. Again, however, the relationship may be more nuanced than this. Shocks may be positive. Will such shocks necessarily improve implementation? They may instead allow governments to disengage from the Fund with the result that programs lapse, as the country no longer needs to draw on IMF resources. Meanwhile, negative shocks may lead the Fund to grant waivers, with the result that programs remain uninterrupted and continue to be fully financed.

A third factor influencing implementation is *adjustment capacity*. In principle, it may be expected that implementation will be superior in economies that are more diversified and flexible, and possess greater scope for economic adjustment. This may be proxied by the *level of economic development*, which is itself proxied by per capita income. It may also be captured by the degree of *trade openness*. Yet again, however, openness may work both ways. From one point of view, economies that are more open may be expected to have higher foreign trade price elasticities, making conventional exchange rate policies more effective. Demand management policies may also have an effect on the current account at a lower cost in terms of reduced domestic economic activity. However, greater openness may also make an economy more vulnerable to exogenous shocks. Moreover, economies that are less open may have greater scope to benefit from trade liberalization.

The fourth and fifth factors that may be expected to influence implementation are the *level of financing from the Fund*, and the *ease with which future programs may be negotiated*. Higher levels of financing should provide greater incentives for governments to complete programs since there is a greater financial reward for accepting the perceived costs of IMF conditionality. More resources will be available to compensate the losers from economic reform. However, things may again be more complex than this simple idea implies. Other things being given, higher levels of financing may encourage governments to substitute out of adjustment. The question is then the extent to which institutional arrangements surrounding conditionality allow them to do this.

Up to now we have covered only economic variables. What are the *political factors* that may, in principle, be expected to exert an impact on implementation and in what way? Once more, for many of them the a priori reasoning is ambiguous and unclear. The theory of policy implementation points to the importance of *special interest groups* (SIGs) or 'veto players' that have sufficient power to block reform (Drazen 2001; Mayer and Mourmouras, 2002, 2004).[1] However, available data only allow imperfect measures to be used in empirical studies. For example, the role of SIGs may not be captured appropriately by simply looking at their number, although in general terms it may become more difficult to push through reform where there are many of them. Opposition may, however, be more effective where there is just one well organized and influential SIG as compared to a large number of disorganized ones. In principle, the strength of SIG opposition need not necessarily be reflected by parliamentary opposition if there are non-proportional voting systems or non-participation by SIGs in the parliamentary process. The opposition may, in any case, be *within* the government rather than outside it, as different ministries may have different views about the design of IMF programs. SIGs may furthermore influence the composition and nature of compliance rather than the level of compliance.

In a *democratic* society, opposition groups will have greater voice and influence and this may make implementation more difficult for an incumbent government as it seeks to enact unpopular policy. At the same time, if democracy implies greater involvement by civil society in policy decision-making and majority support for policy reform, a higher level of ownership may, in principle, make it more likely that programs will be implemented. *Powerful leadership*, whether under a democratic or totalitarian regime, may be more relevant than the political system itself, but again this is difficult to capture empirically.

Regime durability may foster a consistent and coherent approach to economic policy, but it may also make economic reform less likely as special interests become more entrenched and able to resist reform that threatens rents that they may receive under the status quo. Similarly *corruption* may also be anticipated to reduce the chances of implementation as distortions and rent-seeking occur. Although not beyond debate, there is also a broad consensus that corruption has a negative effect on economic growth which in turn makes it more difficult to implement reform.

The *stage of the electoral cycle* may also be expected to exert an effect on implementation, although this is another case where there may be opposing forces at work. Theories of the political cycle suggest that governments seek to pursue expansionary policies shortly before elections in order to raise consumption, reduce unemployment and garner popular support. These policies are likely to be inconsistent with IMF programs. After elections, governments may have to pursue counter-inflationary policies, which can either be blamed on the previous administration where there has been a change in the political party in power, or on the IMF where an IMF program is in place. This would be consistent with a political cycle of implementation based on the timing of elections; implementation would fall when elections are close. However, while incumbent governments may be anxious to demonstrate national sovereignty over policy in the build-up to an election, they may not want to send out the negative signals about economic management that may be associated with the failure to implement IMF programs. Similarly, the IMF may be reluctant to withdraw support shortly before an election for fear of being accused of trying to exert political influence. Much therefore depends on the circumstances in which programs lapse. Of course, if the Fund is seen as an agent of powerful capitalist countries—as it has been by some of its critics—it could be argued that the Fund's position will vary depending on the complexion of the incumbent government. Following an election, a new government may want to negotiate its own program with the Fund, one to which it is committed. If so, this would imply that implementation would not improve immediately after an election, but might improve after a lag of a few months.

The above brief conceptual survey illustrates why a neat, cut and dried theory of implementation is difficult to construct. It also suggests that while both political and economic variables may play a role, the precise nature of this role is often theoretically unclear. One is therefore drawn toward empirical investigation. What factors in practice appear to significantly influence the implementation of IMF programs, and to what extent is it a political rather than an economic phenomenon? However, the above analytical discussion does in some instances lead us to anticipate the sign of particular relationships.

6.6   NEW EMPIRICAL INVESTIGATION

6.6.1   Methodology and Data

We undertake regression analysis based on a pooled dataset in which each program is treated as an independent observation. Since the number of programs varies across countries the panel is unbalanced. Not all data are available for all countries or years and the number of observations for estimation depends on the choice of explanatory variables. The annual data cover the years 1992–2004 and extend to 95 countries that participated in a Fund-supported program. All the variables, their definitions and the data sources are listed in Appendix I.

The macroeconomic data come from the *International Financial Statistics*, *World Economic Outlook* and *World Development Indicators* databases of the IMF and the World Bank. For the political economy data, the *Polity IV Dataset* (Marshall and Jaggers, 2002), the World Bank's *Database of Political Institutions* (Beck et al., 2001) and the *International Country Risk Guide* datasets are used. The inherent subjectivity of some political datasets poses a limitation for the present study.

IMF programs include stand-by and extended programs, as well as programs under the concessionary facilities (Enhanced Structural Adjustment Facility and Poverty Reduction and Growth Facility) for low-income countries. Precautionary programs are excluded from the sample when the disbursement rate is used, since their inclusion would bias downwards the measurement of implementation. As mentioned earlier, in the results reported below we focus on the interruption measure of implementation but we use the disbursement measure to check for robustness. We do not use the MONA based measure because of its inherent shortcomings which we listed earlier.[2]

Many studies of IMF programs encounter potential problems of selection bias, since IMF program countries are not randomly selected. Furthermore, endogeneity, where factors affecting the impact of IMF programs are generated by the programs themselves, and reverse causality, where the causal connections run in the opposite direction to the ones implied can make interpretation difficult. All the countries in our sample have chosen to sign agreements. They thus share this underlying characteristic and selection bias should not be a problem. With regard to endogeneity, it may be that the factors that foster implementation can be encouraged over time via IMF conditionality. To an extent, and in principle, they may therefore be endogenous to the implementation of IMF programs. The implementation of contemporary programs seems unlikely to affect initial economic conditions or primary product producing status. Nor does it seem likely that many of the political variables we include will be affected by contemporary implementation. Nevertheless, implementation of contemporary programs may depend on the incidence of past programs, not just because these have encouraged economic reform but also because a better relationship may have been established between governments and the IMF, leading to a greater commitment to economic reform, or simply because there is a need to keep the IMF on side. By including a measure of past involvement with the IMF, we therefore allow, to some degree, for the possibility of endogeneity and reverse causality, although this variable may also capture the probability, as perceived by governments, that they will be penalized for poor implementation by being excluded from future access to IMF resources. However, to be reasonably confident that endogeneity and reverse causality do not color our results, we need to specify our model in a way that, as best we can, allows for this possibility.

6.6.2 Model Specification

The choice of probit and tobit techniques in our preferred model and robustness checks is guided by the need to make efficient use of the information contained in the implementation measures and by the data available. The interruption proxy used in the econometric analysis is a discrete binary random variable, whereas the disbursement proxy takes values between 1 and 100.

Our strategy is to relate the various indicators of the probability of implementation to the underlying political and institutional factors in the borrowing country, to institutional factors and to initial economic conditions. Although the probability of program implementation is not directly observable, it is related to an observable implementation proxy. The model can be described as follows:

$$y_i^* = \beta' x_i + \varepsilon_i,$$

where y_i^* is the probability of successful program implementation, vector β contains estimated coefficients, matrix x_i contains economic and political economy variables, and ε_i is a stochastic disturbance term. We assume a normal distribution and, hence, estimate the above equation as a probit model when we use the interruption index as the dependent variable and as a tobit model when we use the disbursement index to examine the robustness of our results.[3]

To examine the influence of political and economic conditions on implementation, each of our chosen proxies is regressed on an explanatory variable set containing economic and political variables. To obtain our preferred specification of the model we use a 'testing down' approach. The unrestricted model includes variables that have been identified in the extant literature as significant determinants of implementation. We then sequentially drop regressors that do not have significant coefficients at the 10 percent level. Likelihood ratio tests are employed to test the joint significance of dropped variables. All the economic variables were included at their one year pre-program values in an attempt to minimize the chances of endogeneity and reverse causality. As some of the countries in the sample had multiple programs, there is a strong cross-sectional correlation between observations in the entire sample and this means that a fixed effects model is inappropriate.

The following were included as potential explanatory economic variables: net foreign direct investment as a percent of GDP, the rate of monetary expansion, trade as a percent of GDP, a dummy for primary product exporting countries, real GDP growth, GDP per capita, the central government balance relative to GDP, the rate of inflation, the current account balance relative to GDP, and international reserves in months of imports.

Although there is an array of political variables that could be included in the regression analysis, including most of them at the same time would lead to collinearity problems and a loss of precision. On the other hand, omitting relevant institutional and political variables would lead to biased estimates. The political economy variables we include are: two election year dummies, one for pre-election years, and one for post-election years,[4] the degree of democracy, the quality of the bureaucracy, corruption, ethnic tensions, the representation of special religious, nationalistic, regional and rural interests in parliament, regime durability, and the existence of veto players as captured by new DPI data, details of which are available on the World Bank's web pages.

The last variable is worth a closer examination. The theory of implementation suggests that veto players or special interest groups are key determinants of program implementation. Various indexes have been employed in the literature to capture the influence of those whose agreement is necessary before policies can be changed. For instance, a political cohesion variable has been used in two studies; Joyce (2006) for the period 1975–99 and Ivanova et al. (2003) for the period 1992–98. Ivanova et al. (2003) find it to be significant, while Joyce (2006) finds it to be insignificant. The political cohesion variable takes the value of zero for a one-party government, of one for a coalition government with two parties, of two for a coalition government with three or more parties, and of three for a minority government. Based on Roubini and Sachs (1989), this variable does not distinguish countries according to the effectiveness of electoral checks on government decision-makers. Nor does the variable take into account the degree of parties' control over members. Weaknesses with the political cohesion variable led the World Bank to delete it in versions of its DPI database after 2000.

The veto players (checks) variable in the newer versions of the same database attempts to correct for some of the weaknesses of the political cohesion variable. It counts the number of veto players in a political system, adjusting for whether these veto players are independent of each other, as determined by the level of electoral competitiveness in a system, their respective party affiliations, and the electoral rules.

The veto players (checks) variable has been modified and improved over the years (DPI2000, DPI2004). Earlier versions of it counted parties as veto players as long as they were in the government coalition (in parliamentary systems), even when the party was not needed to give the government the majority of the votes (for example, Albania in the early 1990s, and Finland in 1978 and 1979). The current veto players (checks) variable only allows parties to count as veto players when their votes are needed for the government to sustain a majority. It therefore captures more efficiently the essential characteristic of veto players. The construction of the checks data makes allowance for different political systems and covers both presidential and parliamentary systems as well as systems where legislatures are not competitively elected. Again recent DPI data more effectively identify situations where there is an effective 'check' on the government because it needs the support of veto players to enact policy.

Ivanova et al. (2003) used a variable measuring the strength of special interest groups in parliament by computing the maximum share of seats held by parties representing special interests (religious, nationalistic, regional, and rural). Joyce (2006) used a similar variable; a dummy indicating whether the government party represented a special interest group. We also updated the composite indicator of the strength of special interests used by Ivanova et al., and used it in our own regressions. While it was found to be significant in some of our earlier regressions, the existence of veto players, as calculated using the new DPI database, seems to exert a more significant influence over implementation. This may not be surprising since the number of seats that SIGs have in the parliament does not necessarily translate into effective veto power. On the other hand, the new veto players (checks) variable that we use directly measures effective veto power.

Several IMF-related variables were also included in our regressions to test whether the nature of IMF involvement influences the implementation of programs. The size of IMF credits relative to a country's quota and the incidence of past programs with the Fund were also examined.

6.6.3 Results

Table 6.4 lists the country programs that were included in our study. Table 6.5 summarizes our probit estimation results, but only shows those coefficients that were found to be significant. Simple parameters as well as marginal effects are reported.

From amongst the economic variables included in the regressions, only the volume of trade is found to exert a significant effect. Open economies, as measured by the trade to GDP ratio, have a better chance of having uninterrupted access to IMF resources. This result was confirmed when we examined disbursement as a test for robustness (see Appendix II). The insignificance of past IMF programs implies that our finding is not picking up reverse causality.

The size of programs, as measured by the amount of IMF financing in relation to a country's quota, emerges as exerting a significant effect on program interruption. Larger resources appear to assist implementation and make interruption less likely. However, this finding was not confirmed by the disbursement measure of implementation where the size of IMF loans appeared insignificant. Perhaps in these cases countries are more concerned about receiving the endorsement of the IMF for policy reform than about receiving finance from the Fund, with the consequence that the size of the agreed credit is largely unimportant to them.

Turning to the political dimension of implementation, the veto players variable is significant in explaining interruption. Our robustness test using the disbursement measure confirms this result. Powerful opposition veto players do militate against the implementation of IMF programs. However, none of the other political variables emerge as being significant.[5]

Table 6.5 also reports the predictive accuracy of our preferred model. Overall the model predicts accurately 65 percent of the time. However, it is much better at explaining cases where programs are not interrupted

Table 6.4   Countries and programs

Albania	1993, 1998, 2002	Dominican Republic	1993, 2003
Algeria	1994, 1995	Ecuador	1994, 2000, 2003
Argentina	1992, 1996, 2000, 2003	Equatorial Guinea	1993
Armenia	1995, 1996, 2001	Egypt	1993, 1996
Azerbaijan	1995, 1996, 1996	El Salvador	1993, 1995, 1997, 1998
Belarus	1995	Estonia	1993, 1995, 1997, 2000
Benin	1993, 1996, 2000	Ethiopia	1996, 2001
Bolivia	1994, 1998	Gabon	1994, 1995, 2000, 2004
Bosnia & Herzegovina	1998, 2002	Gambia	1998, 2002
Brazil	1998, 2001, 2002	Georgia	1995, 1996, 2001
Bulgaria	1994, 1996, 1997, 1998, 2002	Ghana	1995, 1999
Burkina Faso	1993, 1996, 1999	Guinea	1997, 2001
Cambodia	1994, 1999	Guinea-Bissau	1995, 2000
Cameroon	1994, 1995, 1997, 2000	Guyana	1994, 1998
Cape Verde	1998, 2002	Haiti	1995, 1996
Central African Republic	1994, 1998	Honduras	1992, 1999
Chad	1994, 1995, 2000	Hungary	1993, 1996
Colombia	1999, 2003	Indonesia	1997, 1998, 2000
Congo	1994, 1996	Jamaica	1992
Congo Democratic Republic	2002	Jordan	1994, 1996, 1999, 2002
Costa Rica	1993, 1995	Kazakhstan	1994, 1995, 1996, 1999
Cote D'Ivoire	1994, 1998	Kenya	1993, 1996, 2000
Croatia	1994, 1997, 2001	Korea	1997
Czech Republic	1993	Kyrgyz Republic	1993, 1994, 1998, 2001
Djibouti	1996, 1999	Lao People's Dem. Rep.	1993, 2001

Table 6.4 (continued)

Latvia	1993, 1995, 1996, 1997, 1999, 2001	Romania	1994, 1997, 1999, 2001
Lesotho	1994, 1995, 1996, 2001	Russian Federation	1995, 1996, 1996, 1999
Lithuania	1993, 1994, 2000, 2001	Rwanda	1998
Macedonia (FYR)	1995, 1997, 2000, 2000, 2003	Senegal	1994, 1994, 1998
Madagascar	1996, 2001	Serbia and Montenegro	2001, 2002
Malawi	1994, 1995, 2000	Sierra Leone	1994, 1994, 2001
Mali	1992, 1996, 1999	Slovak Republic	1994, 1994
Mauritania	1992, 1995, 1999, 2003	Sri Lanka	2001
Mexico	1995, 1999	Tajikistan	1998
Moldova	1993, 1995, 1996, 2000	Tanzania	1996, 2000
Mongolia	1993, 1997, 2001	Thailand	1997
Mozambique	1996, 1999	Togo	1994
Nepal	1992	Turkey	1994, 1999, 2002
Nicaragua	1994, 1998	Uganda	1994, 1997
Niger	1994, 1996, 2000	Ukraine	1995, 1996, 1997, 1998
Pakistan	1993, 1994, 1994, 1995, 1997, 1997, 2000, 2001	Uruguay	1996, 1997, 1999, 2000, 2002
		Uzbekistan	1995
Panama	1995, 1997, 2000	Venezuela	1996
Papua New Guinea	1995, 2000	Vietnam	1993, 1994, 2001
Peru	1993, 1996, 2001, 2002	Yemen	1996, 1997, 1997
Philippines	1994, 1998	Zambia	1995, 1995, 1999
Poland	1993, 1994	Zimbabwe	1992, 1992, 1998, 1999

Table 6.5   Estimation results

	Probit Analysis of Program Interruption		Probit Analysis of Program Interruption (Without Outliers)	
	Coefficients	Marginal Effects	Coefficients	Marginal Effects
Trade Volume to GDP	−0.006 (0.003)*	−0.002**	−0.139 (0.004)***	−0.005***
Veto Players	0.119 (0.063)*	0.046*	0.195 (0.071)***	0.071***
IMF Loans to Quota	−0.172 (0.096)*	−0.067*	−0.490 (0.189)***	−0.067***
Constant	−0.026 (0.339)		0.393 (0.400)	
No. of Observations	145		139	
R-squared (McFadden)	0.061		0.155	
Log-likelihood	−92.622		−93.300	
Prediction success				
Interruption correctly predicted	41%		45%	
Non-interruption correctly predicted	82%		80%	
Total	65%		66%	

Notes:
Standard errors are reported in parentheses.
*** indicates significance at 1 percent; ** indicates significance at 5 percent; * indicates significance at 10 percent level.

than those where they are. Historical descriptive data suggests that about 60 percent of programs proceed without interruption. A straight guess of non-interruption would therefore be accurate about 60 percent of the time. Our model exhibits 82 percent accuracy. We generate considerable additional explanatory power. For interruptions, however, our preferred parsimonious model performs much less well and no better than a straight guess based on past experience. In many cases where openness, veto players and the amount of IMF resources suggest that a program would be implemented without interruption, some other factor gets in the way. However, these other factors are not sufficiently systematic to show up in our large sample regressions.

We use the probit estimation to identify outliers. There are no clear outliers (using our definition of them) in the case of inaccurately predicted implementation. But there are with respect to interruption. To identify them we compare the predicted values for the probability of interruption with our binary indicator of interruption and compute a residual which is the actual value minus the fitted probability.[6] If we define them as cases where the residual is +/− 1.5, we find that the outliers exhibiting unpredicted interruption were Indonesia in 1997, Guyana in 1998, Jordan in 1996, the Philippines in 1998, Kyrgyzstan in 1998 and the Congo in 1996. As would be expected, removing these outliers improves the predictive performance of our model, but certainly does not allow us to conclude that its overall poor performance when predicting interruption is because of the inclusion of a few exceptional cases.

6.6.4 Interpretation and Discussion of the Main Results

The results reported in the previous section may usefully be interpreted in terms of the conceptual framework introduced in Section 5. It would seem that initial conditions, as reflected by a wide range of macroeconomic variables, exert no significant influence over the implementation of IMF programs. This is broadly consistent with what has been found in earlier studies. Relatively large current account or fiscal deficits do not foretell poor implementation. The view that there is a standard or conventional program with similar targets that will be more difficult to achieve where initial conditions are relatively weak is not supported by our evidence. One potential inference is that, in negotiating programs and designing conditionality, the size of the economic disequilibria that need to be corrected is taken into account.

From the economic variables we examine, only trade openness has a significant effect on implementation. This is a robust finding and applies irrespective of whether implementation is measured by interruption or disbursement. It also confirms the findings reported by Joyce (2006). Open economies are more likely to implement IMF programs. So what is going on? It could be that conventional IMF-supported policies have a greater chance of being effective in open economies. Foreign trade elasticities, for example, may be higher making exchange rate adjustment or the management of aggregate demand more effective policy instruments. Or it may be that countries measured as being less open are relying on revenue from tariffs, and that trade liberalization incorporated in IMF programs makes it more difficult for them to achieve fiscal targets. It may also be that, as suggested by Joyce (2006), greater openness reflects a closer proximity between the policy preferences of governments and those of the IMF. Openness has not uncommonly been used as a proxy for economic liberalization more broadly defined. Following this line of argument, our finding is consistent with the claim that implementation depends on commitment and on the degree of ownership of the program. Countries that have open economies may be more likely to accept and endorse the IMF's analysis and therefore carry through agreed programs.

There is, however, a potential downside to openness. Open economies may be more vulnerable to trade shocks. In principle, it could therefore be that open economies are not only more likely to implement IMF programs, but are also more likely to turn to the Fund for assistance. However, studies of the determinants of IMF lending do not identify openness as a significant factor (Bird, 1996). Moreover, in our own regression analysis we tried various measures of exposure to shocks, including the primary product exporter dummy (we also tried a measure of export concentration not reported in this chapter) and we did not find them to be significant in our preferred model. This may imply that the Fund has used waivers and program modifications to protect programs from interruption and to sustain the flow of IMF resources to the affected countries. Of course, as in Section 6.5, shocks can be either positive or negative. In principle, non-disbursement of an IMF credit could be as much to do with a positive trade shock that raises export revenue and reduces the need for IMF support, as with a negative shock that makes it more difficult to comply with the original conditionality. The connection between the incidence of shocks and the implementation of IMF programs is likely to be more subtle and nuanced than we allow for in this chapter. And, as with some of the other variables we find to be systematically insignificant, there may be a more complex story to be told in which factors that are significant idiosyncratically, and in different ways, wash out in large sample regression analysis.

In the short run, the IMF can do little about a country's exposure to shocks apart from encouraging it to pursue a development strategy based on efficient export diversification, although it can, and our evidence suggests that it has, offset the effects of shocks via waivers and modifications. It can also provide further protection against negative shocks by offering supplementary finance in the event of them reoccurring. This is a path down which the Fund is moving in terms of its recently adopted exogenous shocks facility, although experience with the now little used Compensatory Financing Facility is cautionary.

Although our measure of openness is the same as that generally adopted in the literature, its use creates other issues that we need to consider and address as best we can. An underlying problem is that openness may be affected by both structural factors, such as country size, and policy variables, particularly relating to trade liberalization. This means that the statistical association between openness and implementation could reflect a number of potential relationships. For example, it could be that structural openness creates a more conducive economic environment for the implementation of IMF programs. Or it could be that openness reflects the proclivity of governments toward policies of trade liberalization and therefore toward the policies favored by the Fund. Or it could be that the implementation of Fund-backed policies including trade liberalization results in greater openness. Or, as one referee suggested, it could be that, in the context of a 'sudden stop' of capital inflows, trade volumes decline at the same time as it becomes more difficult to implement IMF conditionality.

It is exceedingly difficult to disentangle what is accounting for the statistical association that our results identify. As Pritchett (1996) has demonstrated, there are various measures of outward orientation that attempt to capture the thrust of trade policy, but they are not correlated. This makes it problematic (or even impossible) to unambiguously discern the connection between trade policy and the implementation of IMF programs. However, by lagging the data in the way that we have, and by including a variable to capture past IMF programs, we can at least get an indication of whether we are picking up reverse causality. Since openness emerges as a significant determinant of implementation, as it also does in our robustness test using the disbursement measure of implementation, we remain reasonably confident that it is openness that is affecting implementation and not the other way around. We cannot deduce from our results the extent to which openness reflects structural factors or trade policy.

By lagging our openness variable one year ahead of programs, we also allow for the possibility of there being a contemporary correlation between trade volume and implementation as a result of a sudden stop. In any event, where financial crises involve a sudden stop it is likely that GDP as well as imports will decline and this will neutralize the impact on the trade intensity ratio. Bearing in mind that many countries in our sample are low-income countries that do not have access to private international capital markets and therefore do not experience sudden stops, we conclude that the relationship between trade and implementation is not reflecting endogeneity via the sudden stop route.

Our evidence suggests that the Fund can also affect implementation through the amount of financial assistance it provides or, perhaps more accurately, the amount of finance it stands ready to provide. It is tempting to interpret this finding in a simple fashion. According to this interpretation, IMF resources 'bribe' countries to pursue unpleasant and politically costly policies. The bigger the 'bribe' the bigger the incentive to implement the IMF program, since the losers from the reforms can be better compensated. However, the reality of what is going on may be more complex than this. In other studies of IMF operations, and in particular in some studies of IMF catalysis, it is reported that the significant effect that the size of IMF loans is found to have is conditional upon the loans not being fully used (Mody and Saravia, 2006). It would appear that having the resources in reserve, but also showing that they are not needed, is what is important. The way in which the size of loans affects implementation may again be more subtle than the simple interpretation suggests. This is confirmed by our robustness test based on disbursement where the size of IMF credits is found to be insignificant.

Our results strongly confirm that domestic politics exert a significant influence over implementation whether measured by interruption or by disbursement. This is a robust finding and one that provides evidential support for the theoretical analyses of implementation that emphasize the importance of powerful opposition to the reforms favored in the IMF program. Up until now empirical investigations into the importance of special interest groups (SIGs) have been hampered by poor data. The empirical proxies have only loosely reflected the theoretical ideas. For example, the number of political parties in parliament will be a very imprecise measure of the influence of SIGs. The important question is whether those opposed to the economic reforms embedded in IMF programs possess the power to disrupt implementation; are they 'veto players'. The data we use allow us to come closer than previous studies to capturing the influence of opposition groups by using the 'checks' data recently assembled by the World Bank's *Database of Political Institutions*. As a consequence we find that while conventionally used measures of SIGs generate insignificant results, confirming the results achieved by Joyce (2006) and by Dreher (2003), our measure of veto players is significant; a result that is robust across both the interruption and disbursement measures of implementation. The result not only provides empirical support for the theory of special interests as articulated by Drazen (2001) and others, but it also supports initiatives to promote national ownership. In a related paper, one of us has argued that the political economy of implementation requires the IMF to temper the design of its programs in terms of technical economics (Bird and Willett, 2005) and the findings reported in this study endorse this suggestion. They also suggest that the Fund needs to offer more effective support to governments in explaining the rationale for proposed economic reforms to civil society and opposition groups.

While we find empirical support for the role of veto players in explaining implementation, our results fail to find support for other political variables such as regime durability and the stage of the electoral cycle. Again, however, and given that other studies do report findings to suggest that these factors may be significant, it may be premature to eschew their potential influence at this stage. Regime durability has sometimes been interpreted to capture Olson's claim (Olson, 1993) that as the time in power of the incumbent regime increases, SIGs are better able to identify how they are affected by policy and to organize more effective opposition.

Incumbent governments may find it progressively more difficult to alter the status quo, or may experience a higher degree of policy inertia that limits their ability to implement IMF conditionality. As far as the electoral cycle is concerned, Dreher (2003) finds, albeit limited, support for it. Some of the specifications of our overall model that were statistically less satisfactory and are not reported here also hinted that the election cycle could be significant, although we found that whether an election was imminent or had very recently occurred was insignificant. The implementation of programs instead seemed to improve significantly only after some months had elapsed since an election. Perhaps new governments need a period of time to negotiate their own programs with the Fund. Thus, while our preferred model rejects the systematic significance of the electoral cycle, there may be a remaining suspicion that, on occasion, it may be important and that there may be opposing forces that cancel out in large sample studies.

Overall our results are consistent with what we anticipated. We find that implementation depends on country characteristics (trade openness), the amount of IMF resources made available, and the strength of veto players in opposing reform. Open economies may find it easier to adjust and larger IMF credits create a greater incentive to implement agreed programs. However, implementation becomes more difficult as those opposed to reform have greater political power. Narrow explanations of implementation based exclusively on economic variables fall short. Moreover, some conventional arguments that implementation is adversely affected by the size of initial macroeconomic disequilibria seem to be misplaced. Our findings also offer some value added over simple guesses based on the historical record of implementation. But this applies to non-interruption rather than to interruption. The inference could be that programs may be interrupted for a relatively wide range of reasons that are of idiosyncratic or occasional rather than systematic importance, as well as those that we identify as systematically significant. To investigate this, we returned to the outliers identified by our probit estimation in order to discover what was going on in these cases. In any event, while we fail to provide a 'complete' explanation of implementation, we do discover a range of robustly significant determinants that exert a systematic influence. These in turn have important implications for the design of policy. Our findings suggest that policy initiatives within the Fund are moving in the right direction, but they may not yet have moved far enough.

6.6.5   The Outliers

Although not intended as a major part of our study, one referee to the original version of the chapter encouraged us to offer some description of what was happening in the outliers identified by the probit analysis. Why was interruption not predicted by the model? We therefore offer the following brief commentary.

In July 1998, shortly after national elections, Guyana signed a three year ESAF/PRGF program with the IMF. However, the agreement was followed by political instability associated with claims concerning the reliability of the election results. The main opposition party, the People's National Congress (PNC) alleged electoral fraud. Public demonstrations followed. The Caribbean Community (CARICOM) negotiated an accord between the governing People's Progressive Party and the PNC which called for an international audit of the election results, a redrafting of the constitution, and elections under the new constitution within three years. The pace of structural reform slowed down amidst the political tension and slippages in fiscal and structural reforms pushed the IMF program off track in the first half of 2001, with the consequence that the midterm review could not be completed. After the 2001 elections, Guyana entered into a new three year PRGF arrangement.

The degree of political instability was even greater in the case of the Democratic Republic of Congo (DRC) which (as Zaire) had entered into a three year ESAF program with the IMF in June 1996. By the end of the year substantial progress had been made in implementing reforms. However, the program came to a halt in May 1997 when the Alliance of Democratic Forces for the Liberation of Congo (AFDL), supported by Rwanda and Uganda and led by Laurent Kabilla, overthrew the regime of Mobutu Sese Seko. Kabila declared himself president and renamed the country. The political turmoil was followed by armed conflict which broke out in August 1998, putting relations with the IMF and the World Bank into disarray.

In Indonesia, and under domestic pressures following the East Asian crisis, President Suharto signed a letter of intent with the IMF in October 1997 hoping that the Fund's involvement would restore confidence and help reduce speculative attacks against the rupiah. The three year stand-by agreement aimed at achieving macroeconomic stabilization and structural reform. The program envisaged tight monetary policy, reduced subsidies, tax reform, bank restructuring, import liberalization and the privatization of state-owned enterprises. Although not captured by the measure of SIGs used in our large sample estimation, the program was jeopardized by vested interest groups. The Indonesian government had established the Indonesian Banking Restructuring Agency (IBRA) to manage privatization and bank restructuring, but it achieved only about a third of the intended reform. Moreover, it was popularly claimed that corruption was rife. Deteriorating economic performance led to riots throughout the country and Suharto was forced to resign in May 1998. The IMF program was effectively driven off track by social disturbances and political change. A new EFF program was signed in August 1998 under the newly elected president.

The Philippines also signed an IMF program as the Asian crisis unfolded, and entered into a two year stand-by agreement in April 1998. The program was on track until early 2000. But after that, policy slippages, both fiscal and structural, meant that the last review in March 2000 was not completed. The weakening of the reform process has been attributed to strong political resistance by veto players to key structural reforms (IEO, 2002). The political system in the Philippines required political support from both the executive and legislative branches of government to ensure that reform legislation was enacted. But while the program had been negotiated between IMF staff and the executive branch, the implementation of it stalled when the reforms reached Congress and when they faced judicial challenge.

In the case of Kyrgyzstan, interruption to the 1998 program was associated with a disagreement over tax policy, where the Kyrgyz authorities favored reducing the top rates of tax and the taxation of corporate profits. The issue was eventually resolved and a new program was launched. In Jordan, the EFF begun in February 1996 floundered when there was disagreement between the Jordanian authorities and the IMF over the reliability of key economic and financial data.

In at least four of our six outliers, therefore, it appears that factors associated with political instability and powerful opposition to economic reform lay behind the interruptions that were not predicted by our econometric model. In the other two cases the reasons were rather more idiosyncratic, although tax policy is also political. The conclusion would seem to be not so much that political factors that our econometric model is endeavoring to proxy were unimportant, but rather that they are not being well captured in these cases by the measures that we have used in the large sample estimations.

6.7   CONCLUDING REMARKS

When assessing the effectiveness of IMF programs it is important to take into account that a relatively high proportion of them are not fully implemented. If policy is to focus on trying to raise the rate of implementation, it is necessary to understand as fully as possible the factors that determine it.

Theoretical analysis has identified a range of potential determinants, and empirical investigation is needed to clarify which of these are systematically significant in practice. A relatively small number of studies have provided some preliminary insights, but they have also illustrated the underlying methodological and data difficulties. Results have been conflicting and the messages for policy have therefore been unclear.

This chapter contributes to this growing field of study. It draws on the most recent theoretical work to isolate a group of economic and political factors that may be expected a priori to influence implementation. It goes on to identify empirical proxies for them using the most up-to-date available data and formulates an econometric model based on them. The model is then estimated, using a large dataset covering 95 countries over the period 1992–2004. While focusing on the irreversible interruption of programs as the preferred measure of implementation, the chapter also tests for robustness by examining an alternative measure based on the disbursement of IMF credits and attempts to explain why differences may be found between these two measures.

Most conventional indicators of macroeconomic performance and policy are found to be insignificant. However, trade openness is significant; economies that are more open have a better record of implementation.

Confirming recent theoretical contributions and using the best available data, we also discover that implementation is disadvantaged by the existence of veto players who can effectively block economic reform, although other political factors appear to be systematically insignificant. The probability of interruption is also discovered to vary negatively with the amount of available IMF lending incorporated in programs.

Although the chapter provides value added to our understanding of implementation, it does not as yet allow us to predict, with complete confidence, the probability that individual programs will be interrupted. However, the results reported here do suggest that predictions will be wide of the mark if they fail to include salient political factors. This suggests that the IMF needs to take domestic politics into account when forming a judgment as to whether programs will be implemented. The results also suggest that the Fund has been right to stress the importance of national ownership, although it remains to be seen whether the related policy initiatives, particularly in the form of streamlining will be adequate to improve implementation. Our preliminary results on this issue are not sanguine.

Further research also needs to focus on formulating a more sophisticated political economy approach to implementation. Given the shortcomings of large sample data relating to political variables, this is likely to involve collecting together a series of structured case studies that can more successfully capture idiosyncratic economic and political variables. However, a preliminary examination of the outliers in our study suggests that, although they are not being picked up by the particular proxies adopted in the econometric model, political economy variables are also important in these cases as well.

ACKNOWLEDGMENTS

We are greatly indebted to Anna Ivanova, Alex Mourmouras, Ruben Atoyan and Axel Dreher for very kindly making their databases available to us. They are in no way responsible for the way in which we have used them. We are also grateful to Tim Lane for guiding us through the institutional details and to three referees for their helpful and constructive comments. Again the usual disclaimer applies.[5] For an earlier discussion of the rate of 'veto players' see Tsebelis (2001) and for a theoretical analysis of special interests see Grossman and Helpman (1994, 2001).

NOTES

1. For an earlier discussion of the rate of 'veto players' see Tsebelis (2001) and for a theoretical analysis of special interests see Grossman and Helpman (1994 and 2001).
2. The IEO (2002) finds substantial errors and gaps in the MONA database for tracking performance under programs, especially with regard to data on outcomes. It concludes that 'existing weaknesses in data on how programs have performed are an impediment to efforts to enhance the IMF's ability to learn from experience and to monitor the implementation and impact of its own policies'.
3. To check for the robustness of our conclusions, we use the logit model on the assumption that the cumulative distribution is logistic. The results of the logit regression confirm the findings of the probit regression. The estimated coefficients and marginal effects are very similar, with similar degrees of significance. See Appendix II for a comparison of the results.
4. To control for the influence of elections, an index is used which measures the share of the year which is within twelve months prior to a national (executive or legislative) election. For example, if an election is in February, the pre-election index would take the value of 1/12 and the post-election index would take the value of 10/12.
5. We have also created two other implementation indices by breaking down the disbursement rate into four and five intervals. The first index of implementation classifies program countries as non-compliers for 0 to 25 percent, poor compliers for 26 to 50 percent, weak compliers for 51 to 75 percent and good compliers for 76 to 100 percent. The second index breaks the disbursement rate into 5 intervals; 0–20 percent, 21–40 percent, 41–60 percent, 61–80 percent and 81–100 percent. Using the ordered probit model and following the same procedure of log likelihood tests, we find support for the significance of the veto players variable. It is significant at 1 percent and has a negative coefficient in both specifications.
6. The precise computation of the residual taking account for the variation of the estimator is as follows; $r_i = y_i - \hat{F}_i / \sqrt{1 - h_{ii}}$,

   where $h_{ii} = F(\hat{\beta}'x_i) \lfloor 1 - F(\hat{\beta}'x_i) \rfloor x_i'$ $Est.Asy.Var.$ $\lfloor \hat{\beta} \rfloor x_i$, and $\hat{F}_i$ denotes the fitted probability estimator.

REFERENCES

Beck, T., Clarke, G., Groff, A., Keefer, P., and Walsh, P. (2001). New tools in comparative political economy: The database of political institutions. *World Bank Economic Review*, 15, 165–176.

Beveridge, W.A., and Kelly, M.R. (1980). Fiscal content of financial programs supported by stand-by arrangements in the upper-credit tranches, 1967–78. *IMF Staff Papers*, 27(2).

Bird, G. (1996). Borrowing from the IMF: the policy implications of recent empirical research. *World Development*, 24(11), 1753–1760.

Bird, G. (2007). The implementation of IMF programs: A conceptual framework. *Review of International Organizations*, subsequently published as Bird, G. (2008). The implementation of IMF programs: A conceptual framework. *Review of International Organizations*, 3 (1), 41–64.

Bird, G., and Rowlands, D. (2001). IMF lending: How is it affected by economic, political and institutional factors? *Journal of Policy Reform*, 4(3), 243–270.

Bird, G., and Rowlands, D. (2002). The pattern of IMF lending: An analysis of prediction failures. *Journal of Policy Reform*, 5(3), 173–186.

Bird, G., and Willett, T.D. (2005). IMF conditionality, implementation and the new political economy of ownership. *Comparative Economic Studies*, 46(3), 423–450.

Conway, P. (1994). IMF lending programs: Participation and impact. *Journal of Development Economics*, 45(2), 355–391.

Dollar, D., and Svensson, J. (2000). What explains the success or failure of structural adjustment programs? *Economic Journal*, 110, 894–917.

Drazen, A. (2001). Conditionality and ownership in IMF lending: A political economy approach. *IMF Staff Papers*, 49 (special issue), 36–67.

Dreher, A. (2003). The influence of elections on IMF program interruptions. *Journal of Development Studies*, 39(6), 101–120.

Dreher, A. and Vaubel, R. (2005). Foreign exchange interventions and the political business cycle: A panel data analysis, mimeo, University of Konstanz, University of Mannheim.

Edwards, S. (1989). The International Monetary Fund and the developing countries: A critical evaluation, in *Carnegie-Rochester Conference Series on Public Policy: IMF Policy Advice, Market Volatility, Commodity Price Rules and Other Essays*: 7–68, North Holland.

Edwards, M.S. (2001). Crime and punishment: Understanding IMF sanctioning practices, mimeo, Rutgers University.

Grossman, G.M., and Helpman, E. (1994). Protection for sale. *American Economic Review*, 84, 833–850.

Grossman, G.M., and Helpman, E. (2001). *Special Interest Politics*, Cambridge, MA: MIT Press.

Haggard, S. (1985). The politics of adjustment: Lessons from the IMF's extended fund facility. *International Organization*, 39(3), 505–534.

Independent Evaluation Office (IEO) (2002). Evaluation of the prolonged use of fund resources, Washington, DC: IEO.

International Monetary Fund (IMF) (2001). Strengthening country ownership of Fund-supported programs, Washington, DC: IMF.

Ivanova, A., Mayer, W., Mourmouras, A., and Anayiotas, G. (2003). What determines the success or failure of Fund-supported programs? *IMF Working Paper*, 03/8, Washington, DC.

Joyce, J.P. (2006). Promises made, promises broken: A model of IMF program implementation. *Economics and Politics*, 18(3), 339–365.

Killick, T. (1995). *IMF Programs in Developing Countries: Design and Impact*, New York: Routledge.

Marshall, G.M., and Jaggers, K. (2002). Polity IV Project version 2002.

Mayer, W., and Mourmouras, A. (2002). Vested interests in a political theory of IFI conditionality, *IMF Working Paper*, 02/73, Washington, DC.

Mayer, W., and Mourmouras, A. (2004). IMF conditionality and the theory of special interest politics. *Comparative Economic Studies*, 46(3), 400–422.

Mecagni, M. (1999). The causes of program interruptions, in Bredenkamp, H., and Schadler, S. (eds), *Economic Adjustment and Reform in Low-Income Countries*: 215–276. Washington, DC: IMF.

Mercer-Blackman, V., and Unigovskaya, A. (2000). Compliance with IMF program indicators and growth in transition economies, *IMF Working Paper*, 00/47 Washington, DC.

Mody, A. and Saravia, D. (2006). Catalysing private capital flows: Do IMF programmes work as commitment devices? *Economic Journal*, 116(513), 843–867.

Mussa, M., and Savastano, M. (2000). The IMF approach to economic stabilization, in Bernanke, B.S., and Rotemberg, J.J. (eds), *NBER Macroeconomics Annual 1999*: 79–122. Cambridge, MA: MIT Press.

Nsouli, S., Atoian, R., and Mourmouras, A. (2004). Institutions, program implementation, and macroeconomic performance, *IMF Working Paper*, 04/184, Washington, DC: IMF.

Olson, M. (1993). Dictatorship, democracy and development. *American Political Science Review*, 87, 567–576.

Polak, J.J. (1991). The changing nature of IMF conditionality, *Essays in International Finance*, No. 184, International Finance Section, Department of Economics, Princeton.

Pritchett, L. (1996). Measuring outward orientation in LDCs: Can it be done? *Journal of Development Economics*, 49, 307–335.

Roubini, N. and Jeffrey Sachs, J. (1989). Political and economic determinants of budget deficits in the industrial democracies. *European Economic Review*, 33, 903–938.

Schadler, S., Bennet, A., Carkovic, M., Dicks-Mireaux, L., Mecagni, M., Morsink, J.H.J., and Savastano, M. (1995). *IMF Conditionality: Experience under Stand-by and Extended Arrangements, Part I: Key Issues and Findings*, and *Part II: Background Papers*, IMF Occasional Papers No. 128 and 129, Washington, DC.

Tsebelis, G. (2001). *Veto Players: How Political Institutions Work*, Princeton, NJ: Princeton University Press.

Zulu, J.B., and Nsouli, S.M. (1985). *Adjustment Programs in Africa: The Recent Experience*, IMF Occasional Paper No. 34, Washington, DC.

APPENDIX I: VARIABLE DEFINITIONS AND DATA SOURCES

VARIABLE	DEFINITION	SOURCE
PROXIES FOR THE DEPENDENT VARIABLE OF IMPLEMENTATION		
Disbursement Ratio	Share of committed funds disbursed	IMF Country Reports
Program Interruption	Irreversible Interruption Dummy	Ivanova et al. (2003) Nsouli et al. (2004)
MACROECONOMIC VARIABLES		
FDI	Net Foreign Direct Investment as percent of GDP	WDI
Money Growth	Rate of monetary expansion	WDI
Trade Volume	Sum of imports and exports divided by GDP	WDI
Growth	GDP growth rate	WEO
Government Balance	Central Government Balance/GDP	IFS
Inflation	Inflation	IFS
Current Account	Current Account Balance/GDP	WEO
Reserve/Imports	Reserves to Imports in months	WEO
Primary Product Exporter	Dummy for Primary Product Exporter	WDI
GDP per capita	Initial GDP per capita (constant at 2000)	WDI
IMF RELATED VARIABLES		
Loans to Quota	Approved IMF Credit in relation to a country's quota	Nsouli et al. (2004)
Fund months spent	Number of months spent in IMF-supported programs	Nsouli et al. (2004)
POLITICAL ECONOMY VARIABLES		
Pre-election	Share of the year which is within twelve months prior to a national election	Dreher and Vaubel (2005)
Post-election	Share of the year which is within twelve months after a national election	Dreher and Vaubel (2005)
Veto Players	Number of veto players in the legislature	DPI
Democracy	Indicator of type of regime. Includes measures of (a) competitiveness of political participation, (b) competitiveness of executive recruitment and (c) constraints on the chief executive. Ranges from strongly autocratic (-10) to strongly democratic ($+10$)	Polity IV

VARIABLE	DEFINITION	SOURCE
Strength of Special Interest	Computed as the maximum share of seats in the parliament held by parties representing religious, nationalistic, regional and rural interest groups	DPI
Regime Durability	Regime Durability, the number of years since the most recent regime change	Polity IV
Quality of Bureaucracy	Institutional strength and quality of the bureaucracy measured on a 4 point scale	ICRG
Corruption	Corruption within the political system, 6 points	ICRG
Ethnic Tensions	The degree of tension within a country attributable to racial, nationality or language division. Higher ratings suggest minimal tension, 6 points	ICRG

APPENDIX II: ROBUSTNESS CHECKS

	Probit Analysis of Program Interruption		Logit Analysis of Program Interruption		Tobit Analysis of Disbursement Rate	
	Coefficients	Marginal Effects	Coefficients	Marginal Effects	Coefficients	Marginal Effects
Trade Volume to GDP	−0.006 (0.003)*	−0.002**	−0.010 (0.005)*	−0.002**	0.273 (0.137)**	0.150**
Veto Players	0.119 (0.063)*	0.046*	0.195 (0.102)*	0.047*		
IMF Loans to Quota	−0.172 (0.096)*	−0.067*	−0.306 (0.179)*	−0.074*	−6.650 (2.349)*	−3.673***
Constant	−0.026 (0.339)		−0.001 (0.561)		95.587 (13.205)***	
No. of Observations	145		145		112	
Log-likelihood	−92.622		−92.503		−349.216	

Notes:
Standard errors are reported in parentheses.
*** indicates significance at 1 percent; ** indicates significance at 5 percent; * indicates significance at 10 percent level.

7. The effects of IMF programs on economic growth

7.1 INTRODUCTION

A central part of the IMF's role is to assist member countries in achieving sustainability in their balance of payments. In order to do this some countries periodically negotiate programs with the Fund at times when their balance of payments has become unsustainable. In earlier chapters, and often drawing on our already published research, we have examined the factors that influence participation in such programs, as well as the extent to which they are implemented by the countries that negotiate them. The next question, and the one to which we turn in this previously unpublished chapter, relates to the effects of IMF programs.

There is a large literature examining the impact of IMF programs and we have alluded to this in the introductory chapter of this book. However, the research has not led to unambiguous conclusions. Indeed, those with starkly opposing views can find some evidence to support their arguments if they use the literature and empirical record selectively. Thus some claim that IMF programs have positive effects, some claim that they have negative effects, and some claim that they have no significant effects at all.

The reasons for the lack of clarity are not hard to find. Just to consider a few of them will suffice for our purposes. First, the effect of IMF programs may be assessed either in terms of their influence on key policy variables such as fiscal policy, monetary policy and exchange rate policy, or on economic outcomes such as economic growth, inflation, unemployment and the balance of payments. Since there is a range of both policy variables and economic outcomes, it is possible, or even likely, that a mixed picture will emerge. Focusing on outcomes for example, and given the trade-offs that often exist between them, improved performance in some areas may be matched by deteriorating performance elsewhere. If a case is discovered where an IMF program is associated with falling inflation and a shrinking current account deficit, but also with rising unemployment and a declining rate of economic growth, it is unclear whether this case is one of success or failure unless there is agreement on what weights to attach to the different outcomes.

Things are further complicated by the fact that the effects may change over time. In these circumstances, any assessment depends on the specific time period chosen. A program that appears unsuccessful in the short run may turn out to be beneficial in the long run, and vice versa.

Furthermore, but still in relation to outcomes, if programs are designed with the intention of making foreign investors more inclined to lend, the effects of programs may be judged against the extent to which they exhibit this so-called catalytic effect. We return to this issue in the next chapter.

A second reason for the lack of consensus concerning the effects of IMF programs relates to the methodological problems involved in empirically isolating the part played by a program as opposed to other factors. Once again, we have already discussed this briefly in the introduction to the book.

In one relatively short chapter it is impossible to examine all aspects of the effects of IMF programs. We therefore narrow things down. Since the IMF's Articles of Agreement establish that one of its main purposes is to facilitate balance of payments correction without countries having to pursue policies that are destructive of national and international prosperity, we focus on the effects of programs on economic growth. If it transpires that programs exert an enduring negative effect, there would be prima facie evidence that the Fund is failing to fulfill one of its principal purposes. However, if programs have no significantly adverse effect on economic growth then it would appear that a more sanguine judgment may be warranted.

There are various contingent conditions that might be expected to influence the connection between IMF programs and economic growth. We examine three of them in this chapter. First, we investigate whether the impact of non-concessional programs in middle-income countries differs from that of concessional ones in low-income countries. Second, we explore whether it makes a difference whether the program is completed or not. And third, we test to see whether the amount of resources associated with a program influences its impact on economic growth.

In our empirical examination we attempt to allow for potential selection bias by comparing program and non-program countries that have similar probabilities of participating in an IMF program, based on an appropriate participation model. Since, as we have discussed in earlier chapters, it appears that the determinants of participation by middle-income countries in IMF programs differ from those of low-income countries, it is important to modify the participation model when applying the propensity score matching approach that we use.

The main contribution of the chapter lies in offering a new set of empirical results concerning the effects of IMF programs on economic growth.

However, before presenting these, we briefly consider whether it is possible to establish firm theoretical priors. What effect might we expect IMF programs to have? And might this effect depend on the nature of the program, whether it is completed, and the amount of financial resources involved?

7.2   AN INFORMAL ANALYTICAL FRAMEWORK

What is the basis for expecting that IMF programs could have a significant effect on the variables that are important for economic growth?[1] A difficulty here is that there is no uniform model of growth in developing countries that permits us to specify what these variables are. In principle, growth appears to depend on a range of reasonably well-established factors, but their relative importance varies from case to case. The factors include things such as productivity, the rate of capital formation, the quality of institutions, the quality of economic policies, resource endowments, political stability, the degree of corruption, whether or not a country is landlocked and whether it has a tropical or temperate climate. Establishing the relative importance of these factors has been the subject of considerable disagreement amongst growth theorists and empiricists.

Isolating the effects of IMF programs is even more difficult. An IMF program may affect some of the factors that influence economic growth, but not others. It may have a direct or indirect influence on them. It may exert strong or weak pressure. Some aspects of IMF programs may be beneficial for growth whilst others may be detrimental. How the various elements of a program combine determines the ultimate overall effect. It is a daunting task to precisely capture the routes via which the Fund might, in principle, affect economic growth, let alone to estimate them empirically.

A less ambitious approach is to view economic growth as being potentially constrained by the amount of external finance available and by the quality of economic policies that are pursued. This approach more easily accommodates a potential role for IMF programs. They may help to relax a financing constraint by providing resources either directly or indirectly by catalyzing additional capital inflows. For many LICs that have only limited access to private international capital markets, the potential catalytic effect of IMF programs on foreign aid is likely to be more important. However, the catalytic effect may work in the opposite direction. In circumstances where having an IMF program transmits a negative signal about the size and nature of a country's economic difficulties, the effect on other capital flows—especially private ones—may be negative. This effect could then mean that because of reduced capital inflows IMF programs have a negative rather than a positive effect on economic growth.

As far as economic policy is concerned, IMF programs should have a beneficial effect on economic growth where they improve policy design. Better policies should, after all, lead to better outcomes. Moreover, by helping to generate economic stability and by reducing vulnerability to shocks, for example through creating fiscal space and promoting reserve accumulation, there could be further beneficial growth effects associated with IMF programs.

However, there are ambiguities here as well. Some critics of the Fund have staunchly maintained that the economic policies advocated by the IMF, and embedded in programs, are inappropriate for developing countries and rely excessively on compressing domestic aggregate demand. Consequently the implementation of a Fund program may have a negative effect on economic growth, especially in the short run. It is on the basis of such arguments that IMF programs are sometimes viewed as anti-growth and anti-development.

Once more there may be important temporal distinctions to be made. If the policies favored by the IMF focus on demand compression in the short run and on enhancing aggregate supply in the long run, the effects on economic growth will be time variant. There will be a short run negative effect followed by a long run positive effect. Matters are made more complex where programs involve currency devaluation since, in principle, such a policy has both expansionary and contractionary elements.[2] Once more we find that, even with a less ambitious theoretical framework, it remains difficult to formulate precise analytical priors concerning the likely impact of IMF programs on economic growth.

Further thought merely serves to make things yet more complicated. IMF programs that are potentially beneficial because of the policy reform they incorporate will not realize their potential if the policies are not implemented. However, if the main avenue through which IMF programs encourage growth is via the provision of financing, then their effects will depend on the amount of resources involved and the size of catalysis.

Where does the discussion in this section leave us? While it would be convenient to be able to construct a clear set of principles regarding the effect of IMF programs on economic growth, this is not the case. There are various ways in which the Fund's influence could be beneficial, as it would be if binding financial constraints on growth were to be relaxed, or if appropriate policy reform were to be facilitated. But there are other reasons to believe that the effect could be negative, particularly in the short run where aggregate domestic demand is compressed. Much also depends on the reaction of markets and aid donors to the negotiation of IMF arrangements and these are difficult to predict. Thus, while the analytical framework presented above allows us to identify a number of variables that it is worthwhile investigating empirically, it does not give a clear and unambiguous picture of what we should expect to find.

For illustrative purposes let us consider two hypothetical scenarios. First, take the case of a middle-income country or emerging economy. It negotiates a program with the Fund when it experiences macroeconomic disequilibrium with aggregate demand exceeding aggregate supply. Its balance of payments has become unsustainable because a current account deficit can no longer be financed by running down reserves or by borrowing from international capital markets. This situation may have arisen from macroeconomic mismanagement that has made the country vulnerable to crisis. The mismanagement may have involved excessively large fiscal deficits that have been financed by monetary expansion or by debt accumulation. Referral to the Fund coincides with a capital account crisis and a sudden stop or reversal in capital flows. Policy under the auspices of an IMF program aims to stabilize the economy and strengthen the overall balance of payments. It seeks to regain the country's access to international capital. It does this by attempting to reduce the fiscal deficit, and by raising the rate of interest and reducing the international value of the domestic currency. In the short run, this combination of policies may be expected to have a contractionary macroeconomic effect, particularly if there are important balance sheet effects associated with currency depreciation. In the long run, however, stabilization may facilitate a return to the trend and pre-crisis rate of economic growth. In this case the negative short run growth effects will not persist. Indeed, a country with an IMF program may return to its trend rate of economic growth more quickly than does a non-program country faced with similar economic circumstances.

As a second hypothetical scenario let us consider a low-income country. Here also there may have been elements of macroeconomic mismanagement. But there may also be more pronounced structural deficiencies. There may be weaknesses on the supply side of the economy. Private capital inflows will be less important than they are in the case of a middle-income country, but foreign aid may be more important. Shocks occur via the trade account rather than the capital account and are associated with export shortfalls and import excesses. An IMF program may go hand in hand with foreign aid. In these circumstances, there may be a less pressing need to raise the rate of interest, with more emphasis being placed on currency depreciation as a way of strengthening the current account. The balance sheet effects that are significant for the middle-income country and that contribute to a short run negative effect on economic growth are much less significant in the case of this low-income country. With higher foreign trade price elasticities in the long run than in the short run, the beneficial effects on the current account, and on economic growth, may take time to be felt. In similar vein, economic reform aimed at inducing structural adjustment is unlikely to have an immediate beneficial effect on economic growth, but may have a delayed one. If the IMF program encourages aid donors to contribute more resources than they would have done otherwise, the combination of the additional aid and the IMF resources may be expected to cushion the need for short term adjustment based on compressing domestic aggregate demand. As a consequence of the above factors, the short term negative effect on economic growth may be ameliorated and the longer term growth trajectory improved.

In both of the hypothetical scenarios described above it also seems reasonable to assume that the implementation of program conditionality and the amount of IMF resources provided should make a difference. There seems little a priori reason to assume that there will be significant differences between a country without a program and one that is in similar economic circumstances and has a program that it then fails to implement (unless the up-front provision of IMF resources helps to overcome a financing constraint or the mere act of signing up to a program itself has important consequences for market access—this returns us to the catalytic effect that we examine in the next chapter).

In principle, and with other things remaining constant, additional resources should cushion the need for short run adjustment. However, a large amount of IMF resources may reflect the size of the initial macroeconomic disequilibrium and the adjustment needed. It is therefore feasible that large IMF programs leave a larger financing gap, and in these circumstances the need for short run adjustment will be greater.

7.3   EFFECTS OF IMF PROGRAMS ON ECONOMIC GROWTH: LITERATURE REVIEW

There is a large literature that examines the macroeconomic effects of IMF programs.[3] A number of surveys exist (see, for instance, Bird, 2007). Contributions to the literature vary in terms of the particular macroeconomic variables examined, the sample used and the methodology adopted. With regards to the impact on economic growth results are mixed. However, the weight of evidence seems to suggest that the effects are more often than not negative. Key studies that report a negative effect include Bordo and Schwartz (2000), Przeworski and Vreeland (2000), Hardoy (2003), Hutchison (2003, 2004), Hutchison and Noy (2004), Vreeland (2003), IEO (2002), Barro and Lee (2005), Butkiewicz and Yanikkaya (2005), Dreher (2006), Eichengreen, Gupta and Mody (2008), Marchesi and Sitori (2011), and IMF (2012). Positive or mixed results are reported by Conway (1994), Dicks-Mireaux, Mecagni, and Schadler (2000), Evrensel (2002), Hutchison (2004), and Atoyan and Conway (2006). Some of these studies find that while the short run effects of IMF programs on economic growth are negative, the long run effects are positive. A useful detailed summary of all the main studies is presented in tabular form by Bal Gunduz et al. (2013) and this is reproduced here as Table 7.1.

A number of observations may be made about the existing literature. First, many of the studies do not distinguish between low- and middle-income countries, even though there is substantial reason to believe that the circumstances in which they refer to the Fund differ. LICs have a greater tendency to be prolonged users of IMF resources and undertake the majority of their borrowing under concessional lending windows. Bird et al. (2004) discover that the characteristics associated with prolonged engagement with the IMF are those often exhibited by LICs. In other work we conclude that participation by LICs in IMF programs is determined by factors that differ from those that affect participation by middle-income countries (Bird and Rowlands, 2009b).The differences are also shown by the results presented in Chapter 5, and by the participation models that we report later in this chapter.

Second, the methods used to deal with selection bias may be deficient. In some cases no allowance is made for the possibility that it exists, or only informal techniques are used to deal with it. In other cases there is more formal adjustment using a Heckman two stage procedure or instrumental variables. However, there are problems in finding appropriate instruments; that is, variables that are correlated with participation in IMF programs but not with economic outcomes such as growth. There is evidence from studies into the catalytic effect that results are sensitive to the technique used to deal with selection bias (Bird and Rowlands, 2009a).

Third, for studies that adopt a propensity score matching (PSM) approach—an approach that we use in the empirical section of this chapter—results will depend on the accuracy of the underlying participation equation upon which the probability of IMF programs is calculated. This means that a participation equation derived from a dataset that includes middle-income countries may be inappropriate when applied to LICs and vice versa. Since the clear majority of IMF programs are with low-income countries, it is worthwhile to take a close look at their involvement with the Fund. As just noted, in this chapter we use different participation equations for middle-income and low-income countries when calculating propensities to have IMF programs.

There is a sub-set of the literature that concentrates on LICs. Some of these studies deal more directly with the specific facilities under which programs have been arranged; particularly the now defunct PRGF and its predecessor the ESAF (see, for example, Schadler et al., 1993; Bredenkamp and Schadler, 1999; Dicks-Mireaux et al., 2000; Ghosh et al., 2005; Hajro and Joyce, 2004; Botchwey et al., 1998; Gupta et al., 2002; and Bird and Mosley, 2006).

Other studies examine the overall effects of programs in low-income countries. Dicks-Mireaux et al. (2000) find some evidence that IMF programs in LICs have had positive macroeconomic effects, including that of benefitting economic growth, but their results fail conventional tests of statistical significance. Bird and Mosley (2006) find evidence that suggests that the PRGF and the ESAF helped recipient countries to increase their rate of economic growth, and also to redirect government expenditure in a pro-poor way and increase social capacity, but their results rely on a relatively small number of examples and their non-program control group is only relatively informally established.

A recent study published by the IMF (Bal Gunduz et al., 2013) uses a PSM approach to address many of the problems that have beset earlier research into the effects of IMF programs. It provides evidence to support the argument that long running involvement by LICs with the IMF, as well as short run engagement associated with shock-related drawings, have a beneficial effect on economic growth. Although this study represents an important step forward, the effects of standard IMF concessional programs are not investigated and remain moot. Moreover, the participation model used to calculate propensities is largely related to shocks of one form or another.

In this chapter we attempt to add value to the existing literature by investigating the effects of concessional IMF programs on economic growth in low-income countries as well as the effects of non-concessional programs on growth in middle-income countries. We also test to see whether the completion of programs and the amount of resources made available makes a difference to their impact on economic growth.

7.4 ASSESSING THE EFFECTS OF IMF PROGRAMS ON ECONOMIC GROWTH: METHODOLOGY

In estimating the effect of IMF programs on economic growth we use the propensity score matching approach as a way of dealing with potential selection bias; this method seeks to allow for the possibility that countries that turn to the IMF differ in important ways from those that do not. The PSM approach identifies countries with broadly equivalent probabilities of signing an IMF program based on a specified participation or selection equation. The estimating procedure (in this case conducted using the software program

Table 7.1 Summary of literature on the impact of IMF programs, 2000–12

Outcome variables	GDP growth	Inflation	Fiscal deficit	Current Account balance	Monetary growth	Gini coefficient	Education spending
Bordo and Schwartz (2000)	−	+		+			
Dicks-Mireaux, Mecagni, Schadler (2000)	+*	−					
Garuda (2000)						+*/−*a	
Przeworski and Vreeland (2000)	−*						
Evrensel (2002)	+*b	−		+*	+/−		
Hardoy (2003)	−						
Hutchison (2003)	−*						
Vreeland (2003)	−*						
Dreher and Vaubel (2004)			−*		−*		
Hutchison (2004)	+						
Independent Evaluation Office (2002)	−*/−d						
Barro and Lee (2005)	−*						
Butkiewicz and Yanikkaya (2005)	−*						
Easterly (2005)	0e		−			−	
Atoyan and Conway (2006)	+/−		−*	+*			
Dreher (2006)	−*						
Nooruddin and Simmons (2006)							−*

Health spending	Poverty	Period	Countries	Type of programs	Selection Correction	Method
		1973–1998	14 EMs	SBA EFF	No	
		1986–1991	61 LICs	ESAF	No	
		1975–1991	39 countries	Mixed	Yes	PSM
		1970–1990	79 countries	Mixed	Yes	Heckman
		1971–1997	91 countries	Mixed & by program	No	
		1970–1990	109 developing countries	Mixed	Yes	PSM PSM (DID)
		1975–1997	67 countries	SBA EFF	Yes	Heckman[c]
		1961–1993	110 countries	Mixed	Yes	Heckman
		1975–1997	94 countries	Mixed	No	
		1975–1997	25 EMs	SBA EFF	Yes	PSM Heckman
		1975–1999	82 Prolonged vs temporary users	Mixed & by program	Yes	IV
		1975–1999	130 countries	SBA EFF	Yes	IV
		1970–1999	100 developing countries	Mixed	Yes	IV
		1980–1999	20 repeated users	Mixed	Yes	IV f
		1993–2002	95 developing countries	Mixed	Yes	PSM Heckman
		1970–2000	98 developing countries	SBA EFF	Yes	IV
–*		1980–2000	98 countries	Mixed	Yes	

Table 7.1 (continued)

Outcome variables	GDP growth	Inflation	Fiscal deficit	Current Account balance	Monetary growth	Gini coefficient	Education spending
Eichengreen, Gupta, and Mody (2008)	−*						
Marchesi and Sitori (2011)	−*g						
IMF (2012)h	−i	−	+		0		
Clements, Gupta, and Nozaki (2013)							+*
Oberdabernig (2013)						+*j	

Notes:
Heckman = Heckman two-step estimator for correcting selection bias; IV = Instrumental variable estimator; PSM = Propensity Score Matching; DID= Difference-in-difference; EMs = Emerging Markets; EFF = Extended Fund Facility; ESAF = Enhanced Structural Adjustment Facility; LICs = Low-Income Countries; MICs = Middle-Income Countries; SAF = Structural Adjustment Facility; SBA = Stand-By Arrangement. +* Significantly positive; −* Significantly negative; + Positive but insignificant; − Negative but insignificant; 0 Very close to zero.
a   Countries with low propensity scores show improvement, while for those with high propensity scores inequality deteriorates.
b   Significant only for SAF/ESAF, positive but insignificant in mixed sample.
c   This study applies Heckman correction to growth equation, however, the inverse mills ratio (IMR) turns insignificant. The author notes that his participation equation is not strong. Therefore, it is difficult to know whether the insignificance of the IMR is because a stable participation equation is not identified or participation is random.
d   Finds significant negative effect for prolonged users only, while the impact on growth is insignificant for temporary users.
e   Results from IV regressions are very close to zero.
f   Easterly (2005) notes that his instruments are weak.
g   They report a significantly positive impact from the interaction of IMF and World Bank programs.
h   Based on descriptive comparison vis- à -vis the control group constructed by the PSM, therefore, significance level is not reported.
i   Positive effect is reported for years following the initiation of programs.
j   The findings are reversed for the period 2000–09 with IMF programs leading to lower poverty and lower inequality.

Source: Draws on Steinwand and Stone (2008), expanded by authors to include selected key aspects of previous studies as well as recent literature.

Health spending	Poverty	Period	Countries	Type of programs	Selection Correction	Method
		1980–2003	24 countries with sudden stops	SBA EFF	Yes	Heckman
		1982–2005	128 developing countries	Mixed	Yes	IV
		2002–2011	44 MICs	SBA EFF	Yes	PSM
+*		1985–2009	LICs and MICs	Mixed & by program	Yes	
	+*j	1982–2009	LICs and MICs	Mixed	Yes	IV

Stata) then generates five PSM methods which use different techniques for identifying comparable cases of program and non-program countries. It tests for statistically significant differences in the averages of comparable groups. Four standard measures in Stata are stratification, nearest neighbor, kernel and radius. The fifth propensity score (PS) matching method enforces a more rigorous balancing requirement than the other four, and requires that the propensity equations are modified to drop sequentially the explanatory variables in the selection equation that differ too widely between the program and non-program countries. This last method sometimes generates instability in the results and we report only the ones that reflect the most typical results whilst preserving the most balanced selection equation.

In what follows we start off by investigating the effects of non-concessional programs on economic growth in 80 middle-income countries, defined by the World Bank to be lower-middle income and upper-middle income countries. We therefore conflate the categories that we adopted in Chapter 5 when analysing participation in more detail. We then move on to examine the effect of concessional programs in 66 low-income countries, defined as countries that are eligible for concessional IMF programs.

After this we examine the effects of program completion and of the amount of resources made available. For program completion we use what has become a standard proxy measure; programs are considered as having been completed if 80 percent or more of the available resources have been drawn down by the end of the arrangement. This is not an ideal measure of completion or the implementation of conditionality, since it does not distinguish between those programs that are not completed as a result of economic circumstances improving to a degree that makes an IMF program no longer necessary, and those that are blown off course by adverse external shocks or because there is a governmental decision not to deliver on policy commitments.

Programs may be completed in the sense of meeting all the performance criteria but without the country necessarily drawing all the resources. Alternatively, via modifications to the program or the use of waivers, a country may be allowed to draw the full amount of the IMF credit without meeting all the performance criteria spelt out in the original letter of intent. Whilst acknowledging these limitations, the completion measure is reasonably well correlated with another measure of implementation that has been used in the literature and that is based on the irreversible interruption of a program, and we deem it adequate for our purposes. It is also superior to one based on the MONA database. Chapter 6 provides more information on program implementation.

When testing the effects of the amount of financing, we first examined the distribution of total IMF financing available as a share of the country's GDP. We then split the sample into the large and small program categories to reflect a reasonable division of this financing-to-GDP ratio.

As noted in our prior discussion, the effects of IMF programs are likely to vary with the degree of policy implementation and the amount of IMF support. The data we have are typically at a very highly aggregated level and are available only on a rather crude annual level, making it empirically difficult to identify any subtle changes in the effects over time. In addition, the window to examine the effects of IMF programs is often fairly small, since it is unusual for countries in the sample to avoid exogenous shocks that complicate the analysis for subsequent years, or for countries not to sign an IMF agreement in a subsequent year if it had failed to do so when predicted. Therefore we are forced to do the best we can and limit our analysis to the year the agreement is signed and the subsequent two years for those countries in the sample with an agreement, and to a similar three year period for non-signing countries.

The tables of results provide the propensity score matching results for the five different tests for the year of signing the agreement, and the following two years. Positive (negative) numbers in the table indicate that the IMF programs are associated with a positive (negative) effect on economic growth relative to non-signing countries, with the quantity indicating the estimated differential effect on growth as a percentage of GDP.

Table 7.2   Participation models (probit equations for signing IMF agreements)

Variable name	Non-concessional agreements in middle-income countries		Concessional agreements in low-income countries	
	Coefficient estimate	Z-score	Coefficient estimate	Z-score
Past IMF program exposure	0.0508***	9.96	0.0230***	5.39
Real GDP per capita	0.124***	3.91	–	–
Growth (previous year)	−0.0547***	−6.27	–	–
Growth (long-term average)			0.0438*	2.43
Domestic Bank Credit growth	−0.00415***	3.11	–	–
Real exchange rate depreciation	0.00160***	3.37	–	–
Current Account deficit >3% of GDP	0.279***	2.58	–	–
Big reserve loss (fixed exchange rate country)	–		–	
Big reserve loss	0.487***	3.39	–	–
Debt–service payments to exports ratio	0.790**	2.42	0.0116**	2.56
Past rescheduling	−0.623***	−3.70	–	–
Imminent official debt rescheduling	–	–	0.927***	6.94
Imminent rescheduling	0.790***	4.72	–	–
Elections	–	–	0.343**	2.51
Metals price index	–	–	−0.00845***	−2.73
Constant	–	–	−1.32***	−5.04
Number of observations	1382		691	
Pseduo-R^2	0.264		0.189	
Probability that all coefficient estimates = 0	0.00		0.00	

Note: ***, **, *, † identify coefficient estimates that are significant at the 1, 2.5, 5 and 10 percent two tailed test levels of significance, respectively.

7.4.1   Results for Middle-Income Countries

Table 7.2 presents the participation equations that form the basis for estimating the propensity scores that we use to deal with selection bias. These are closely related to the models reported in Chapter 5, although the samples used are not exactly comparable. In the participation model we use here, for example, we combine all middle-income countries together.

From Table 7.3 we see that performance in terms of economic growth in middle-income countries is relatively poor for IMF program countries

Table 7.3   Effect of non-concessional IMF program on middle-income country growth

Propensity Matching Procedure	Year of signing	One year after signing	Two years after signing
Stratification	−1.20***	−1.07[a]	0.37[a]
Nearest Neighbor	−1.15**	−1.68†	0.30
Kernel	−1.24***	−1.11[a]	0.41[a]
Radius	−2.17***	−1.63*	n/a
PS match	−1.13*	−0.70	0.82

Notes:
***, **, *, † identify coefficient estimates that are significant at the 1, 2.5, 5 and 10 percent two tailed test levels of significance, respectively.
a: no standard error was available, so significance levels could not be ascertained.
n/a: the program could not provide results.

in the year of signing. The estimates suggest that middle-income countries that sign on to an IMF program have a growth rate that is just over 1 percent lower than similar non-signing comparator countries in the year of signing. These results are consistent with an interpretation that IMF programs have an immediate contractionary effect on program countries. It is also possible, however, that signing countries are significantly worse off than non-program countries in a manner that is not being fully captured by the participation equation. It is difficult to establish the extent to which the result reflects the trajectory of economic growth associated with the signing of programs and to distinguish this from the effects of the programs themselves. Therefore we cannot reach firm conclusions about the effects of programs for the year in which they are signed. Either there appears to be a negative effect on economic growth, or if there is any immediate positive growth effect it is insufficient to overpower the poor economic conditions that led to the programs in the first place.

Overall, the full sample results suggest that any negative growth effects of program signings, controlling for the signing propensities, declines gradually. Two years after the year of signing there is weak evidence that the growth effect is, on average, positive relative to non-program countries. For the year after and two years after, however, the dispersion of the growth effects is too large to suggest statistical significance. Therefore, while on balance the growth effects of non-concessional IMF programs in middle-income countries seem to become more benevolent over the two years that follow the signing of the program, these effects are neither universal, nor statistically significant. Clearly other variables must be

Table 7.4   *Effect of non-concessional IMF program on middle-income country growth by program size*

Propensity Matching Procedure	Average (Treatment) Effect on Growth of IMF programs					
	Year of signing		One year after signing		Two years after signing	
	Small program	Large program	Small program	Large program	Small program	Large program
Stratification	−0.60	−2.60***	−1.03a	−1.16[a]	0.23[a]	0.71[a]
N. Neighbor	−0.65	−2.23**	−1.90†	−1.19	−0.33	0.29
Kernel	−0.64	−2.62***	−1.17[a]	−1.09[a]	0.13[a]	1.00[a]
Radius	−1.34***	−4.01***	−2.49**	−n/a	n/a	n/a
PS Match	−0.53	−0.16	−1.01†	−0.067	0.12	1.16

Table 7.5   *Effect of non-concessional IMF program on middle-income country growth by program completion*

Propensity Matching Procedure	Average (Treatment) Effect on Growth of IMF programs					
	Year of signing		One year after signing		Two years after signing	
	Incomplete	Complete	Incomplete	Complete	Incomplete	Complete
Stratification	−1.25*	−1.38**	−1.01a	−1.37[a]	0.08a	0.38
N. Neighbor	−1.15	−1.40†	−0.64	−2.70†	0.96	−0.38
Kernel	−1.20†	−1.49**	−0.94[a]	−1.48[a]	0.23[a]	0.38[a]
Radius	−2.08***	−2.47***	−2.37†	−1.06	n/a	n/a
PS Match	−0.98	−1.19	−1.02	−0.95	0.35	−0.23

intervening in determining the growth patterns that emerge after signing an IMF program.

The results are consistent with the notion that, having initially created macroeconomic stability, probably by compressing domestic aggregate demand, this establishes a foundation upon which subsequent growth may be built.

In Tables 7.4 and 7.5 we examine contingent factors. One is the amount of IMF resources associated with the program. The earlier theoretical discussion was somewhat ambivalent about what might be expected. Our results suggest that larger programs are associated with worse growth performance in the year of signing. The relationship is less clear cut for subsequent years. It would appear that the IMF might be providing more resources where economic problems are more severe, but not

Table 7.6   Effect of concessional IMF program on low-income country
*   growth*

Propensity Matching Procedure	Year of signing	One year after signing	Two years after signing
Stratification	0.75	0.50	0.91†
Nearest Neighbor	0.66	1.56	0.94
Kernel	0.73	0.45	0.90†
Radius	0.74	0.13	0.46
PS match	0.97	0.50	0.15

proportionately more resources. As a consequence, the compression of domestic aggregate demand, along with a negative effect on economic growth, is more pronounced in the short term for large programs. It may also be that where large programs are heavily drawn upon, there is a negative signal transmitted to capital markets. There is then a negative catalytic effect that is also detrimental to growth. This possibility is further examined in the following chapter.

Turning to the effects of program completion, the results are presented in Table 7.5. It seems that the negative effects of IMF programs on economic growth are slightly larger in the year of signing for programs that are eventually completed. This may mean that, where countries need to draw heavily on the IMF, a negative signal is transmitted to capital markets. The markets may prefer situations where, although a relatively large amount of resources is available from the IMF, the resources do not have to be used. Overall, however, the results in Table 7.5 do not justify firm conclusions about the impact of program completion in determining the effects of IMF programs on economic growth in middle-income countries.

7.4.2   Results for Low-Income Countries

When we examine the effects of IMF programs on economic growth in low-income countries, we discover a rather different set of results. The key results are presented in Table 7.6. The first observation to be made is that nothing particularly significant from a statistical point of view emerges. This is reasonably consistent with what might have been expected. It would have been somewhat surprising to find that IMF programs had highly significant effects on economic growth over a relatively short time span, given the often fairly deep-seated and fundamental issues that influence economic growth and the structural problems often encountered in LICs. Having said this, there is some evidence that suggests that IMF programs

Table 7.7   *Effect of concessional IMF program on low-income country growth by program size*

| Propensity Matching Procedure | Average (Treatment) Effect on Growth of IMF programs | | | | | |
| | Year of signing | | One year after signing | | Two years after signing | |
	Small program	Large program	Small program	Large program	Small program	Large program
Stratification	1.03†	0.29	0.51	0.49	0.88	1.04
N. Neighbor	0.98	−0.30	1.69*	0.09	0.78	2.08**
Kernel	0.95†	0.32	0.42	0.54	0.94	0.93
Radius	0.82	0.07	−0.28	0.93	n/a	n/a
PS Match	0.82	0.89	0.72	0.39	0.80	2.51**

Table 7.8   *Effect of concessional IMF program on low-income country growth by program completion*

| Propensity Matching Procedure | Average (Treatment) Effect on Growth of IMF programs | | | | | |
| | Year of signing | | One year after signing | | Two years after signing | |
	Incomplete	Complete	Incomplete	Complete	Incomplete	Complete
Stratification	0.20a	0.92	n/a	0.93	n/a	1.46**
N. Neighbor	−0.45	1.23	0.20	1.96	0.09	1.47
Kernel	0.29	0.89	−0.58	0.85	−0.46	1.47***
Radius	−0.26	0.81	−1.18†	0.79	n/a	n/a
PS Match	−0.88	0.48	0.01	0.82	0.74	1.62†

in LICs exert a beneficial influence on economic growth. The result only becomes significant two years after programs are signed, and even then only at the 10 percent level. Unlike in the case of MICs, it appears that in LICs there are no significant short term adverse effects on economic growth.

The results reported in Tables 7.6, 7.7 and 7.8 are consistent with some of the theoretical ideas that we discussed earlier in the chapter. Perhaps in the year of signing, the additional resources associated with an IMF program, either directly, or by influencing the willingness of donors to provide more aid, allow adjustment to be cushioned and to place less emphasis on compressing domestic aggregate demand, thereby protecting economic growth. Two years after the year in which programs are signed it may be that the effects of structural reform on economic growth are beginning to be felt, along with the expansionary effects of currency depreciation. However, these growth benefits may be sacrificed if the program is not completed. To enjoy the improvement in their economic health it seems that LICs need to finish the course of treatment.

Perhaps more interesting is the absence of evidence that IMF programs have a detrimental effect on growth in low-income countries, at least in the initial years of a program. While not statistically distinct from zero, the countries with IMF programs exhibit uniformly higher rates of growth on average than the non-program comparator countries.

Taken as a whole, our findings show that it is unfounded to make sweeping generalizations about the effects of IMF programs on economic growth in emerging and developing economies. Certainly we find little empirical support for the idea that IMF programs are systematically associated with an enduring reduction in the rate of economic growth. For middle-income countries there is an immediate negative effect that may be the consequence of the macroeconomic stabilization embedded in IMF programs. But even here it is difficult to be certain that we have eliminated the possibility that this effect is the result of the weak economic circumstances that drive countries to the Fund for assistance. When examining growth performance two years after a program has been signed the negative effect has disappeared. There is even a hint that, having created macro stability, countries begin to experience an albeit insignificant increase in the rate of economic growth by comparison with broadly similar non-program countries. For LICs, and for the entire period from the year of signing a program to two years afterwards, the growth effects appear to be fairly benign and may even be modestly beneficial.

It is interesting that while much of the literature suggests that IMF programs are particularly inappropriate for low-income countries, that they impair economic growth and are antagonistic toward development, our results seem to suggest something different. In large measure it appears that IMF programs do not lead to policies being adopted that are destructive of national prosperity. The severe criticisms of IMF conditionality in LICs seem unwarranted. Moreover, for LICs, it also appears that economic growth can be better protected where the IMF provides relatively large amounts of finance and where governments complete the programs to which they agree when they sign the letter of intent.

7.5   CONCLUDING REMARKS

Given its complex nature and the myriad of factors that exert an influence on economic growth, it may be expected that the involvement of the IMF is unlikely to have large and highly significant effects in either direction, once other factors are taken into account. Having said this, a substantial portion of the existing empirical literature has found evidence to suggest that IMF programs have a negative effect on economic growth. More often than not the mechanisms through which this effect materializes are not investigated. But it may be assumed that the supporting argument would be that the Fund systematically encourages policies that compress aggregate demand, resulting in a form of deflationary overkill, and that this has an enduring detrimental effect on economic growth. In these circumstances the Fund would be operating in a way that is largely at odds with its purposes as laid down in the Articles of Agreement.

While it is not possible to specify a model that precisely captures all the ways in which IMF programs may affect economic growth, it is possible to think of some ways in which the effect might be positive rather than negative. Under the auspices of conventional non-concessional programs in middle-income countries, and by facilitating stabilization through the pursuit of broadly appropriate policies, as well as by providing short term finance in circumstances where this is unavailable from other sources, the Fund may help to speed recovery from a crisis and foster a return to trend rates of economic growth. The evidence we present in this chapter is largely consistent with this claim. To the extent that there is any significant negative effect this seems to be short term in duration.

Our evidence is consistent with a scenario where middle-income countries turn to the IMF in severe economic distress and where domestic aggregate demand exceeds aggregate supply. IMF programs initially have the effect of slowing down the rate of economic growth by comparison to broadly equivalent non-program countries. However, by two years after signing the negative effect has been ameliorated, and although not statistically significant, program countries are beginning to experience a positive effect on economic growth by comparison with non-program countries.

For low-income countries using concessional IMF facilities it appears from the evidence we present that any potential adverse short term effect on economic growth associated with macroeconomic stabilization is neutralized by the resources provided by the Fund and by the additional foreign aid that often accompanies IMF involvement. In the two years that follow the signing of an agreement the effect on growth appears to be increasingly positive and may even improve the growth trajectory. In part, this could be to do with the structural economic reforms that programs encourage. The positive longer term effects are particularly apparent where programs are completed and where they are well resourced.

While the results presented in this chapter do not suggest that IMF programs always have a large, important, and highly significant positive effect on economic growth they do suggest that claims that programs impose an enduring and systematically negative effect are unfounded. They also underline the need to avoid over-generalization. The effects of IMF programs on economic growth differ in important ways between sub-groups of countries. While it is insecure to claim that our results support specific causal connections, they are consistent with reasonably coherent theoretical expectations of the ways in which IMF programs influence economic growth.

NOTES

1. Bird (2004) provides an account of the IMF's policies toward economic growth and poverty reduction and links this to recent research into the causes of economic growth in poor countries.
2. Much depends on the relationship between economic growth and the balance of payments. One possibility is that there is a negative relationship. Here, in order to strengthen the current account, it is necessary to sacrifice economic growth, since this will tend to lower the demand for imports below what it would otherwise have been. If the Fund's top priority is to strengthen the current account then it follows that economic growth may be adversely affected. However, if the balance of payments strategy is based on expenditure switching devices such as devaluation rather than on expenditure reduction, then the negative growth effect may be reduced.
3. In addition to the studies that examine the macroeconomic effects of IMF programs, there are also studies that investigate more directly their effects on poverty and income inequality (Bird, 2004; Bird and Mosley, 2006; Hajro and Joyce, 2004; IEO, 2004; Oberdabernig, 2013; Vreeland, 2003).
4. Notes for tables: ***, **, *, † identify coefficient estimates that are significant at the 1, 2.5, 5 and 10 percent two tailed test levels of significance, respectively.
   [a] : no standard error was available, so significance levels could not be ascertained.
   n/a: the program could not provide results.

REFERENCES

Atoyan, R., and Conway, P. (2006). Evaluating the impact of IMF programs: A comparison of matching and instrumental-variable estimators. *Review of International Organizations*, 1(2), 99–124.

Bal Gunduz, Y., Ebeke, C., Hacibedel, B., Kaltani, L., Kehayova, V., Lane, C., Mummssen, C., Mwase, N., and Thornton, J. (2013). The economic impact of IMF supported programs in low income countries, *IMF Occasional Paper*, 13/277, Washington, DC: International Monetary Fund.

Barro, R. and Lee, J-W. (2005). IMF programs: Who is chosen and what are the effects? *Journal of Monetary Economics*, 52(7), 1245–1269.

Beck, T., Clarke, G., Groff, A., Keefer, P., and Walsh, P. (2001). New tools in comparative political economy: The database of political institutions. *World Bank Economic Review*, 15(1), 165–176.

Bird, G. (2004). Growth, poverty and the IMF. *Journal of International Development*, 16, 621–636.

Bird, G. (2007). The IMF: A bird's eye view of its role and operations. *Journal of Economic Surveys*, 21(4), 683–745.

Bird, G., and Mosley, P. (2006). Should the IMF discontinue its long-term lending role in developing countries?, in Ranis, G., Vreeland, J., and Kosack, S. (eds), *Globalization and the Nation State: The Impact of the IMF and the World Bank*. London, Routledge.

Bird, G. and Rowlands, D. (2009a). The IMF's role in mobilizing private capital flows: Are there grounds for catalytic conversion? *Applied Economics Letters*, 16(17), 1705–1708.

Bird, G., and Rowlands, D. (2009b). A disaggregated empirical analysis of the determinants of IMF arrangements: Does one model fit all? *Journal of International Development*, 21, 915–931.

Bird, G., Hussain, M., and Joyce, J. (2004). Many happy returns: Recidivism and the IMF. *Journal of International Money and Finance*, 23(2), 231–251.

Bordo, M.D., and Schwartz, A.J. (2000). Measuring real economic effects of bailouts: Historical perspectives on how countries in financial distress have fared with and without bailouts. *Carnegie-Rochester Conference Series on Public Policy*, 53(1), 81–167.

Botchwey, K., Collier, P., Gunning, J-W., and Hamada, K. (1998). *External Evaluation of the Enhanced Structural Adjustment Facility*. Washington, DC: IMF.

Bredenkamp, H., and Schadler, S. (eds) (1999). *Economic Adjustment and Reform in Low Income Countries: Studies by the Staff of the International Monetary Fund*. Washington, DC: IMF.

Butkiewicz, J.L., and Yanikkaya, H. (2005). The effects of IMF and World Bank lending on long-run economic growth: An empirical analysis. *World Development*, 33(3), 371–391.

Conway, P. (1994). IMF lending programs: Participation and impact. *Journal of Development Economics*, 45(2), 365–391.

Dicks-Mireaux, L., Mecagni, M., and Schadler, S. (2000). Evaluating the effect of IMF lending to low income countries. *Journal of Development Economics*, 61, 495–526.

Dreher, A. (2006). IMF and economic growth: The effects of programs, loans and compliance with conditionality. *World Development*, 34(5), 769–788.

Dreher, A. and Vaubel, R. (2004). The causes and consequences of IMF conditionality. *Emerging Markets Finance and Trade*, 40 (3), 26–54.

Easterly, W. (2005). What did structural adjustment adjust? The association of policies and growth with repeated IMF and World Bank adjustment loans. *Journal of Development Economics*, 76, 1–22.

Eichengreen, B., Gupta, P., and Mody, A. (2008). Sudden stops and IMF-supported programs, NBER Chapters, in *Financial Markets Volatility and Performance in Emerging Markets*: 219–266. Cambridge, MA: NBER.

Evrensel, A. (2002). Effectiveness of IMF-supported stabilization programs in developing countries. *Journal of International Money and Finance*, 21(5), 565–587.

Ghosh, A., Christofides, C., Kim, J., Papi, L., Ramakrishnan, U., Thomas, A., and Zalduendo, J. (2005). The design of IMF-supported programs. *IMF Occasional Paper*, No 241, Washington, DC: International Monetary Fund.

Gupta, S., Plant, M., Dorsey, T., and Clements, B. (2002). Is the PRGF living up to expectations? *Finance and Development*, 39(2), 17–20.

Hajro, Z., and Joyce, J.P. (2004). A true test: Do IMF programs hurt the poor? *Applied Economics*, 41(3), 295–306.

Hardoy, I. (2003). Effect of IMF programs on growth: A reappraisal using the method of matching. *Institute for Social Research Paper*, 2003:040.

Hutchison, M.M. (2003). A cure worse than the disease? Currency crises and the output costs of IMF-supported stabilization programmes, in Dooley, M. and Frankel, J.A. (eds), *Managing Currency Crises in Emerging Markets*: 321–359. Chicago, IL: University of Chicago Press.

Hutchison, M.M. (2004). Selection bias and the output costs of IMF programs. *EPRU Working Paper Series* 04-15, Economic Policy Research Unit, Department of Economics, Denmark, Copenhagen.

Hutchison, M.M., and Noy, I. (2003). Macroeconomic effects of IMF-sponsored programs in Latin America: output costs, program recidivism and the vicious cycle of failed stabilization. *Journal of International Money and Finance*, 22, 991–1014.

Ilzetzki, E.O., Reinhart, C.M., and Rogoff, K. (2004). Exchange rate arrangements into the twenty-first century: Will the anchor currency hold? Unpublished.

IMF (2012). *2011 Review of Conditionality-Background Paper: Outcomes of IMF Supported Programs*. Washington DC, International Monetary Fund.

Independent Evaluation Office (IEO) (2002). *Evaluation of Prolonged Use of IMF Programs*. Washington, DC: IMF.

Independent Evaluation Office (IEO) (2004). *Evaluation of Poverty Reduction Strategy Papers and Poverty Reduction and Growth Facility*, Washington, DC: IMF.

Marchesi, S., and Sitori, E. (2011). Is two better than one? The effects of IMF and World Bank interaction on growth. *Review of International Organizations*, 6(3), 287–306.

Oberdabernig, D.A. (2013). Revisiting the effects of IMF programs on poverty and inequality. *World Development*, 46, 415–429.

Przeworski, A., and Vreeland, J. (2000). The effect of IMF programs on economic growth. *Journal of Development Economics*, 62(2), 385–421.

Schadler, S., Rozwadowski, F., Tiwari, S., and Robinson, D.O. (1993). Economic adjustment in low income countries: experience under the enhanced structural adjustment facility,' *IMF Occasional Paper*, No 106, Washington, DC: International Monetary Fund.

Steinwand, M.C., and Stone, R.W. (2008). The International Monetary Fund: A review of the recent literature. *Review of International Organizations*, 3(2), 123–149.

Vreeland, J. (2003). *The IMF and Economic Development*. Cambridge: Cambridge University Press.

APPENDIX: DEFINITIONS AND SOURCES

Dependent Variable

Non-concessional agreements (for the middle-income countries estimations): A binary variable (0 or 1) indicating that a stand-by agreement (SBA) or extended financing facility agreement (EFF) was signed in a particular year. Source: IMF *Annual Report* (several years).

Concessional agreements (for the low-income countries estimations): A binary variable (0 or 1) indicating that a structural adjustment facility (SAF), enhanced structural adjustment facility (ESAF) or poverty reduction and growth facility (PRGF) agreement was signed in a particular year. Source: IMF *Annual Report* (several years).

Independent Variables

Note: To avoid problems of simultaneity, all variable values are calculated from the previous year unless otherwise indicated.

Past IMF program exposure: The number of months in which a country was operating with an IMF program in the previous three years. IMF *Annual Report* (several years).

Real GDP per capita: The level of real per capita GDP as calculated using the chain method, in thousand $US. Source: Center for International Comparisons *Penn World Tables*.

Growth (previous year): Annual rate of economic growth, as a percentage. Source: World Bank, *World Development Indicators*.

Growth (long-term average): Average rate of growth for the previous three years, as a percentage. Source: World Bank, *World Development Indicators*.

Domestic bank credit growth: Average annual rate of growth of domestic bank credit, as a percentage. Source: World Bank, *World Development Indicators*.

Real exchange rate depreciation: The real exchange rate depreciation experienced by a country over the previous three years, calculated with the nominal exchange rate depreciation against the US dollar, adjusted for the county's consumer price inflation relative to that of the United States, expressed as a percentage. Source: World Bank, *World Development Indicators*.

Current account deficit > 3 percent of GDP: A binary variable with the value 1 if a country experienced a current account deficit larger than 3 percent of GDP. Source: World Bank, *World Development Indicators*.

Big reserve loss (fixed exchange rate country): A binary variable with the value 1 if a country experienced a drop in its foreign reserves of more than 25 percent in a single year, and it had a fixed exchange rate. Source: World Bank, *World Development Indicators* and the Reinhart and Rogoff exchange rate data (from Ilzetzki, Reinhart, and Rogoff, 2004).

Big reserve loss: A binary variable with the value 1 if a country experienced a drop in its foreign reserves of more than 25 percent in a single year. Source: World Bank, *World Development Indicators*.

Debt–service payments to exports ratio: The ratio of a country's debt service payments to its exports, expressed as a ratio. Source: World Bank, *World Development Indicators*.

Past rescheduling: A binary variable with the value of 1 if a country was identified as having had a portion of its debt rescheduled in the previous year. Source: World Bank, *World Development Indicators*.

Imminent official debt rescheduling: A binary variable with the value of 1 if a country was identified as requiring a portion of its official debt to be rescheduled in the next year. Source: World Bank, *World Development Indicators*.

Imminent rescheduling: A binary variable with the value of 1 if a country was identified as requiring a portion of any debt to be rescheduled in the next year. Source: World Bank, *World Development Indicators*.

Elections: A binary variable taking the value of 1 if a country held an election in the current year. Source: Beck et al. (2001).

Metals price index: The World Metals price index value. Source: IMF *World Economic Outlook*.

8. IMF programs and private capital flows

8.1 INTRODUCTION

A central issue in discussions about the world's financial system is the nature of the relationship between the International Monetary Fund (IMF) and private international capital markets. On the one hand they may be viewed as substitutes, with the IMF becoming involved in countries that have little access to private capital, or where private capital outflows have created a short-term external financing vacuum. Those who subscribe to the idea of creditor moral hazard go further and claim that the prospect of future IMF lending in the event of a crisis encourages private lenders to underestimate risk and to over-lend, which in turn ultimately generates the crisis and IMF intervention. Viewed as complements, on the other hand, IMF lending is claimed to have a catalytic effect on private capital market lending. In this case, the IMF is presented as bailing in private capital through signaling, coordination, or coercion. Through catalysis the IMF can facilitate balance of payments adjustment with fewer of its own resources. The nature and size of the catalytic effect is therefore of considerable importance. If catalysis is overestimated it will lead to insufficient financing and excessive balance of payments adjustment.

Increasing attention has been paid to the catalytic effect of IMF programs on private capital flows. The survey of the literature by Cottarelli and Giannini (2002) traces the evolution of the concept, analyses its possible operational mechanisms, and evaluates the available empirical evidence of its existence. In this chapter we use more recent theoretical insights to guide an empirical examination of the IMF's potential catalytic effect. We also undertake a detailed and disaggregated investigation into catalysis to examine the extent to which the effect varies between different sets of circumstances.

8.2   CATALYSIS: THEORETICAL UNDERPINNINGS

In their review of the catalytic effect, Cottarelli and Giannini (2002) claim that there are five channels through which it may work: policy design, information, commitment, screening, and insurance. IMF programs may lead to the design of superior policies that improve a country's future economic performance. Agreements may also reveal information about policies and performance otherwise unavailable to private capital markets. Programs may signal a government's commitment to reform, and reduce the chances that there will be policy slippages, or they may screen out governments that are not serious about reform. Finally, the IMF may provide insurance by acting as a lender of last resort, though possibly at the risk of creating moral hazard.

Early studies focused on conditionality as the principal modality for catalysis (Rodrik, 1996; Bird and Rowlands, 1997). The anticipation is that the catalytic effect of IMF agreements will be stronger when policy conditions are well designed and their implementation credible. However, when private markets believe that IMF programs will lead to recession or financial difficulties, or that good policies will not be implemented, then catalysis will be weak, non-existent or, in the extreme, negative. For example, 'conventional' IMF programs often lead to interest rate increases and exchange rate devaluation (Bird and Rowlands, 1997). According to the asset market approach this policy combination might induce capital inflows by raising the return on invested capital and reducing future exchange rate risk. However, rising interest rates may also send a negative signal, which in credit rationing models might precipitate reduced capital inflows due to higher default probabilities and lower expected returns. Devaluation may also signal lower commitment to defending the value of the currency, raising the specter of future exchange rate risk. Consequently Bird and Rowlands (1997) argue that the sign of the catalytic effect associated with IMF conditionality is theoretically unclear and that its true nature is essentially an empirical question.

In the aftermath of the East Asian crisis, researchers began to place more emphasis on the IMF as a provider of short-run liquidity, thereby inducing a stronger commitment to adjustment by making associated policies more sustainable politically and overcoming collective action problems that might otherwise lead to default. The consequent reduction in default risk could in turn encourage private capital inflows. Of course, in the absence of conditionality, IMF liquidity may also allow governments to relax adjustment efforts, raising default probabilities and discouraging investment. The withdrawal of private capital would in turn be facilitated by the provision of IMF resources. In this context a number of papers have investigated the logic of partial as opposed to complete bailouts, with models of the former frequently generating multiple equilibria and an incentive for private creditors to foreclose and bring about default and crisis. When creditors are not coordinated, only a full bailout that completely fills the financing gap will restore confidence (Zettelmeyer, 2000; Frankel and Roubini, 2001; Jeanne and Wyplosz, 2001).

Recent contributions to the theory of catalytic finance have concentrated on the impact of IMF lending on the probability of default. Morris and Shin (2006) continue the focus on IMF lending and default probabilities, using a global games framework to analyse the behavior of three players: short-term creditors, the IMF and debtor governments. In this coordination game with limited uncertainty, IMF lending may be necessary and just sufficient to supplement the financial resources a debtor country obtains from adjustment efforts, thereby encouraging short-term creditors to roll over their debt despite initial concerns about liquidity. Where a country has strong fundamentals and a government committed to stabilize the economy, there is no risk of illiquidity, no need for additional resources, and no role for IMF-induced catalysis. Where economic problems are fundamental and commitment to adjustment is weak, the IMF's relatively small resource contribution is unlikely to induce significant additional adjustment, and will thus fail to persuade creditors to roll over debts. Catalysis is therefore unlikely to exist here either, and the Fund's resources may be wasted. Catalysis may occur where countries on the margin of default receive just enough IMF resources and incentives to adjust to restore market confidence. Consequently, the catalytic effect will display context-specific non-linearities.

Similar conclusions emerge from Corsetti, Guimaraes, and Roubini (2006). In their model, crises are caused by the interaction between poor fundamentals, self-fulfilling creditor runs, and the policies of investors, governments and the IMF. The model shows that the IMF can prevent a scramble for liquidity by coordinating agents' expectations and by increasing the number of creditors willing to lend for any given set of fundamentals. As in Morris and Shin (2006), IMF lending may induce stronger economic adjustment efforts. The Fund's influence increases with its lending level and the precision of its information, and default may be avoided even if IMF lending only partially fills the external financing gap.

In a related model, Penalver (2004) suggests that it is the implicit subsidy on IMF resources that encourages borrowing countries to exert adjustment effort and to avoid default. By preventing default, IMF lending increases the marginal rate of return to investment thereby encouraging capital flows. Penalver's analysis therefore builds an analytical bridge between debt rollovers and new capital flows.

This 'new wave' of finance models highlights the well-established observation that the IMF's catalytic effect relies largely upon its ability to reduce uncertainty and increase the probability of superior economic performance, either through lending (as these new models accentuate), or via conditionality. For countries with fundamental economic problems, IMF involvement is unlikely to alter the perceptions of private capital markets and may indeed trigger an outflow of private capital, facilitating its substitution with official resources. For more sound economies, IMF involvement will have either no impact or may transmit a negative signal to private capital markets. For countries between these extremes, IMF involvement may reduce uncertainty and provide assurances that the added liquidity and adjustment effort will be sufficient to move the economy forward. It is in these situations that, a priori, catalysis may be expected to be relatively strong. Where earlier informal approaches focused on return and risk as the underlying determinants of international capital movements, these newer models usefully demonstrate how catalysis may be contingent on the nature and seriousness of the economic problems faced by IMF clients.

However, different types of capital will have different risk and return profiles, and may respond differently to IMF programs. Progress here is impeded by the fact that the theory of capital movements is too imprecise to exploit these differences in a large sample econometric model. Much of the literature on the determinants of foreign direct investment, for example, focuses on decision-making within multinational enterprises; there is no well-established theory of FDI viewed from the perspective of the recipient country, nor do good data exist for dyadic flows. We also lack a well-established theory of bank lending, bonds or portfolio investment upon which estimations of IMF catalysis may be confidently based.

Yet informal theorizing does suggest some hypotheses. For example, bank lending is likely to be short or medium term in nature, pro-cyclical, and influenced by proximate economic variables such as short term interest rates and liquidity. In contrast, foreign direct investment will depend more on the long term prospects for economic growth, policy relating to the repatriation of profits, and political stability. Portfolio investment may share some of the features of both of the above. Bond market responses are likely to vary with their maturity profile and the extent to which they are credibly guaranteed.

If the determinants of private capital flows are complex and differentiated, it follows that IMF programs may be expected to affect different types of capital in different ways. To the extent that stand-by arrangements (SBAs) are associated with increased macroeconomic stability they may be expected to have a positive effect on all capital flows, as theories of catalysis frequently assume. However, while the rise in interest rates and the elimination of currency overvaluation (thereby diminishing the likelihood of future devaluation and associated adverse balance sheet effects) might exert a positive effect on bank lending, a negative effect of programs on economic growth (or even the expectation that this will be the effect) might discourage FDI. Moreover, the infusion of credit associated with an SBA may be expected to be more relevant for public and publicly guaranteed (PPG) bank lending and bonds than for non-guaranteed inflows such as FDI.

The IMF's Extended Fund Facility programs (EFFs) might, in contrast, be expected to have more profound effects on longer term flows. To the extent that such programs are seen as correcting structural deficiencies and exerting a positive effect on long run economic growth, they should have a positive impact on FDI. However EFFs may also be interpreted as signaling the need for fundamental economic reform. Here, a previously good record of implementation may be required to encourage catalysis.

This discussion allows us to formulate a number of testable propositions about the relationship between IMF programs and private capital flows.

The *first* proposition is that the catalytic effect will vary across different types of private capital flow. For example, short-term creditors may be more concerned about macroeconomic stability and liquidity while long-term investors may look for evidence of structural adjustment.

Second, IMF programs are more likely to be successful if initial conditions are not severely adverse. The catalytic effect will therefore tend to be weak in situations where economic fundamentals are very poor, and may be negative if capital outflows are facilitated by IMF financing. For countries with relatively strong fundamentals, IMF arrangements may again exert little catalytic effect, and may even deter capital inflows by transmitting a negative signal. It is between these two extremes that a positive catalytic effect may be expected to be strongest. Consequently, it will depend non-linearly on the initial country conditions.

Third, catalysis should be stronger if IMF conditionality is well designed and effectively implemented. As examined elsewhere in this book, there is a large literature and extensive debate about the design of IMF programs. Critics suggest that conditionality emphasizes policies favored by international capital markets.[1] If so, the key uncertainty for catalysis pertains to implementation, which is affected by a complex mixture of economic and political factors (see Chapter 6). Creditors may thus be expected to wait to see whether governments keep to their policy commitments, and there may be no signaling-related catalytic effect. Alternatively, capital markets may consider a country's past track record of implementation as a reasonable guide to the future.

Fourth, there is a reasonable presumption that the prolonged use of IMF resources implies either the existence of intractable economic or political problems, or a serial reluctance to implement programs. It follows that the catalytic effect will be weaker for prolonged users of IMF resources.

Fifth, the type of facility under which resources are borrowed from the Fund may in principle give a further indication of the nature of the economic problems being encountered. SBAs tend to be associated with short-term stabilization, while EFFs are associated with more fundamental and longer-term structural adjustment. Indeed, EFF agreements are generally seen as having more extensive conditionality as they often include both stabilization and adjustment elements. It follows that SBAs may be expected to exhibit a stronger catalytic effect on shorter term flows, while EFFs may have a greater impact on longer-term flows such as FDI. A rider to this is that, as we discovered in Chapter 3, the actual economic differences between countries using SBAs and EFFs have become increasingly difficult to discern econometrically.

Sixth, where countries encounter problems of illiquidity, it may be expected that catalysis will be stronger when IMF lending is large relative to a country's financing needs, particularly in the case of short term lending. With IMF credits being conditional, the incentive to implement programs may also be expected to be higher in these cases, further enhancing catalysis. However, it may be a country's precautionary borrowing potential that is important; the actual use of these resources may negatively affect catalysis.

What support for the above propositions exists in the empirical literature?

8.3 EXISTING EVIDENCE ON CATALYSIS

The existing empirical evidence on the catalytic effect has been summarized at some length elsewhere (Bird and Rowlands, 2002; Cottarelli and Giannini, 2002; Hovaguimian, 2003). The methodologies used have included large sample econometric estimation, case studies and attitude surveys of market participants. The general consensus from this body of research is that there is relatively little evidence in support of the catalytic effect of IMF lending on private capital flows, at least not as a universal, strong and positive phenomenon. Individual studies do, however, discover evidence of a significant positive effect on some flows in specific circumstances. These conflicting results raise questions as to when the catalytic effect may be positive and when it may be negative. Unfortunately the existing literature does not include a comprehensive disaggregated analysis of catalysis and it is this that we attempt to provide in this chapter.

The propositions in the previous section systematically identify the circumstances in which a catalytic effect may be expected to be at its weakest or at its strongest. Some of the existing empirical research is relevant in this context. In a study of the bond market, Mody and Saravia (2006) find evidence that countries with weak fundamentals do not experience catalysis while those where the fundamentals are less weak encounter a significant positive catalytic effect. Bordo, Mody, and Oomes (2004) report similar results, but find a 'dip and recovery' pattern. They conclude that IMF programs are most valuable 'for countries in vulnerable, as distinct from extreme distress, situations' (Bordo, Mody, and Oomes, 2004: 444). In contrast, but still focusing on bond markets, Arabaci and Ecer (2014) claim that there is a positive catalytic effect that on average becomes stronger as the macroeconomic fundamentals of a country improve. Jensen (2004) and Edwards (2006) find results less favorable to catalysis for foreign direct investment and portfolio flows respectively. Bird and Rowlands (2002) also find that disaggregation across time periods, samples, individual lending facilities, and the degree of conditionality, previous experience with the IMF and types of capital flow, make a difference. They recount a complex story for the effect of IMF programs on private flows. However, while these studies have shed important light on the catalytic effect, they do not set out to test specific propositions such as those formulated in the previous section. The remainder of this chapter attempts to fill this gap.

8.4 ESTIMATIONS, METHODS AND DATA

In estimating the catalytic effect, the challenge is to isolate the impact of the IMF so that observed changes in capital movements can be attributed to its involvement. For example, countries experiencing some form of economic crisis may be expected to turn to the IMF for assistance. They may also be expected to experience a capital outflow. It is, however, unsafe to draw a direct causal connection between the IMF's involvement and the loss of capital. There is a potentially serious selection problem.

As discussed at length in Chapter 5, countries are generally anticipated to go to the IMF for a program when their balance of payments is unsustainable. The distribution of program and non-program countries is non-random; the fragile economic conditions that drive a country to the Fund will also affect independently its subsequent economic performance and ability to attract new capital. Consequently, the estimated magnitude of the catalytic effect will be biased downwards if uncorrected for non-random selectivity. Earlier empirical work on catalysis avoided formal selection correction procedures (Bird and Rowlands, 1997, 2002; Rowlands, 2001), occasionally adopting less formal approaches instead (Bird and Rowlands, 2002). More recent work, for example Mody and

Saravia (2006) and Edwards (2006), has incorporated formal selection corrections for some aspects of catalysis, however, the correction procedure
and the extent of any bias is itself open to debate.

There is mixed evidence about the necessity of selection correction
procedures. For example, while Vreeland (2003) finds that the selection
problem introduces bias when studying the effects of the IMF on growth
and inequality, the results reported by Edwards (2006) when examining the
catalysis of portfolio flows appear much less sensitive to it.

There is also the question of how to model empirically the selection bias;
an issue that we have already discussed in Chapter 5. In this chapter we use
a treatment effects model as the primary estimation procedure. We use the
signing of an IMF program as the treatment, allowing us to focus on the
initial signaling effect of a new agreement while correcting for the endogenous choice of entering such an agreement. For the primary estimations
we use a maximum likelihood procedure that provides for robust variance-
covariance estimation by permitting observations on each country to be
treated as potentially dependent. The treatment effects model is related to
the propensity score matching approach that we use elsewhere in the book.

The data used for the estimation are unbalanced panels of between 1048
(1985–2006) and 1523 (1975–2006) observations (depending on the selection equation) on 80 different middle-income countries (as currently defined
by the World Bank) that were eligible to sign an IMF. By ending the data
in 2006 we avoid the effects of the global economic and financial crisis that
erupted toward the end of the 2000s. Low-income countries are excluded
from the study as the catalytic effect for them is traditionally dominated by
official flows, and the evidence suggests that the influences on their participation in IMF programs differs significantly from middle-income countries
(Bird and Rowlands, 2007, 2009). We further discuss catalysis in the context
of low-income countries in the final section of this chapter.

The dependent variable measuring the catalytic effect is a country's net
private capital flow as a proportion of gross domestic product (GDP). We
use net flows rather than gross flows since our concern is with the impact
of IMF programs on countries' overall external financing positions and
the consequences for the resulting speed of economic adjustment; gross
flows are affected by exogenous repayment schedules while net flows are a
more accurate reflection of whether investors wish to increase or decrease
their exposure.

We examine various categories of capital flows: total flows, short-term
debt, foreign direct investment, portfolio flows (bond, equity and total),
public and publicly guaranteed (PPG) debt flows (bank, bond, other
private, and total), and private non-guaranteed (PNG) debt flows (bank,
bond, and total). The averages for these different flows are summarized in

Table 8.1   *Average annual net flow-to-GDP percentages 1975–2006*

Type of capital flow	All middle-income countries that could sign an IMF agreement	All middle-income countries that could sign an IMF agreement but did not	All middle-income countries that signed an IMF agreement
All private net flows	5.94	6.36	4.16
Private short term net flows	0.62	0.67	0.43
Net foreign direct investment	3.44	3.69	2.42
Net portfolio flows	0.51	0.56	0.32
Net Portfolio Bonds	0.40	0.43	0.25
Net Portfolio Equity	0.12	0.12	0.07
Net PPG total debt	0.92	0.98	0.68
Net PPG bank debt	0.37	0.39	0.26
Net PPG bond debt	0.33	0.36	0.20
Net PPG other private debt	0.23	0.23	0.21
Net PNG total debt	0.43	0.46	0.32
Net PNG bank debt	0.36	0.38	0.27
Net PNG bond debt	0.07	0.08	0.04
Number of Observations	1491	1204	287

Table 8.1 for all eligible countries in the sample, and for those that signed, or did not sign an IMF agreement the year before. The basic data suggest that inflows into IMF eligible countries are lower in the following year for the group that signs an IMF agreement than for the group that does not. This observation does not take into account the conditions associated with signing an agreement, however, and thus cannot be linked causally to the actual IMF agreements themselves.

The IMF treatment variable is an indicator of the signing of any conditional IMF program. In the largest estimation sample (1523 observations) there is a total of 325 cases where at least one program is signed. In total there are 233 SBAs, 57 EFFs, 4 Structural Adjustment Facility agreements (SAFs) and 38 Enhanced Structural Adjustment Facility or Poverty Reduction and Growth Facility agreements (ESAF/PRGFs) signed; in seven of these cases multiple agreements are signed in the same year. While our main interest is in the non-concessional SBA and EFF agreements, we estimate using all conditional lending facilities to avoid the problem of predicting that an IMF agreement is expected but a concessional SAF, ESAF or PRGF agreement is signed in place of the SBA or EFF agreements that are more typical of the middle-income country group.[2]

To take into account the potential selection bias, a secondary estimation of the dichotomous treatment variable is specified using a set of explanatory variables commonly found in the literature estimating IMF program participation. This literature is summarized in Chapter 5. These economic and political variables are all lagged one year from the year the agreement is signed to minimize endogeneity. The explanatory variables include economic growth, reserve adequacy, indicators of recent debt rescheduling and impending debt rescheduling, and indicators of recent IMF agreements in preceding years. Two additional versions of the underlying economic model are also estimated. The first adds an indicator of legislative elections; this version is the selection equation used for the main base model estimations reported in the chapter. The next adds both the indicator for legislative elections and a measure of a country's UN voting proximity to the United States. As discussed in Chapter 5 this has become a popular variable in IMF selection equations because of its interpretation as a measure of US influence over Fund decisions (Thacker, 1999; Dreher, Sturm, and Vreeland, 2009).[3] Its inclusion therefore allows us to see whether there are political influences on the catalytic effect of IMF programs as captured by this variable.

The results of these three probit equations for selection are presented in Table 8.2, and they perform reasonably well with pseudo-R^2 values above 0.23.[4] In general, countries with current debt rescheduling needs (which are linked institutionally to the need for an IMF program) and a history of IMF involvement tend to sign agreements with the Fund. Countries that are growing more rapidly, have relatively high reserves, and that have recently rescheduled debt, are less likely to adopt an IMF program. On the political side, a legislative election is associated with a higher propensity to sign an agreement the next year, and there is weak evidence that voting at the UN in a manner similar to the United States is also positively associated with IMF agreements.

The explanatory variables included in our capital flows equations reflect basic economic conditions, and are lagged by one year to reduce the likelihood of endogeneity. They include: per capita GDP, the investment rate, the export to GDP ratio, real international interest rates, real exchange rate depreciation, reserve adequacy, debt–service ratio, and the ratio of PPG debt to GDP. We selected these variables because they have been commonly included in the empirical literature on capital flows. The expectations about how they should affect capital inflows are relatively clear and we do not discuss them in detail; those variables that suggest robust economic conditions should attract capital, while indicators of difficulty or weak fundamentals will presumably deter additional inflows. The precise definitions of all variables appear in the Appendix.

Table 8.2   Probit results for estimating the propensity scores

Explanatory Variable	Model 1	Model 2	Model 3
	Coefficient estimate (Normal statistic)	Coefficient estimate (Normal statistic)	Coefficient estimate (Normal statistic)
GDP growth (lag = 1)	−0.0304*** (−3.73)	−0.0342*** (−4.21)	−0.0423*** (−4.00)
Reserve adequacy (lag = 1)	−2.08*** (−3.21)	−2.10*** (−3.21)	−1.56*** (−2.74)
Debt Rescheduled (lag = 1)	−0.830*** (−5.69)	−0.780*** (−5.23)	−0.724*** (−3.87)
Debt Rescheduled	1.10*** (8.09)	1.00*** (7.29)	1.05*** (5.77)
Past IMF program (lag = 1)	0.675*** (4.51)	0.648*** (4.01)	0.584*** (3.52)
Past IMF program (lag = 2)	0.305* (2.23)	0.297* (2.02)	0.303 (1.79)
Past IMF program (lag = 3)	0.210 (1.79)	0.186 (1.54)	0.189 (1.32)
Legislative election (lag = 1)	– –	0.229*** (2.55)	0.244*** (2.43)
UN voting behavior	– –	– –	0.105 (1.80)
Constant	−1.09*** (−11.62)	−1.06*** (−10.91)	−1.25*** (−10.76)
Number of observations	1700	1493	1177
Pseudo R-squared	0.233	0.232	0.246
Years in sample	1974–2006	1976–2006	1984–2006

Note: Robust normal test statistics appear in parentheses. ***, **, and * indicate statistical significance at the 2%, 5%, and 10% levels for two-tailed tests.

In order to examine various other dimensions of how IMF programs may affect capital flows, three Fund-related explanatory variables are included in the primary capital flow equation. First, we examine the amount of resources drawn from the IMF as a share of imports and debt service payments, in order to separate out the effects of program conditionality and signaling from any associated liquidity effects. Second, we examine the number of months in which a country was previously under an agreement (weighted more heavily for more recent years) to determine whether or not past program experience induces or deters additional capital flows. Third, we include a measure of the number of recently incomplete IMF programs to see if a history of poor implementation affects capital flows.[5] Finally, in addition to estimating the standard treatment effects model, we also estimate a fixed-effects version of the treatment effects model by including dummy variables for each country in the sample (and suppressing the constant).

8.5 RESULTS

The full results of the treatment effects estimation (using the second selection equation as the base model) on total net flows appear in the first results column of Table 8.3. For brevity we present only the results for the sample that includes legislative elections in the selection equation but not UN voting. In addition we do not restrict the sample by excluding cases where there were particularly high capital flows relative to GDP.[6] The results of the fixed-effects version of the base treatment effects model appear in the last column of Table 8.3.

Table 8.4 presents the coefficient estimates for the IMF signing treatment variable derived from the different capital flow equations, and presents some summary statistics for the performance of the equations. The last three columns of Table 8.4 present these statistics for sub-samples of countries identified in the selection equation as having a low, medium, or high propensity to sign an agreement.

To focus our analysis we examine in detail only those variables that shed light on the propositions outlined previously. The results of the estimations are presented in two stages. First, we examine the main estimations and selection equations to see how well they perform relative to our prior expectations. Second, we present the results in terms of the six propositions presented in Section 8.2.

8.5.1 Equation Performance

From Tables 8.3 and 8.4 we can see that with the exception of the portfolio equity flows and PPG and PNG bond flows, all equations have an acceptable level of joint coefficient significance for the full sample estimations; in the smaller sub-samples reported in Table 8.4 some other categories of flows also have poorly performing equations.

In terms of goodness of fit, the equations perform reasonably well.[7] For total net flows (Table 8.3) three of the non-IMF variables have statistically significant coefficient estimates, indicating that higher investment levels, more exports, and lower global interest rates are all associated significantly with higher net capital inflows.[8] The estimation results of the fixed-effects version of the model are largely comparable to those of the

Table 8.3   Base-line treatment effects estimation results on total net flows

Explanatory Variable (lagged one year)	Model 1 (main model)	Model 2 (fixed-effects version)
GNI per capita	0.226	0.540***
	(1.26)	(2.84)
Investment	0.219***	0.187***
	(4.62)	(3.69)
Exports/GDP	0.0583***	0.0238
	(2.56)	(0.82)
Real LIBOR	−0.486***	−0.370***
	(−5.13)	(−4.39)
Depreciation	0.00228	0.00361
	(1.17)	(1.72)
Reserve adequacy	−0.0179	−0.0218***
	(−1.15)	(−2.80)
Debt Service	0.0609	0.0277
	(1.57)	(0.98)
Debt/GDP	−0.00789	−0.00531
	(−1.44)	(−1.01)
IMF Flows	−0.297***	−0.202**
	(−2.68)	(−2.38)
Past IMF months	0.156***	0.109*
	(3.29)	(2.11)
Failed IMF programs	−0.515	−0.558
	(−0.81)	(−0.81)
IMF Treatment	−5.50***	−5.65***
	(−3.42)	(−3.69)
Constant	−2.52	–
	(−1.48)	

Selection equation for IMF agreement signings (lagged 2 years)

GDP growth	−0.0392***	−0.0406***
	(−5.17)	(−4.97)
Reserve adequacy	−0.0221***	−0.0214***
	(−2.93)	(−2.93)
Past rescheduling	−0.757***	−0.729***
	(−4.86)	(−4.34)
Imminent rescheduling	1.02***	0.981***
	(6.38)	(5.41)
Past IMF program (lag 2)	0.661***	0.659***
	(4.03)	(4.09)
Past IMF program (lag 3)	0.311**	0.289*
	(2.29)	(2.19)
Past IMF program (lag 4)	0.151	0.165
	(1.25)	(1.37)

Table 8.3 (continued)

Explanatory Variable (lagged one year)	Model 1 (main model)	Model 2 (fixed-effects version)
Legislative election	0.213**	0.231***
	(2.30)	(2.58)
Constant	−1.00***	−1.00***
	(−8.13)	(−8.33)
No. of obs.	1339	1339
P(all βs = 0) (χ^2 test)	0.00	0.00
ρ	0.349	0.394
P(ρ = 0) (χ^2 test)	0.00	0.00

Notes:
Robust normal test statistics appear in parentheses. ***, **, and * indicate statistical significance at the 2%, 5%, and 10% levels for two-tailed tests.
The parameter ρ is the covariance between the estimating and selection equation. If ρ = 0, then the selectivity correction is not statistically important.

standard treatment effects estimation, though the exports-to-GDP variable no longer has a significant coefficient estimate, while the coefficient estimates for income per capita and reserve adequacy become statistically significant.

For the most part, the equations correcting for selection perform consistently well. The diagnostic tests generally indicate that correcting for selection is important statistically in most of the full sample equations except for short term debt (Table 8.4, full sample). As noted earlier, past studies such as Edwards (2006) raise questions about the statistical importance of selection in affecting estimations of the catalytic effect. For several of the smaller sub-samples in the last three columns of Table 8.4, selection corrections do not seem necessary.

8.5.2 Evidence on the Propositions

Proposition 1 suggests that different types of capital flow are motivated in different ways and that IMF arrangements may therefore exert different degrees of catalysis across them. We find ample evidence to support this proposition. Though not reported in detail, the estimating equations on the different capital flows reveal some variation in terms of important explanatory variables. For example, while high real international interest rates are generally associated with lower net inflows of capital, the estimated coefficient for this variable is not statistically significant for

Table 8.4   *Estimated coefficients for the IMF treatment variable for different capital flow categories and different agreement signing propensities*

Variable	Full sample	Low Probability of signing	Medium Probability of signing	High Probability of signing
Total flows	−5.50***	−6.41**	9.83***	−0.476
	(−3.42)	(−2.20)	(2.85)	(−0.16)
	(1339,0,0)	(1035, 0, 0.03)	(204, 0, 0.0054)	(93, 0, 0.75)
Short term debt	0.062	−0.118	*−0.93*	8.91
	(0.14)	(−0.19)	*(−0.85)*	(1.04)
	(1339, 0, 0.39)	(1035, 0, 0.0.73)	*(191, 0.76, 0.57)*	(113, 0, 0.021)
FDI	−2.26**	−1.41	2.27	−3.13***
	(−2.43)	(−0.98)	(1.31)	(−4.83)
	(1339, 0, 0)	(1035, 0.002, 0.13)	(191, 0.02, 0.31)	(113, 0, 0)
Portfolio	−0.77**	−1.02**	0.365	−1.49***
	(−2.39)	(−2.26)	(0.47)	(−3.30)
	(1339, 0, 0)	(1035, 0.08, 0.07)	(191, 0, 0.97)	(113, 0, 0)
Bond	−0.608*	−0.84**	−1.36***	0.032
	(−2.18)	(−2.08)	(−5.56)	(0.57)
	(1339, 0, 0)	(1035, 0.08, 0.07)	(191, 0.0, 0.05)	(116, 0.02, 0.52)
Equity	*−0.161**	−0.168	*0.103*	−0.215***
	(−2.09)	(−1.81)	*(0.46)*	(−3.84)
	(1339, 0.22, 0.02)	(1035, 0.07, 0.05)	*(191, 0.37, 0.68)*	(113, 0, 0)
PPG debt	−1.08***	−1.01	3.64***	0.879
	(−3.43)	(−1.75)	(4.76)	(0.62)
	(1339, 0, 0.0)	(1035, 0, 0.03)	(191, 0, 0)	(116, 0, 0.81)
Bank	−0.544***	−0.346	2.84***	−0.106
	(−2.79)	(−0.64)	(5.40)	(−0.06)
	(1339, 0, 0.01)	(1035, 0, 0.37)	(191, 0, 0)	(113, 0, 0.91)
Bond	*−0.517*	−0.752*	−1.19***	0.457
	(−1.91)	*(−1.97)*	(−5.27)	(0.99)
	(1339, 0.13, 0.01)	*(1035, 0.31, 0.07)*	(191, 0, 0)	(113, 0.08, 0.24)
Other	−0.102	−0.115	0.197	−0.615**
	(−0.97)	(−0.60)	(0.77)	(−1.78)
	(1339, 0, 0.01)	(1035, 0, 0.06)	(191, 0.01, 0.67)	(113, 0, 0)

Table 8.4   (continued)

Variable	Full sample	Low Probability of signing	Medium Probability of signing	High Probability of signing
PNG debt	−0.621**	*−0.749*	−0.334	0.596
	(−2.36)	*(−1.57)*	(−0.90)	(0.88)
	(1339, 0.05, 0.02)	*(1035, 0.20, 0.38)*	(191, 0, 0.35)	(113, 0, 0.28)
Bank	−0.545**	*−0.675*	−0.232	0.607
	(−2.36)	*(−1.61)*	(−0.86)	(1.13)
	(1339, 0.04, 0.03)	*(1035, 0.24, 0.39)*	(191, 0, 0.34)	(113, 0, 0.13)
Bond	−0.0963	*−0.085*	−0.426***	*−0.123****
	(−1.63)	*(−0.92)*	(−4.87)	*(−1.16)*
	(1339, 0.16, 0.01)	*(1035, 0.106, 0.40)*	(191, 0, 0)	*(113, 0.71, 0.04)*

Notes:
Robust normal test statistics appear on the right in parentheses. ***, **, and * indicate statistical significance at the 2%, 5%, and 10% levels for two-tailed tests. Figures in the second parentheses are, respectively, the sample size, the probability that the hypothesis that all regressors are jointly insignificant is falsely rejected, and the probability that the hypothesis that the parameter $\rho = 0$ is falsely rejected.
If $\rho = 0$, then the selectivity correction is not statistically important. Probabilities marked as 0 imply the probability is less than 0.005. Estimations where the hypothesis of all regressors being jointly insignificant is falsely rejected have their results in italics and must be treated with caution.

portfolio equity flows, PPG bank and other private debt flows, and PNG bond flows. Higher per capita income levels are associated with private bond lending and portfolio inflows, but not other capital flows. Short-term debt inflows are affected by exchange rate depreciation, while other flows are not. Bond flows generally seem less affected by economic fundamentals such as investment rates, exports, and debt obligations.

In terms of the catalytic effect, the first results column of Table 8.4 indicates that for the full sample estimations, signing an IMF agreement is generally associated with lower capital inflows in the following year. The magnitude of the catalytic effect varies from insignificant for short-term and 'other' PPG debt flows, to weakly negative for PNG and PPG bond flows, to significantly negative for total flows (−5.5 percent of GDP), and the sub-components of foreign direct investment (−2.3 percent), portfolio flows (−0.8 percent), PPG debt (−1.1 percent), and PNG debt (−0.6 percent). The negative effect on FDI is consistent with that found by Jensen (2004). Because of these differential effects, it appears that IMF agreements are not only associated with a decline in net private capital inflows, but also a restructuring of them. In short, IMF agreements are associated with varied and nuanced effects on different types of private capital flow.

Proposition 2 claims that the strength of the catalytic effect should vary non-linearly with the strength of a country's economic fundamentals. Specifically, net capital flows to countries with either relatively weak or relatively strong fundamentals may not be catalyzed, and in the latter case there may even be a negative effect arising from an unexpected signal of problems. For countries experiencing some difficulties but not yet in distress, the IMF may have a favorable catalytic effect. We tested the proposition by splitting our sample into three groups on the basis of their estimated probability (or propensity scores) of signing an IMF agreement in order to reflect the extent of economic difficulties.[9] The summary catalytic effects appear in the last three columns of Table 8.4.

We find evidence of the non-linearities suggested by proposition 2. For countries that sign an IMF agreement despite a low predicted probability of doing so the results indicate a large and statistically significant negative catalytic effect, which then reverses and becomes strong and positive for countries with medium signing propensities. Where proposition 2 fails is in predicting negative catalysis for countries with a high predicted probability of an agreement; the associated coefficient is negative, but it is fairly small and statistically quite insignificant. These results are somewhat sensitive to the sample used in the estimation. Most notably, decreasing slightly the signing probability that divides the medium and high probability samples yields a large and positive catalytic effect for the latter group, suggesting that the main positive catalytic effect is observed primarily for a few cases around this cut off value.

By and large this pattern is reflected in the different components of total capital flows. For all of the different components the low signing probability samples exhibit negative catalysis, although only two of these are statistically significant. The groups with medium and high predicted probabilities of signing exhibit considerable variation across the different capital flows categories, with some of the results being sensitive to the chosen boundaries for these groups. For the medium probability group, IMF agreements seem to repel bonds but attract PPG bank debt. It is interesting to note that the results for the bond estimations are broadly consistent with those reported in Mody and Saravia (2006), who focus on bonds alone.

In addition, some countries on the boundary between these categories experience large short-term capital inflows, though the associated coefficient is not statistically significant. Finally, while the overall negative catalytic effect for countries with a high probability of signing is statistically insignificant, there are several categories of flows that have statistically significant negative coefficients on the IMF signing variable.

Given the small sample sizes for some of the estimations and the sensitivity of some results to the choice of differentiating between groups with medium and high probabilities of signing, some caution is warranted in interpreting the results. In general, however, proposition 2 receives significant support from our analysis.

Proposition 3 suggests that poor program implementation will weaken the catalytic effect. It is difficult to test all of the interpretations of this proposition, as implementation is complex and difficult to measure (see Chapter 6). Here we focus on the general effect that weak implementation has on catalysis by examining the estimated coefficient for the indicator of recent incomplete programs. Following the literature, we interpret substantial non-completion as an indication of program failure (Killick, 1995; Bird, 2007). In the total net flows estimation the estimated coefficient for our measure of program incompletion is negative as expected. However, it is not statistically significant. For PNG bank flows, PPG bank flows and portfolio bond flows, the estimated coefficient for past incomplete programs is negative and statistically significant as expected. While none of the other estimated coefficients for this variable are statistically significant, and most are negative, there is weak evidence that PPG bank flows may actually and paradoxically react positively to past incomplete programs.

Interacting program failure with the indicator of an IMF program signing did not generate any compelling evidence of a change in the catalytic effect. Overall, then, the non-completion of previous IMF programs does not appear to have a strong or consistent effect on subsequent capital flows, and proposition 3 cannot be accepted on the basis of the tests conducted here.

Proposition 4 suggests that a lengthy history of IMF programs, even when completed, will reduce the catalytic effect by signaling structural difficulties. Recidivism is generally associated with poorer countries (Bird, Hussain, and Joyce, 2004), so here, and given our focus on middle-income countries, we examine this proposition by looking at a shorter three-year history. The estimations for aggregate net flows reported in Table 8.3 do not support the proposition. In fact, in most equations the presence of recent IMF programming in a country is associated with higher current inflows, including total flows, short term debt, foreign direct investment, and PNG bank debt. Consequently there is some evidence to suggest that private lenders may value the Fund's ongoing involvement with a country.

In the other categories of capital inflow there was no statistically

Table 8.5　Estimated coefficients for the IMF, SBA and EFF treatment variables for different net capital flow categories

Variable	All IMF	Concessional	SBAs and EFFs	SBAs only	EFFs only
Total	−5.50***	5.04	−6.17***	−5.96***	−4.70**
	(−3.42)	(1.27)	(−3.94)	(−3.90)	(−2.48)
Short term	0.062	−0.173	0.253	0.373	−0.560
	(0.14)	(−0.27)	(0.61)	(0.88)	(−1.37)
FDI	−2.26**	9.16***	−2.84***	−2.86***	−1.49
	(−2.43)	(4.75)	(−3.79)	(−4.01)	(−1.45)
Portfolio	−0.770**	−0.442	−0.787*	−0.839**	−0.247
	(−2.39)	(−1.75)	(−2.13)	(−2.27)	(−0.64)
Bond	−0.608**	−0.415	−0.615	−0.662*	−0.174
	(−2.18)	(−1.81)	(−1.90)	(−2.02)	(−0.49)
Equity	*−0.161**	−0.0643	*−0.169**	−0.183**	*−0.084*
	(−2.09)	(−0.88)	*(−2.13)*	(−2.32)	*(−0.88)*
PPG debt	−1.08***	−1.27***	−1.06***	−1.02***	−1.06*
	(−3.43)	(−2.86)	(−3.10)	(−2.92)	(−2.03)
Bank	−0.544***	1.73***	−0.526***	−0.481**	−0.820**
	(−2.79)	(4.04)	(−2.73)	(−2.53)	(−2.49)
Bond	*−0.517*	*−0.380*	−0.521	*−0.579*	*−0.056*
	(−1.91)	*(−1.77)*	(−1.65)	*(−1.82)*	*(−0.16)*
Other	−0.102	−0.358**	−0.101	−0.0470	−0.249
	(−0.97)	(−2.44)	(−0.76)	(−0.32)	(−1.07)
PNG debt	−0.621**	3.41***	−0.699**	−0.710**	*−0.656**
	(−2.36)	(5.20)	(−2.43)	(−2.38)	*(−2.07)*
Bank	−0.545**	3.05***	−0.620**	−0.638**	*−0.566**
	(−2.36)	(5.49)	(−2.45)	(−2.42)	*(−1.97)*
Bond	*−0.0963*	−0.193	*−0.102*	*−0.0951*	*−0.178*
	(−1.63)	(−0.19)	*(−1.60)*	*(−1.53)*	*(−1.07)*
Number of signings	311	35	276	222	56

Notes:
Robust normal test statistics appear in parentheses. ***, **, and * indicate statistical significance at the 2%, 5%, and 10% levels for two-tailed tests.
Estimations where the hypothesis of all regressors being jointly insignificant is falsely rejected have their results in italics and must be treated with caution.

significant coefficient estimate except for a negative one for other private PPG debt, and then only at 0.075 one-tailed level of significance. In the total flows equation, an additional month of IMF programming in the previous year is associated with an increase in capital inflows equivalent to

0.16 percent of GDP. Subsequent tests interacting past IMF programming and current signing of an IMF agreement, and looking at a longer time horizon (previous six years), do not alter these findings.

Proposition 5 suggests that catalysis may vary with the type of IMF agreement. Short term investors may be looking for the stabilization policies associated with SBAs, while longer term investors are looking for the more numerous conditions and longer-term structural adjustment focus of EFFs. The results for all agreements (311 cases), all non-concessional agreements (276 cases) and SBAs (222 cases) are all essentially the same, reflecting the dominance of the stand-by arrangements. The only notable difference appears for the estimation of the EFF catalytic effect, which is similar to the other non-concessional agreements except for the absence of a statistically significant negative catalytic effect on FDI and portfolio flows. The sign of the coefficient estimate also becomes negative for short term flows, though it remains statistically insignificant. So there is some evidence that EFF agreements are less repellent to the non-debt flows.

There are also 35 cases in our sample of middle-income countries signing concessional agreements. The estimated catalytic effects for these arrangements differ significantly from the non-concessional ones, and indeed provide the only evidence of positive catalysis. Three categories of capital flows appear to respond positively to concessional arrangements: FDI, and both PPG and PNG bank debt. These responses are generally large in magnitude: the coefficient on FDI indicates an inflow of 9 percent of GDP. Overall, PPG debt responds negatively to concessional agreements, due to outflows of PPG other debt and, of marginal statistical significance, PPG bond debt. Proposition 5 is therefore generally supported by our results. If we consider that one of the main differences between these agreements is the stringency and nature of their conditionality, then a reasonable though complex story can be told about how the conditions of key IMF agreements affect differentially each specific type of capital flow.

Proposition 6 suggests that the liquidity effects of IMF programs may catalyze, in particular, short term capital, although there may be a difference between used and unused access to IMF resources. When the liquidity measure is taken as actual drawings in a year, the results indicate a substitution effect between IMF credit and almost all other capital flows. Measuring IMF resource use as drawings from the IMF, expressed as a proportion of imports and total debt service payments, gives a sense of the extent to which these resources are financing external outflows.[10] As these current account outflows are on average about 50 percent of GDP for the countries in the sample, the magnitude of the effect on total capital flows is that for every ten dollars of IMF credit used there is about a six dollar decline in other private flows, or a substitution effect of about −0.6.[11] This substitution effect is consistently negative across the different categories of capital flow, except for PPG bank and other private debt (insignificant and small positive coefficient estimates), and reflects particularly strong negative substitution effects for portfolio and PNG debt flows.

Since the direct substitution effect is less than one, it follows that, in total, additional financial resources are made available (especially to the government) when borrowing from the Fund occurs (though the effect may be offset or enhanced by the additional separate effects of new agreements, old ones, or the record on failed implementation). However, there is little to suggest that the provision of IMF liquidity induces additional capital inflows from other private sources, and the IMF may need to lend considerably more than a country's anticipated capital shortfall in order to support the desired blend of adjustment and financing. This result could be seen as being consistent with the claim by Mody and Saravia (2006) that private capital markets may, in some cases, want to see a Fund program in place irrespective of the amount of Fund credit involved, but they do not want to see countries having to use that credit.[12] On balance our results do not support proposition 6; the biggest negative responses to IMF inflows are for portfolio bond and PNG debt flows; other flows are not affected significantly. IMF resources tend to bail out rather than bail in private capital.

8.5.3 Sensitivity of the Results

The basic results for the IMF effects reported above are reasonably robust across a range of sensitivity tests that we conducted. Alternative versions of the selection equation and the capital flow equation produce similar results (see, for example, the results reported in the last column of Table 8.3).

Our first formal diagnostic procedure is to make sure that our data are stationary. We test each of the dependent and independent variables in the capital flows equation for stationarity using the test developed by Levin, Lin, and Chu (2002) for panel unit roots.[13] The hypothesis of non-stationarity is rejected for all variables except per capita income. Re-estimating the equations without this variable does not yield any significant changes in our results.

Our second test for robustness splits the sample into early (pre-1991) and late (post-1990) periods.[14] We find that the later sample period leads to a negative coefficient estimate for the IMF variable that is larger in magnitude (−5.31) and statistically very significant. By contrast the earlier period still has a fairly large negative coefficient estimate for the IMF signing variable (−2.13), but it is not statistically significant. Therefore the negative association between IMF programs and private capital flows seems to be a more recent phenomenon.

We also split the data on the basis of income per capita. The effect of signing IMF agreements on private capital flows into the poorer middle-income countries remained negative but was smaller in magnitude and statistically insignificant once GDP per capita dropped below approximately \$5700 (approximately the median). In contrast the negative catalytic effect was much stronger in magnitude, and the associated coefficient estimate (−7.54) is statistically significant, for the higher income portion of our sample. Consequently the negative effects of IMF agreements on private capital flows seem largely confined to wealthier countries in the sample, and the processes determining capital inflows into poorer countries appear to be distinct from those of the wealthier group. This result also holds true for levels of political and civil freedom. Dividing the countries into 'more free' and 'less free' (Freedom House, 2011) indicates that the negative estimated coefficient on the IMF agreement signing variable is statistically significant only for 'freer' countries. Finally, splitting the sample by relative economic size (GDP as a share of all middle-income country GDP) indicates that negative catalysis is particularly problematic for middle-sized countries that are relatively large, but not the largest. The estimations on the small and very large middle-income country groups have negative coefficient estimates for the IMF signing variable, but these coefficients are not statistically significant.

One problem with the data is its low frequency relative to developments in capital markets. Annual data obscures the reaction to IMF programs by treating programs signed early in a calendar year in the same way as programs signed at the end. To investigate whether this artifice of the data introduces a bias, we perform two sets of tests. First we re-weight the dependent variable as a blend of inflows over two years. For example, for an agreement signed in February the inflows of the first year would be weighted 10/12 while those of the second year would be weighted 2/12. The results are comparable regardless of whether we use inflows from the year of signing and the following year, or the following two years. The magnitude of the negative catalytic effect is larger for the weighted flows of the two years after an agreement (−5.21) than for the weighted flows of the year of the agreement and the following year (3.99); both estimated coefficients are statistically significant.

This result is reinforced by the second test in which we run the main estimation on two separate samples: those where countries sign early in a calendar year, and those where they sign later in the year. The estimated coefficient on the IMF agreement variable again remains negative and strongly significant statistically in both cases, and the magnitude of the effect is somewhat larger for agreements signed earlier in a year. These results suggest that the negative effect of the agreement grows stronger for a period after the agreement is signed, rather than having an immediate and large negative effect that then begins to dissipate.

To test whether program size affects catalysis we split the sample into two according to program size relative to GDP and estimate the base treatment effects model on each. For both samples the estimated coefficient for the IMF agreement variable remains negative, statistically significant, and roughly the same magnitude (though the larger agreements have a slightly smaller negative effect). Our conclusion is that the size of the agreement is not particularly important in determining the catalytic effect.

We also test whether catalysis was affected by the political interests of the United States, as measured by the similarity of a country's votes on key UN resolutions to the voting of the US. The base model equation (which does not include UN voting in the selection equation) is estimated on two samples, one where the country votes frequently the same way as the US, and a second where voting similarity is very low. The estimations for the two groups both indicate strong and statistically significant negative catalysis, though interestingly the magnitude of the estimated coefficient is much larger for countries that vote less often with the US than for those which vote with the US (-6.6 versus -3.75).

Finally, we re-estimate the basic capital flows equations but include the lagged dependent variable. The results are reasonable and largely comparable to those already reported. For example, the lagged dependent variable coefficient estimates are all positive and statistically significant for all the different categories of capital flow, except for short term debt flows where the relationship is negative and statistically significant. The estimated coefficients for the IMF signing indicator generally remain comparable to the main results reported in Table 8.4, though their size and level of statistical significance are generally somewhat smaller and, in the case of PNG debt flows, there is evidence of positive catalysis.

Overall, therefore, our results raise serious doubts about the existence of a general and positive catalytic effect associated with the signaling effect of a newly signed IMF program. In fact, it appears that the effect on subsequent capital inflows of signing such agreements is generally negative for middle-income countries. Just as important, however, are the variations in this effect across different types of flows, time, and the economic state of the country.

8.6   CONCLUDING REMARKS

For many years the IMF has claimed that an important part of its role is to catalyze others to lend either by relieving immediate liquidity crises or by allowing governments to signal their commitment to reform through conditionality. Early empirical evidence seemed to be inconsistent with this claim. However, these studies were often not strongly grounded in theory and did not formally correct for selection bias. More recent research has dealt more formally with selection, but has focused on individual components of capital flows (such as bonds, portfolio flows, and FDI) in isolation. As their results point in different directions, generalizations on the basis of any one of them is unsatisfactory. Formal theoretical models suggest that the degree of catalysis should depend on specific factors such as a country's economic fundamentals, while less formal theorizing has identified other factors that may influence the nature of catalysis. These theoretical insights have not been systematically explored in empirical analyses.

This chapter has attempted to provide a comprehensive empirical analysis of catalysis that is guided by both formal and informal theoretical insights. The analysis corrects for selection bias and also acknowledges the limitations of doing so. Using a treatment effects estimation procedure to deal with selection problems, the chapter explores the empirical connection between IMF arrangements and private capital flows in middle-income countries. Unlike other recent studies it examines catalysis across a wide range of private capital flows as well as across IMF facilities. Rather than simply presenting the resulting evidence, we relate it to a series of propositions concerning catalysis.

Our findings confirm that it is unwarranted to generalize from a subset of results. While there are some combinations of circumstances (such as economic fundamentals in the borrowing country, particular IMF facilities, and specific types of capital flow) in which catalysis seems to occur, there are others in which it does not, or in which the effect is negative. Indeed, on the whole there is much stronger evidence that catalysis is generally negative rather than positive. However the highly nuanced nature of the results points to the dangers of attempting to make general conclusions, especially on the basis of examining only partial evidence.

Given the importance attached by the IMF and others to catalysis, and given that a belief in its efficacy has consequences for IMF lending and resources, the policy implications of our findings are important. First, policy needs to be much more subtle and cognizant of the circumstances in which IMF programs are either more or less likely to exert a catalytic effect on different types of capital inflows. Second, the limitations of catalysis need to be fully taken into account in the design of IMF programs and in thinking about alternative ways of mobilizing external capital in support of economic adjustment, as discussed in Bird and Rowlands (2004). Third, reforms to conditionality, such as those introduced following the global economic and financial crisis in 2008, need to be informed by the impact they may or may not have on private capital flows. The results reported in the chapter illustrate just how complex catalysis is. Simplistic assumptions about it are theoretically and empirically unjustified, and policies based on these assumptions are unlikely to be effective.

Finally, there is a sharp contrast between low-income and better off developing economies when it comes to talking about the influence of IMF programs on other capital flows. A number of studies have identified a significant positive relationship between IMF programs and foreign aid (Bird and Rowlands, 2007, 2009, and Bal Gunduz and Chrystallin, 2014). We do not explore this relationship in any detail in this book. However, the results that we derive from estimating participation equations as reported in Chapter 5 also pick up a positive relationship between IMF programs and aid. This is unlikely to reflect catalysis in the conventional sense. IMF programs and aid are joint products with both the IMF and donors together attempting to assemble an appropriate package of finance and policy reform. Aid donors are delegating the design of economic adjustment to the IMF, and the provision of additional aid is conditional on the satisfactory negotiation of an IMF program.

NOTES

1. See Bird (2007) for a review.
2. For the most part eligibility is determined by income cutoffs associated with eligibility for International Development Association concessional lending. Some countries received concessional arrangements from the IMF despite having fairly high per capita income levels, especially former Soviet Republics or Yugoslav states in transition. We also do the analysis using only SBA and EFF agreements while excluding from the sample instances where a concessional program was signed; the results are qualitatively very similar to those reported here, though the magnitude of the (negative) catalytic effect is even larger than when concessional programs are included in the treatment.
3. Using the UN voting patterns reduces the sample by 300 observations, as the data are only available starting in 1983. The inclusion or exclusion of the UN variable (and of the various political variables we tried) had no significant effects on the core results, and in most cases the estimated coefficient for the UN variable remained insignificant. A useful and current review of the literature on the geopolitical dimensions of IMF behavior appears in Dreher and Vreeland (2011).
4. By contrast, recent studies such as Moser and Sturm (2011) report pseudo R^2 measures that are below 0.15 even for much smaller samples, and often below 0.1.
5. The variance inflation factors and bivariate correlations indicate no serious multicollinearity amongst the variables in the main estimating equation. In the selection

equation there is evidence of some multicollinearity between the two variables measuring impending and past rescheduling, and amongst the lagged variables indicating
past IMF program. When variables with possible multicollinearity are removed the
results of the selection equation and the main treatment effects equation do not change
significantly.

6. We did conduct estimations on samples restricted to cases where the capital flows are
   not excessive. In the full sample there are only a few cases of very large capital flows
   (over 75 percent of GDP). However even when we restrict the sample to cases where
   capital flows are less than 10 percent of GDP, the key results remain qualitatively
   unchanged.

7. In one of the robustness checks we estimated the equations using panel data techniques
   (random effects, though the fixed effects model yielded comparable results). The resulting R^2 values were between 0.12 and 0.13 for the total net flow equations.

8. In order to allow sufficient space to focus on catalysis we do not discuss here the magnitude of the effects that the non-IMF variables have on capital flows.

9. For comparability the boundaries for these sub-samples were kept the same as much
   as possible. Countries for which the estimated probability of an IMF agreement (as
   predicted by the selection equation) was less than 0.41 were identified as 'low probability' (column 3 in Table 8.4). When this probability was between 0.41 and 0.585 the
   country was regarded as having a medium probability of signing (column 4), while the
   high probability cases were those above 0.585 (column 5). These levels were determined
   by trying to create the most balanced sample sizes for which the estimations converged.
   In ten cases the hypothesis of jointly insignificant estimated coefficients could not
   be rejected, and the results (marked in italics in Table 8.4) must be viewed with some
   caution. In cases where convergence was not achieved, the sample was varied slightly to
   generate an equation from which inferences could be drawn with at least some confidence in their statistical properties; the extent of sample size variance can be seen from
   the reported number of observations for each sample. Due to the non-linearity of the
   estimation and the small sample sizes, the results in the last three columns should be
   treated with some caution. In the cases of short-term debt and FDI the results for the
   high probability cases were sensitive to rather small variations in the sample. Most of
   the other cases appeared fairly robust.

10. Estimations using the size of the original agreement as a percentage of GDP, indicating
    potential borrowing from the IMF, had the same qualitative effect. This result is not
    really surprising, as most of the countries do draw on their agreements very quickly, and
    these drawings will typically be a fixed proportion of the actual agreement size.

11. The calculation comprises the −0.297 IMF flows coefficient in Table 8.2 multiplied by 2
    to reflect the sample average ratio of GDP to exports and debt service payments.

12. Mody and Saravia (2006) argue that having the Fund's resources available is seen as
    a positive signal by bondholders, but that actually drawing on the resources is indica-
    tive of financial problems that may discourage lending. Of course there is interesting
    endogeneity here: if the positive response to an agreement induces only limited capital
    inflows, a government may need to draw on its agreement and thereby possibly discour-
    age further lending.

13. The test requires a balanced and continuous panel, and was therefore conducted on 840
    observations, the largest such dataset we could construct.

14. This division conveniently coincides with the pre- and post-Cold War periods, a test fre-
    quently of interest to international relations scholars. Whether the increasingly negative
    effect of IMF program signings indicated by the results is related to the end of the Cold
    War, the subsequent growth in private capital flows after the Brady Plan resolution of
    the middle-income country debt crisis, or other factors, is difficult to disentangle.

REFERENCES

Arabaci, M., and Ecer, S. (2014). The International Monetary Fund and the catalytic effect: Do IMF agreements improve access of emerging economies to international financial markets? *The World Economy*, 2014, 1575–1588.

Bal Gunduz, Y., and Chrystallin, M. (2014). Do IMF supported programs catalyze donor assistance to low income countries. *IMF Working Paper*, WP/14/202, Washington, DC: IMF.

Bird, G. (2007). The IMF: A bird's eye view of its role and operations. *Journal of Economic Surveys*, 21, 683–745.

Bird, G., and Rowlands, D. (1997). The catalytic effect of lending by the international financial institutions. *The World Economy*, 20, 967–991.

Bird, G., and Rowlands, D. (2002). Do IMF programs have a catalytic effect on other international capital flows? *Oxford Development Studies*, 30, 229–249.

Bird, G., and Rowlands, D. (2004). Financing balance of payments adjustment: Options in the light of the elusive catalytic effect of IMF-supported programs. *Comparative Economic Studies*, 46, 468–486.

Bird, G., and Rowlands, D. (2007). The IMF and the mobilization of foreign aid. *Journal of Development Studies*, 43, 856–870.

Bird, G., and Rowlands, D. (2009). Financier or facilitator? The changing role of the IMF in low-income countries, in Boughton, J., and Lombardi, D. (eds), *Finance, Development, and the IMF*: 113–133. Oxford: Oxford University Press.

Bird, G., Hussain, M., and Joyce, J.P. (2004). Many happy returns? Recidivism and the IMF. *Journal of International Money and Finance*, 23, 231–271.

Bordo, M.D., Mody, A., and Oomes, N. (2004). Keeping capital flowing: The role of the IMF. *International Finance*, 7, 421–450.

Corsetti, G., Guimaraes, B., and Roubini, N. (2006). international lending of last resort and moral hazard: A model of IMF catalytic finance. *Journal of Monetary Economics*, 53, 441–471.

Cottarelli, C., and Giannini, C. (2002). Bedfellows, hostages or perfect strangers? Global capital markets and the catalytic effect of IMF crisis lending. *IMF Working Paper* 02/193. Washington, DC: IMF.

Dreher, A., and Vreeland, J. (2011). Buying votes and international organizations. Centre for European Governance and Economic Development Research Discussion Paper Number 123, May 2011.

Dreher, A., Sturm, J-E., and Vreeland, J. (2009). Global horse trading: IMF loans for votes in the United Nations Security Council. *European Economic Review*, 53(7), 742–757.

Edwards, M.S. (2006). Signalling credibility? The IMF and catalytic finance. *Journal of International Relations and Development*, 9, 27–52.

Frankel, J., and Roubini, N. (2001). The role of industrial country policies in emerging market crises. NBER Working Paper No 8634.

Freedom House (2011) *Freedom in the World*. Washington: Freedom House. Data retrieved from www.freedomhouse.org/report-types/freedom-world (last accessed September 29, 2015).

Hovaguimian, C. (2003). The catalytic effect of IMF lending: A critical review. *Financial Stability Review*, 15, 160–169. London: Bank of England.

Jeanne, O., and Wyplosz, C. (2001). International lender of last resort: How large is large enough? *IMF Working Paper* 01/76. Washington, DC: IMF.

Jensen, N.M. (2004). Crisis, conditions and capital: the effect of International Monetary Fund agreements on foreign direct investment inflows. *Journal of Conflict Resolution*, 48, 194–210.

Killick, T. (1995). *IMF Programmes in Developing Countries—Design and Impact.* London: Routledge.

Levin, A., Lin, C-F., and Chu, C-S.J. (2002). Unit root tests in panel data: Asymptotic and finite sample properties. *Journal of Econometrics*, 108, 1–24.

Mody, A., and Saravia, D. (2006). Catalyzing capital flows: Do IMF-supported programs work as commitment devices? *Economic Journal*, 116(513), 843–867.

Morris, S., and Shin, H.S. (2006). Catalytic finance: When does it work? *Journal of International Economics*, 70, 161–177.

Moser, C., and Sturm, J-E. (2011). Explaining IMF lending decisions after the Cold War. *The Review of International Organizations*, 6(3/4), 307–340.

Penalver, A. (2004). How can the IMF catalyse private capital flows? A model. *Bank of England Working Paper* No 215. London: Bank of England.

Rodrik, D. (1996). Why is there multilateral lending? In M. Bruno, B. and Pleskovic (eds), *Annual World Bank Conference on Development Economics 1995*: 167–193. Washington, DC: World Bank.

Rowlands, D. (2001). The response of other lenders to the IMF. *Review of International Economics*, 9, 531–546.

Thacker, S. (1999). The high politics of IMF lending. *World Politics*, 52, 38–75.

United States Department of State (various years) Voting Practices in the United Nations. Washington, DC: United States Department of State.

Vreeland, J.R. (2003). *The IMF and Economic Development*. Cambridge: Cambridge University Press.

Zettelmeyer, J. (2000). Can official crisis lending be counterproductive in the short run? *Economic Notes*, 29, 12–29.

APPENDIX: DATA DEFINITIONS AND SOURCES

The mean and standard deviation for the main sample of 1339 observations appear in parentheses. Source is the World Bank's *World Development Indicators*, unless stated otherwise.

Dependent Variables (all original data in current $US)

All flows: The total of all net PPG, PNG, Portfolio, FDI and short-term debt flows as a percentage of a country's GDP (5.57, 8.51).

Short-term debt: Net short-term debt flows as a percentage of GDP (0.583, 4.15).

FDI: Net foreign direct investment into a country as a percentage of GDP (3.13, 5.01).

Portfolio (total): Purchases of shares and related assets by foreigners as a percentage of a country's GDP (0.542, 1.90) (bonds only: 0.425, 1.76) (equity only: 0.117, 0.587).

PPG debt (total): Net public and publicly guaranteed debt flows as a percentage of GDP (0.841, 2.78) (PPG bank debt: 0.289, 1.67) (PPG bond debt: 0.347, 1.68) (PPG debt from other private sources: 0.206, 1.30).

PNG debt (total): Net private non-guaranteed debt flows as a percentage of GDP (0.476, 2.06) (PNG bank debt: 0.398, 1.82) (PNG bond debt: 0.0784, 0.476).

Capital Account Equation Explanatory Variables (all lagged one year except for real LIBOR)

GDP per capita: Real GDP per capita in constant thousands of 2005 $US prices (Chain series). Source: Penn World Tables (6.61, 3.80).

Investment: Investment share of real GDP per capita as a percentage. Source: Penn World Tables (25.2, 9.10).

Exports/GDP: Ratio of exports to GDP (all in current $US) (38.1, 21.1).

Real LIBOR: The London Interbank Offered Rate on US 6 month Treasury Bills (annual average) minus the rate of US CPI inflation, as a percentage value. Source: IMF, *IMF Financial Statistics* (1.73, 1.98).

Depreciation: The percentage annual change in the official number of domestic currency units per $US multiplied by the ratio of the US consumer price index to the country's consumer price index (2.84, 54.2).

Reserve adequacy: Total foreign reserves divided by total imports of goods and services and debt service obligations (all in current $US), as a percentage (33.2, 34.5).

Debt service: Total long-term debt service payments divided by total exports of goods and services (all in US dollars), as a percentage (20.8, 17.1).

Debt/GDP: Total public and publicly guaranteed debt, divided by GDP (both in current $US), as a percentage (41.4, 52.4).

IMF Flows: Net borrowing from the IMF divided by imports and total debt service payments, as a percentage (0.759, 2.19).

Past IMF months: Weighted number of months of the past three years in which a stand-by or EFF agreement is in effect (weighted 1, 0.75, and 0.5 for 1, 2 and 3 years previously, respectively). Source: IMF, *IMF Annual Report*, various years (6.01, 8.23).

Failed IMF Programs: The number of agreements in the past two years which were 'incomplete' according to the methodology of Killick, that is agreements with more than 20 percent of the commitment undrawn by the country at the time of expiry. Source: *IMF Annual Report*, various years (0.146, 0.386).

IMF: A binary variable indicating if an IMF program has been in operation in the country in the previous year. Source: IMF, *IMF Annual Reports* (0.232, 0.422).

Selection Equation Explanatory Variables (all lagged two years)

GDP growth: Annual GDP growth rate (4.08, 6.41).

Reserve adequacy: Total foreign reserves divided by GDP (both in current $US) (14.8, 16.3).

Past rescheduling: A binary variable indicating how many debt reschedulings it has undertaken in the previous two years (0.173, 0.379).

Imminent rescheduling: A binary variable indicating that debt rescheduling occurred in the current or coming year (0.238, 0.426).

Past IMF: A binary variable indicating that an IMF program was operational for at least one month of the previous year. Source: IMF, *Annual Report*, various issues. Two year lag (0.319, 0.466); three year lag (0.350, 0.477); four year lag (0.355, 0.479).

Legislative elections: A binary variable indicating that a country had a legislative election in a given year. Source: World Bank, *Database of Political Institutions* (0.211, 0.408).

UN voting behavior: The number of times a country voted the same way as the United States on a key vote divided by the number of key votes in which it voted differently from the United States, abstained, or was absent. Source: United States Department of State, Voting Practices in the United Nations, various years (0.841, 0.821).

9. Conclusions

Casual reference to the IMF's *Annual Report* provides information about the status of IMF lending and the countries that have IMF programs. Apart from the Fund's systemic role, a role that we have not discussed in any detail in this book, the pattern of IMF lending raises a number of questions that are important in any debate about the operations of the Fund, the way it works and the scope for and direction of future reform. It is these questions that we have sought to address.

Many commentators have firmly held views about the IMF. These views often contrast sharply. At one end of the spectrum there have been suggestions that the Fund should be closed down or at least that it should curtail much of its lending and severely restrict its operations. At the other end, there are proposals to expand the IMF into a more fully fledged international lender of last resort, with substantially greater lending capacity. Similarly there have been ongoing debates about the design and effects of IMF programs. Critics have argued that the Fund is a purveyor of austerity programs that have seriously adverse effects on economic growth and development. Meanwhile the Fund has emphasized the need for stabilization as a precursor to sustained economic growth and has claimed that its programs play an important and significant role in encouraging international capital markets to lend more than they otherwise would have done, with this additional financing then allowing adjustment to be pursued at a less rapid and more appropriate speed.

Debates about how best to reform the IMF need to be informed by evidence. To what extent are the contradictory claims that are made about the Fund supported empirically?

In the space of a relatively slim volume it is not possible to examine all aspects of the IMF's activities, and the contents of this book do not provide a comprehensive analysis of the IMF. Our focus has instead been fairly narrow. We have concentrated on what may be seen as the 'life cycle' of IMF programs. In essence we have investigated the circumstances in which countries participate in programs, the factors that influence whether programs are implemented, and the effects of programs on economic growth and other capital flows. While these issues are fairly well defined and focus on the IMF's bilateral relationship with member countries, they do have implications for the Fund's multilateral role. For example, by affecting economic policy in individual countries the IMF may be able to exercise some influence over global imbalances and thereby beneficially influence the stability of the world economy. All of these facets of the IMF program life cycle, therefore, affect important dimensions of economic performance at both the national and global levels. The purpose of this final chapter is to draw together in fairly broad terms the policy implications that emerge from the results we report in the main body of this book.

From its inception, many of the IMF's operations have been based on the quotas that member countries have. The formula upon which these quotas are calculated has been periodically modified. To IMF outsiders (as well as some insiders) quota reform appears to be a somewhat arcane issue but it remains central to many of the Fund's operations. Attempts to undertake fundamental reform of the quota system have proved largely unsuccessful. Instead there has been a tendency to tinker with quotas in an attempt to deal with some of the worst deficiencies. Thus, for example, countries have been allowed to exceed their quota limits when making drawings on the Fund. However, the underlying problem is that quotas are being used to help determine the subscriptions that countries make to the Fund, the amount they can draw from it, their allocation of SDRs and perhaps most significantly from the viewpoint of governance their voting rights within the institution. Advanced economies have proved reluctant to see their share of votes reduced by increasing the voting rights of emerging economies. However, as emerging economies account for an increasing proportion of global economic activity, the gulf between their global economic significance and their voting rights within the IMF may threaten the legitimacy and effectiveness of the institution. At some stage policymakers may be forced to recognize that it is not possible for one formula to act as the basis for determining disparate aspects of the Fund's operations. What worked when the Fund was set up may not continue to work in the twenty-first century even when modified in an ad hoc way. The Fund is no longer a credit union in any meaningful sense. Subscriptions to it that provide its resources and affect its lending capacity, the ability to draw from it in the event of a balance of payments need, and the allocation of votes need to be based on different factors and this requires a more substantial break from a universal quota system.

Moreover, there are strong grounds for moving away from relying too heavily on quotas as a basis for determining the Fund's lending capacity. Experience in the late 1990s during the East Asian crisis and in the late 2000s during the global economic and financial crisis illustrates how calls on IMF support can increase suddenly. In these circumstances it is important that the Fund can respond in a speedy and flexible fashion; this flexibility may entail giving the IMF greater recourse to borrowing from international capital markets and thus acting as an international financial intermediary between these markets and the ultimate borrowers of the resources involved, which is in effect what the World Bank does in the context of medium and long term development finance.

Under what facilities should the IMF be making loans to member countries? There has been a tendency for the Fund to respond to new challenges by modifying the range of its lending facilities. As a result and over the years they have proliferated. Indeed to an outsider it is quite difficult to keep up with the changes that have been made and to fully understand their relevance. Following the global crisis at the end of the 2000s numerous changes were made over a short space of time to the range and design of facilities under which high-, middle- and low-income countries can negotiate programs. In some ways the new suite of lending facilities has certain symmetry of structure, with both the concessional and non-concessional options that target (respectively) poorer and wealthier member countries being structured around the ideas of pre-emptive, emergency short-term, and sustained lending programs. What seems logical and symmetric from the IMF's current perspective, however, may not fit the reality of its member states, and there is little reason to believe that a steady state has been achieved in terms of lending windows. In contemplating reform it is important to assess the extent to which separate facilities perform distinct functions. This means that the Fund should not allow itself simply to believe its own rubric relating to each facility but instead analyse whether they are in practice meeting different needs. This implies that it will be important to evaluate the success of the reforms introduced in the aftermath of the global crisis.

Understanding the factors that affect participation in IMF programs is important for a number of reasons. Apart from the intellectual challenge of explaining participation, an understanding of it will help in designing an appropriate portfolio of lending windows. The circumstances in which countries turn to the IMF differ significantly, and such differences need to be reflected in the structure of the Fund's lending facilities. Furthermore, information concerning the determinants of participation helps in calculating the adequacy of the Fund's overall lending capacity. A better grasp of participation also allows us to make a more informed judgment concerning the claims that have often forcefully been made that IMF lending is dominated by political factors and in particular by the interests of the US and other advanced economies. Finally, from an analytical perspective, well-fitting participation models are also needed in order to deal with the selection problem involved in evaluating the effects of IMF programs.

Our empirical examination of participation leads us to conclude a number of things. First, while there are factors that seem to exert a systematic effect on participation there is much that we still cannot explain by using large sample analysis. Methodologically, large sample regression analysis needs to be accompanied by well-structured case studies. When outliers are examined in detail, it is often relatively straightforward to explain why they deviate from the base model of participation. Second, the shortcomings of large sample models do not seem to be associated with the omission of any one particularly important variable, but rather because there are country specific differences. Third, however, it remains feasible to distinguish between different groups of countries when examining the pattern of participation. Low-income countries do differ from middle-income countries in this respect and it is therefore important for the Fund to meet their specific needs. Fourth, given that participation is driven by different factors for different groups of countries, it is important to use appropriate participation models when evaluating the effects of IMF programs using a propensity score matching methodology. In particular, in order to evaluate the effects of an IMF program it is important to use participation models tailored to the specific program and the specific sample of countries for which the program is relevant. Fifth, there is a pattern of serial usage of IMF resources. This long-term reliance may imply that the Fund is falling short in achieving the objective set in its Articles of Agreement that its resources should be used on a temporary and revolving basis. The notion that countries come to the IMF when in crisis, and that Fund assistance helps them to resolve the crisis such that they can graduate from the Fund and not need to borrow from it again, is not a picture that is supported by the evidence. Analysis instead shows that turning to the IMF once is a reasonably good predictor of turning to it again. Even though IMF programs may work in some respects they frequently do not work well enough to avoid the need for further referrals. Finally, the swings in IMF lending that occur are difficult to predict. For example, empirical examination shows that the pattern of IMF lending was disturbed in the case of the surge of lending to East Asian countries at the end of the 1990s and it would almost certainly confirm it as being disturbed again in the case of lending to Greece, Portugal and Ireland during the Eurozone crisis at the end of the 2000s and beginning of the 2010s. The inability to predict with any degree of accuracy the near term demand for IMF programs has important implications for the Fund's resource management and efforts to stabilize the global economy. The need for more flexible resource availability can be achieved by introducing either an automatic formula that creates a connection between the need for IMF resources and their availability, or a greater degree of discretionary flexibility in increasing the Fund's lending capacity when needed, by borrowing directly from international capital markets.

Although we find limited evidence that Fund lending is driven narrowly by the interests of its richer members in general and the US in particular, ways of granting the institution a greater degree of independence and reducing the scope for political manipulation are worthy of study. If such initiatives are to be followed they will also need to be accompanied by measures that offset the public choice critique; namely that the IMF's operations would then be used to serve the interests of its senior management. In a similar vein, a move toward enhanced borrowing from private capital markets would need to protect against the possibility of regulatory capture by market operators.

Having signed up to an IMF program there is then the question of the extent to which it is actually implemented. The IMF illustrated its concern with implementation by embarking on a 'streamlining' initiative at the beginning of the 2000s and its major overhaul of conditionality during global economic and financial crisis at the end of the decade. Our investigation of implementation reveals that this concern is justified. Programs are frequently not carried through to completion. The effects of programs, particularly with regard to economic growth in low-income countries, do appear to depend on whether or not they are completed. We also discover that implementation depends on the ability of powerful special interest groups to veto reform. This veto power is more likely to be exercised in the case of structural conditionality where the record of implementation is weaker than it is in the case of macroeconomic conditionality. Special interest groups are likely to oppose reforms that erode the rents that they have formerly enjoyed.

There are a number of policy responses that could be followed in an attempt to improve the record on implementation. The first is for the IMF to recognize more explicitly the political constraints on conditionality and implementation that exist and design programs accordingly. It may be better for the Fund to advocate what it perceives as a second best program of policy reform from a technical perspective if there is a much stronger chance that it will be supported domestically and therefore more fully implemented. The second is for the Fund to make a greater effort to garner support for its preferred programs by better explaining their underlying rationale and by pointing out their advantages relative to other options. This effort may entail engaging more directly with those who are opposed to reform. The third option is to provide more resources in support of programs. Enhanced financing would increase the marginal benefits from implementation and would allow adjustment to be pursued less rapidly. There may then be scope for better compensating the losers from policy reform. We discover some evidence that suggests that implementation may improve as more resources are made available by the Fund.

In response to the global economic and financial crisis at the end of the 2000s the Fund has moved in these directions. Indeed, it was already moving in some of them before the crisis erupted. It has abandoned the use of structural conditions as performance criteria, has increased its lending capacity and has tried to engage more fully with 'civil society'. However, there are potential problems with this strategy. On many of the occasions where countries turn to the IMF for assistance structural reform may be vitally important for improved economic performance. Superior performance will in the long run reduce the need for further IMF support. Notionally there is an optimum amount of conditionality. Reducing it in order to make it more acceptable politically may in turn reduce some of the beneficial economic impacts of IMF programs. A balance has to be struck. Aware of these dangers, the Fund has stated its intention to be parsimonious with structural conditionality by focusing only on the structural reforms that are central to improved macroeconomic performance. Time will tell whether the reforms introduced after the global economic crisis achieve the right balance between program design and political acceptability.

The acid test of IMF programs is the effects that they have. Some influential commentators have argued that IMF programs have systematically negative effects on economic growth; it has almost become the conventional wisdom. The argument presents the IMF as forcing countries to pursue policies of economic austerity. In contradiction, we find little empirical support for this argument, although in middle-income countries and for the year in which the agreement is signed IMF programs do seem to have a negative effect on economic growth. For low-income countries we find that involvement in IMF programs has generally had a positive effect on economic growth in the two years that follow the signing of the program. This finding has important implications for the IMF. It suggests that the Fund has been relatively successful in complying with its Articles of Agreement that direct it to assist with economic adjustment without forcing countries to rely on measures that damage national prosperity. This record could potentially be adversely affected by the reforms introduced at the end of the 2000s. If positive growth effects are associated with structural reform, then modifying the design of conditionality to reduce the emphasis on such reform may be counter-productive. Since it is largely through economic growth that countries can graduate away from the Fund anything that weakens the effect of programs on economic growth will also impede their ability to make this graduation. In turn, an inability to sustain growth will mean that countries have to borrow from the IMF on a more prolonged basis; something that is inconsistent with the Fund's Articles of Agreement directing it to provide only temporary support.

The IMF has presented its relationship with its low-income country members as one of the key challenges it faces. Some critics have argued that the Fund is ill equipped to assist LICs and that IMF programs have been anti-development. They go on to claim that the Fund should largely withdraw from its involvement with LICs, including curtailing lending to them. Our results suggest that the IMF has generally played a more constructive role in poor countries. Since we have also discovered that IMF programs and foreign aid are positively related, it would appear that the Fund performs a useful function in facilitating an inflow of resources that then allows adjustment to be pursued less rapidly and with less emphasis on compressing aggregate demand and more emphasis on increasing aggregate supply. The Fund should therefore be seeking to strengthen its role in LICs rather than abandon it. Of course this relationship is itself politically influenced by the major aid donors, and could presumably be modified to break the link with the IMF. Advocating such a reform, however, ignores the reason why donors find it useful to involve the IMF. Presumably they find it advantageous to delegate the responsibility for designing and monitoring programs of macroeconomic stabilization and adjustment to the IMF.

In terms of some of the other effects of its programs, the IMF has for a long time claimed that it catalyzes additional financial flows from private capital markets. To the extent that this is the case the need for IMF resources is reduced. Although we discover nuances in the relationship, our results show that generally the catalytic effects of IMF programs in middle-income countries are more likely to be negative than positive. IMF resources act as a substitute for private capital and seem more likely to bail out private capital than bail it in. This finding has important policy implications. If the Fund works on the assumption that there is a positive catalytic effect whereas in practice there is not, then it follows that IMF programs will tend to be under-resourced. As a consequence they will have to place greater emphasis on relatively rapid economic adjustment and on a correspondingly stronger emphasis on compressing aggregate demand than would otherwise be the case. This emphasis on rapid adjustment makes it more likely that there will be a dampening effect on economic growth, certainly in the short term. It also means that there may be more political resistance to reform, which could exert a negative effect on implementation.

In these circumstances it may be better for the IMF to borrow directly from capital markets and on-lend to client countries. If this augmentation of resources enables programs to be more adequately financed and better designed, it may also enable implementation to be improved, which will enhance the reputation of the IMF and make it easier for the Fund to borrow from capital markets. There could be a virtuous circle as opposed to the vicious one that is associated with inadequate financing.

The chapters in this book contain other important messages. First, they show that when studying the IMF, scholars need to be prepared to cross traditional disciplinary boundaries. The IMF's operations involve both economic and political elements. Serious analysis of the IMF requires a genuinely political economy approach. Second, there is no universally appropriate research methodology for studying the IMF. Large sample regression analyses run the risk of missing out significant nuances, whereas qualitative analyses based on case studies run the risk of failing to capture systematic patterns and relationships. The two approaches should be seen as complementary.

Although we have focused on large sample analysis, we have attempted throughout to disaggregate the samples that we use. By doing this we discover different patterns and generate different conclusions than would have been the case if we had taken a more aggregative approach. We have sometimes used the large sample analysis to help identify outliers that we have examined in more detail. We have found this research methodology to be instructive.

Finally, the book emphasizes the complexities of the IMF. While it would be appealing to be able to make clear and unambiguous statements about the Fund, a careful analysis of the empirical evidence suggests that these are likely to be wrong. This complexity has of course not prevented some people from making such broad statements. Our investigations lead us to stress the nuances in many aspects of the IMF's operations. Although less dramatic, we believe that guarded and contingent statements about the IMF are generally more accurate.

Ambiguities relating to its operations create problems for the reform of the Fund. It would be much more convenient to have simple answers to straightforward questions. However, a greater problem would be to base the reform of the institution on claims that are not substantiated by the evidence. With this in mind our hope is that this book makes a contribution to the ongoing debates about the IMF.

Name index

Subject index